The Back-Country Kitchen

*Camp Cooking for Canoeists,
Hikers and Anglers*

by Teresa Marrone

Northern Trails Press
Minneapolis, Minnesota

THIRD REVISION

The Back-Country Kitchen:
Camp Cooking for Canoeists, Hikers, and Anglers

Also by Teresa Marrone:
Wild Berries and Fruits Field Guide—A series of photographic ID guides
    featuring wild berries and fruits in different regions. Currently available:
    MN-WI-MI, IA-IL-MO, IN-KY-OH, and Rocky Mountain states; more
    to come. There is also a companion cookbook for each region.
    (Published by Adventure Publications, Cambridge, MN)
Abundantly Wild: Collecting and Cooking Wild Edibles in the Upper Midwest
    (2004; Adventure Publications)
The Seasonal Cabin Cookbook (2001; Adventure Publications)

For information, contact:
Northern Trails Press, 5353 Oliver Avenue South, Minneapolis MN 55419.
www.northerntrailspress.com

Printed by CG Book Printers, Mankato, MN; text pages printed with
vegetable-based inks on 10% post-consumer recycled paper.

Library of Congress Catalog Card Number: 96-92024
ISBN-13: 978-0-9651535-0-8
ISBN-10: 0-9651535-0-9

What this book is about

This is a book of techniques and recipes for anyone who camps, but primarily for those who need to pack lightweight, yet tasty and nutritious, meals. Some recipes use ingredients that are easily purchased at a grocery store or camping-supply store, while others require home drying in a dehydrator or home oven. Fresh and canned foods are included in some of the recipes, but the vast majority don't rely on canned goods. Full, detailed instructions are given for home-drying vegetables, fruits, meats, sauces, and other foods.

Unlike many other camping-food books, *The Back-Country Kitchen* contains mostly unique, never-before-published recipes – not the same recipes you may have seen in other books time and again. Although some of those popular recipes are also included, this book attempts to venture into new territory, and includes brand-new ideas as well as original camping adaptations of international favorites.

Canoeists, backpackers, hikers, and cross-country bikers will find this book indispensible. As a unique addition, a special chapter includes back-country recipes written to take advantage of freshly caught fish, as well as recipes for back-country hunting camp that feature gamebirds and venison.

All cooking methods are explained thoroughly, so even the novice cook can be assured of success. Helpful photos show specific techniques for preparing trail mixes at home, as well as at-camp cooking techniques. The following keys are used throughout the book to identify each recipe's level of difficulty, whether it uses store-bought ingredients or home-dried foods, and special cooking situations that are needed at camp, such as campfires or baking accessories.

 Recipe is very easy to prepare at camp, and requires minimal equipment (often only one pot).

 Recipe is moderately easy to prepare at camp, and may require two or more bowls or pots.

 Recipe is complicated, and may take a fairly long time and a number of bowls and pots to prepare at camp.

 Recipe uses readily available ingredients that can be purchased at the grocery store, camping-supply store, or health-food store.

 Recipe requires home-dried ingredients.

 Recipe requires campfire or charcoal grill for cooking; cannot be cooked on a campstove.

 Recipe uses canned food item(s).

 Recipe requires use of a camping oven.

 Recipe is baked at home (breads, cookies etc.)

Table of Contents

Introduction

I was raised in a Chicago suburb, in a family that had more interest in the opera, politics and theology than in the White Sox, camping or fishing. I remember being totally awestruck when, during a summer trip to visit relatives in Colorado, my Uncle Bob showed me how to catch cutthroat trout out of a mountain stream. But that was the total of my "wilderness experience" until I attended college in northern Wisconsin.

One thing that I did grow up with, however, was an appreciation for good food. I remember going to my Italian grandmother's house, where you could slip into the bedroom and admire the homemade, hand-cut noodles she had spread out to dry on a towel on the bed (her kitchen was so very small, yet she prepared such incredible meals in it!). My Italian grandfather made a traditional Abruzzi pasta sauce every Sunday, laden with garlicky meatballs, beef chuck and pork country-style ribs. On the other side of the family, my German grandmother was known all over town for her wonderful, flaky pies, her hot potato salad, and special "bidits," a delightful German pastry she laboriously prepared every Christmas. And although my mother claims that she hates to cook, I remember her fixing a variety of interesting dishes, from veal scaloppine, to eggs scrambled with onions and matzohs, to the most wonderful, thick lentil soup I've ever had. From all of these talented cooks, I was put on the culinary trail at an early age.

While in college, I became interested in fishing, and later, hunting. I added things like fresh walleye with morel mushroom sauce, antelope loin seared with black cherries, and ruffed grouse with duxelles to my repertoire. I learned to make game sausages, and to smoke all sorts of foods, both domestic and wild. But please don't get the impression that all I fix is "fancy" foods. I get just as much pleasure from a plate of well-prepared macaroni and cheese as I do from a tureen of bouillabaisse ... well, almost as much!

When I first started camping, naturally, I wanted to bring as much of this good stuff with me into the wilderness as possible. I searched out interesting and exotic-sounding pre-packaged freeze-dried dinners. But after trying a few of them, they all seemed rather similar; and the flavors and textures were blander than I liked. I realized there had to be something that was better, that would still be easy to prepare on the trail but also flavorful and satisfying, more suited to my taste and style of cooking.

So I bought every book I could find that had camping recipes in it. Although a few were very helpful, I was surprised and disappointed when I realized many of them simply contained regular recipes like pot roast, whole roast turkey, and casseroles that had to be cooked for *hours* on a campfire.

That sure didn't fit with my idea of camping – or with my camping schedule! Others relied almost exclusively on canned food ("pour a can of tomato soup, a can of corn, and a can of beef stew into a pot, and cook for 20 minutes…"), which didn't match my style of cooking at all. Still others were really backyard-barbecuing cookbooks; interesting, but not what I was looking for.

I finally decided to pack my own lightweight recipe pre-mixes. A few of the books were very helpful at the beginning, and I soon developed my own repertoire of camping foods that are easy to pack, easy to cook at camp, and delicious. As time went on, I even expanded my list of camping mixes to include adaptations of some international favorites.

Much of the camping we do is associated with fishing or hunting trips. Sometimes, we have access to conveniences like ice, unlimited water, and charcoal grills. On these trips, food weight is generally not much of a problem, and we can carry perishable foods with relative ease. Other trips are more restrictive; we need to pack a week's worth of food into a rucksack, and heavy, fresh food has to be eliminated or severely reduced. Many of our trips are into Minnesota's Boundary Waters Canoe Area Wilderness, where cans and bottles are not allowed; dried foods are the staple, augmented with fresh fish and possibly some foraged fruits, greens or mushrooms.

My style of outdoor cooking changes to suit the needs of the particular trip. When we're fishing, I plan most meals around fresh fish, but I pack a "contingency" meal in case the fish aren't cooperating. For big-game hunting trips, I generally plan on a meal of tenderloin for the first night in deer or antelope camp, and base the other dishes around that; if grouse, ducks or whatever are the quarry, the meal plan changes accordingly and I'll pack the makings for grouse à la king over biscuits, grilled pheasant breast skewers, or whatever strikes my fancy at the time. Since the weather is as unpredictable as the fishing, I always pack alternate meals that can be cooked very quickly over the portable stove or a minimum fire, in case of rain or cold, windy weather; at times like that, I don't want to stand under a flapping tarp for an hour in driving sleet, trying to make a complicated dish! Other times, we have a more leisurely schedule, and it's fun to concoct a more elaborate meal.

Whether the recipe is simple or complex, I do as much of the ingredient preparation at home, in advance, as I can. Even if the recipe simply involves combining various staples with, for example, dry soup mix, I'll do this at home and re-package the ingredients into plastic zipper-style bags, or seal them with a vacuum food-packaging system. There are several good reasons for this. First, it allows me to doctor the seasonings to my taste: to use more or less of that soup mix, add a little curry powder or dried herbs, or whatever seems appropriate. Second, re-packaging organizes the ingredients and prevents me from forgetting a key ingredient – ground beef stroganoff is pretty dull without some hearty dried mushrooms, for example, and if you have forgotten to pack some, you're out of luck. Third, and perhaps most importantly, it eliminates unnecessary packaging, which adds bulk and weight, and creates trash that either needs to be burned or packed out. The foil packages that most freeze-dried camping dinners come in are bulky to pack out, and are pretty tough to burn, even if fires are allowed where you are camping. The zipper bags I use are handy for many things around camp after the food is gone; they're lightweight and easy to transport out in the bottom of the food pack; and I re-use them on other camping trips over the course of the season. When they finally get punctured or too beat up to use again, I take them to the plastic-bag recycling bin at the grocery store, where they eventually find another life as a molded park bench, trash container, or other useful item. Vacuum bags can be re-washed and used several times, although they get shorter each time because the end of the bag is melted together during sealing and must be cut off to empty the contents.

Throughout this book, you'll find a variety of recipe styles. It's my hope that there's plenty here for everyone, from the angler who usually doesn't go near the kitchen, to the experienced gourmand who enjoys tinkering with ingredients and tailoring recipes to taste. Some recipes use ingredients that are readily available at the grocery store or outdoor specialty store; these recipes are marked with the shopping-cart "convenience" symbol. Others require home dehydrating, either in your oven or a purchased dehydrator; these recipes are marked with the "dehydrating" symbol (see pages 22-41 for complete, detailed dehydrating instructions and information). Other symbols with each recipe give additional information. They tell you if the dish is very easy to prepare at camp, or if it is somewhat complex. You'll be able to tell at a glance if the recipe has to be cooked over a campfire or charcoal grill, or if a special camper's oven is needed. And if a recipe requires that you carry canned food, a symbol will alert you to that.

This is a cookbook, so doesn't deal with pitching tents, portaging a canoe, fishing techniques, or any of that. There are lots of books that deal thoroughly with those subjects; I wanted to concentrate strictly on recipes and outdoor cooking techniques. You *will* find information in this book on things like selecting and using camp stoves, how to build and cook with a campfire, how to pack food and kitchen gear efficiently, and other things that directly relate to the back-country kitchen.

Whether you're hiking, canoeing, fishing, or just picnicking, I think you'll find a special satisfaction from preparing and eating your own home-packaged meals. After all, when you're out enjoying the great outdoors, shouldn't your dinner be as good as the scenery?

Chapter One

Planning the Back-Country Menu

Practical meal planning is one of the primary keys to an enjoyable camping trip. Being outdoors all day seems to increase the appetite, and in fact, unless your regular occupation requires a lot of physical exertion, you'll need more calories during your camping trip than you do in your usual daily routine. Complex carbohydrates like those found in grains, pasta, rice, vegetables, and fruits are the body's best source of energy and stamina. Sugar provides simple carbohydrates, which give a burst of short-lived energy but little staying power; use sweets in moderation, or as an emergency energy booster. Protein provides long-lasting energy; sources include meat, cheese and other milk products, fish, legumes, nuts, and eggs. Fat is a very dense source of calories, and some fat is necessary to keep bodily systems functioning smoothly; during cold weather, additional fat provides the calories needed to stay warm. Camping food, especially dried, is generally low-fat; the majority of the fat in the camper's diet will come from cooking oil and butter, nuts, cheese, bacon, sausage, and peanut butter.

Variety is important in the camper's menu, both for enjoyment and nutritional balance. Build your menu on complex carbohydrates, with some protein and a little fat. Vegetables and fruits, in addition to providing complex carbohydrates, supply needed vitamins and fiber, and add variety to the menu; they're also necessary to properly regulate many bodily functions.

If your trip is short, or weight is not a factor (as in car camping), you can include fresh vegetables, fruits, meat, and even canned goods in your daily menu plan. I've seen lots of books supposedly written for campers that simply tell you how to combine various cans of this and that to make a meal. Unfortunately, this doesn't generally work with my style of camping. Weight of the canned goods is often a problem; cans make bulky, messy, bear-attracting garbage; and cans are not allowed in the Boundary Waters Canoe Area (a common destination for us). Plus, I don't particularly like to cook that way; there are only a few canned staples I use at home, and I don't want to lower my eating standards just because I'm out in the back country. Canoeists and other campers who need lightweight, non-refrigerated foods often bring fresh meat and vegetables for the first night out, and rely primarily on dried foods (commercially packed freeze-dried meals as well as home-dried foods) and a few hardy vegetables for the remainder of the trip. Home-drying is a great way to add variety to your camping menu, because you can dry foods that aren't usually available in freeze-dried form. Home-dried foods also cost less than freeze-dried foods, although many take longer to re-hydrate. See Chapter 2 for instructions on home-drying vegetables, fruits, and meat.

When you're planning each meal, also consider the number and type of cooking pots you have, as well as the time and fire it will take to cook each dish. If you're traveling light and have only a medium skillet, a 2-quart pot, and a small teapot, don't plan on having fried fish and hash browns at the same meal; your single medium skillet won't do the job. Instead, plan on cooking the fish in foil over a campfire; then, the skillet will be free for the hash browns. If you won't be having a campfire, use the skillet to fry the fish, and prepare a hearty potato chowder, or maybe a pasta dish, in the 2-quart pot. Some suggestions for menus that work well together are given on pages 20-21.

The majority of the camping I do is related to fishing trips, and during a fishing trip I always plan on fresh fish for some meals. But I also bring along contingency dishes, in case fishing is lousy. I can always bring back the unused food, and since it's lightweight, it isn't a big deal to carry an extra bag or two; but it usually isn't convenient to run to the local store to pick up a some hamburger if the walleyes weren't cooperating. And I hate going to bed hungry! Weather is another unknown, and I always pack a few meals that are easy to pull together in bad weather. It's terribly frustrating to have an elaborate dish planned for dinner, and to have to deal with it during a raging gale or a snowstorm because you don't have a simpler choice available.

Packing Recipe Pre-Mixes

Some of the camper's cookbooks I've bought that rely on dried foods advocate simply bringing along various foods in bulk, so while you're on your trip you can whip up whatever strikes your fancy at the moment. While this sounds romantic, I don't believe it's practical except perhaps for a large group or an extended trip. I prefer to figure out a complete menu plan in advance, and to pack specific recipes into individual, labeled bags. That way, I know I'll have exactly what I need for each meal, and I won't be carrying around extra staples I won't use. There are certain foods I *do* carry in bulk – cooking oil, butter, maple syrup, lemonade mix, coffee, a little sugar and flour, and seasonings. But because I've made a specific and detailed menu plan, I know approximately how much of these staples I'll need.

I recommend packing the dried ingredients for individual dishes in plastic zipper-type bags or special vacuum-sealed bags. Freezer-weight zipper bags and vacuum bags are heavier than regular-weight plastic bags, and are more resistant to punctures. Plus, they won't melt when you pour boiling water into them, and so are an ideal container for reconstituting dried vegetables (see page 155). Write the name of the recipe and trail instructions on the empty bag with a fine-point permanent marker (Sanford Sharpies work well; check at an office-supply store). Sometimes, a recipe in this book will call for additional ingredients like seasonings that are placed into a small plastic bag and sealed with a twist-tie (I use Baggies sandwich bags); add this sealed bag to the zipper or vacuum bag with the rest of the ingredients so everything is together. If using a zipper bag, roll it up from the bottom (label-side out) to squeeze out as much air as possible before sealing the zipper top; the rolling also provides an additional layer or two of plastic around the food, making punctures and spills less likely. Vacuum bags are sealed with a special vacuum machine (page 55). The rolled or vacuumed bags stow easily in the food pack.

You may want to further organize your food pack by putting all of the prepared bags into three differently colored nylon stuff sacks – one each for breakfasts, lunches or snacks, and dinners. That way, you can find the proper bag fairly easily, without strewing the other pre-mixed meals all around the campsite (this is particularly helpful when the weather is nasty; you don't have to expose all your food bags to the rain while you dig for the one you want).

Carrying Fresh Meat, Vegetables, and Fruits

If you plan on bringing fresh meat for the first day or two of your trip, buy it several days in advance of your departure. Re-package the meat to eliminate styrofoam trays, cardboard boxes, or other unnecessary and bulky packaging. Vacuum packing (page 55) is ideal for this, or you can use freezer paper and other common supplies. Wrap steaks, chops and the like in freezer paper (shiny side in) and seal with freezer tape; pack ground meats or loose items like chicken thighs in a plastic zipper bag, and overwrap with freezer paper. Freeze the meat in a single layer in the coldest part of your freezer for at least a day. Wrap the frozen meat well in several layers of newspaper, and tuck it into the center of your food pack just before you leave. Depending on the weather and the time of your departure, the meat will be thawed and ready for cooking by your first night's camp, or possibly the next day. Beef or venison keeps better than pork; chicken and turkey are more prone to spoilage than either beef or pork. Fish and seafood are the most perishable of all meats. Whole cuts like steak retain their wholesomeness longer than ground meat.

Smoked meat keeps better than untreated fresh meat, so you can carry bacon, *real* smoked ham (not the stuff that's been injected with smoke flavoring; might as well not eat ham!), Canadian bacon, and cold-smoked sausages like hard salami longer than plain meats. Note that raw "fresh" sausages like pork links spoil as quickly as hamburger. Jerky keeps without refrigeration for a month or more, and can be used to provide meat on a lightweight, non-refrigerated trip; however, you need to soak it for a long time if you plan to cook it rather than just eating it out-of-hand. Smoked fish doesn't keep as long as dry salami, unless it is smoked to the point of becoming fish jerky (actually, salmon jerky is wonderful if you can find it).

Some fresh vegetables and fruits travel better than others. Hard, non-refrigerated vegetables like potatoes, onions, and winter squash work well if weight isn't a problem. Carrots travel well, but become limp after a few days in warm weather if unrefrigerated. Broccoli, corn-on-the-cob, cauliflower and the like are OK for the first night out, but wilt and get funky after that. Cucumbers travel surprisingly well if bleach-treated first (see below) and stored in a crush-proof container like your coffeepot. Apples and oranges are good fresh fruits for campers (again, if weight and bulk aren't a problem); soft fruits like bananas and peaches are a disaster, and shouldn't be considered unless you're car-camping or living in a mobile camper. Another tip: buy your fruits and vegetables unrefrigerated (or grow them yourself); they'll last longer than produce that came from a refrigerated case.

I first read about treating fresh vegetables with bleach in Cliff Jacobson's *Boundary Waters Canoe Camping With Style*, and it really works! He recommends it for tomatoes and green peppers, and I've also used it very successfully with cucumbers. His formula is to simply immerse washed, whole vegetables in a sinkful of cold water to which you've added about one-eighth cup of regular chlorine bleach. Soak the vegetables for a few minutes, then dry before packing (I air-dry the vegetables on a rack to avoid removing the bleach water; he dries them with a towel). Wrap each vegetable in a piece of paper toweling and pack in a crush-proof location; wash before using. Vegetables treated in this way will last a week or more on a camping trip; untreated vegetables get soft spots and begin rotting in about two days.

Eggs, Cheese, and Other Proteins

At least once on each camping trip, I like to indulge myself with a breakfast of bacon and real eggs. I also usually carry fresh eggs to use as a wash for pan-fried fish. Fresh eggs last for a week on the trail with no further treatment, unless it is extremely hot; then, I wouldn't push it beyond two or three days. If you can buy eggs unrefrigerated directly from a farmer (or take them from your own hens!) so much the better; like fruits and vegetables, eggs that have never been refrigerated last longer than those that have been chilled.

I've read about coating eggs with vegetable oil or paraffin wax, and also about dipping them in a sodium silicate solution (known as water glass; available at winemaking supply stores and at some pharmacies). These methods seal the shell, preventing spoilage by air. I've never tried any of these techniques, but if you're going to be out in hot weather and really want fresh eggs, you might want to give one of them a shot.

Carry fresh eggs in the original container if it's cardboard; the container can be burned after the eggs are gone. Styrofoam containers shouldn't be burned, and have no place in the wilderness. Camping-supply stores also sell little plastic "egg safes" that carry 6 or 12 eggs. These work well, but once they're empty, they are sort of a nuisance to carry. For safety, place the cardboard container or the egg safe in a plastic zipper bag; if one of the eggs breaks, you'll be glad you did. If I'm packing for a shore lunch away from base camp and I want an egg for fish breading, I'll wrap the egg in a paper towel, then place it in the water cup of my nesting cook kit until lunchtime.

Egg shells don't burn very well in a campfire unless it's extremely hot. Rinse them and crush finely, then scatter well away from camp in an area where birds can find them. Or pack out the empty shells with your other garbage.

Powdered eggs are available at camping-supply stores; they're also called "scrambled eggs". I use them not only for omelets, but also in many recipes in this book. The taste and texture are no match for the real thing, but the convenience is unbeatable. Once a package of powdered eggs has been opened, keep it refrigerated and try to use it fairly soon, to retain optimum quality.

Cheddar, Colby, Swiss, Gouda, real Parmesan and other hard cheeses travel well, and are rich in protein and flavor. Many hikers and canoeists rely almost exclusively on a quick lunch of cheese, bread, and salami. Soft cheeses like cream cheese, cottage cheese, and Brie spoil very quickly, and should be carried only if refrigeration is available. Hard cheeses can tolerate a week in an unrefrigerated pack, and some actually improve in flavor. Wrap the cheese very well in plastic wrap, and place in a freezer-weight zipper bag; or, seal the cheese in daily portion sizes with a vacuum sealer. Unrefrigerated cheese tends to lose its shape and become oily on the surface after a day or two, but it's perfectly OK to eat. If you're near a cold stream, you can put the wrapped cheese in another plastic bag or two and submerge it in the water to cool it down before you eat it; this improves its texture. (Don't be tempted to leave it in the stream overnight, or even unattended during the day! Raccoons and other woodland critters are as fond of cheese as humans are.)

If the only Parmesan cheese you've ever had is the shelf-stable stuff sold in cardboard canisters, do yourself a favor and try the real thing. A hunk of real Parmesan or Romano will keep for weeks unrefrigerated, and is spectacular when shaved with your pocket knife or grated onto pasta, chili, lentils, soup, vegetables, and lots of other back-country foods. Authentic Parmesan doesn't keep well unrefrigerated if pre-grated, which always makes me wonder what they do to that shelf-stable stuff in the green cans. Anyway, look for real Parmesan and Romano at a deli specializing in Italian or Greek food; the cheese departments of most large grocery stores also carry it. Buy a decent-sized chunk; it's expensive, but worth it. You can also buy pre-wrapped triangles of Parmesan and Romano in the refrigerator case of many grocery stores; Stella and Kraft are two brands I see frequently. They're worlds better than the shelf-stable stuff, but not as good as the real thing.

For a great option to freeze-dried meats, look for "imitation" chicken, beef, and turkey. If you've ever had mock duck at an Asian restaurant, this is the same kind of stuff. It's made from wheat gluten and flavorings, and works extremely well for camping. The ones I've used are formed into rough chunks which really do look like cooked meat, and the texture is a distinct improvement over the tiny freeze-dried meat chunks. Because it can be hard to find, I didn't call for it in any recipes; but you can substitute ⅓ cup of this wonderful stuff in any recipe calling for an ounce of freeze-dried meat. If you're interested, try an internet search for "imitation chicken"; you'll find it at sites that cater to vegetarians, as well as sites that sell supplies for emergency preparedness. It's also occasionally available at Asian markets.

Peanut butter provides both protein and fat in generous doses, and is a camping staple for many people. Cashew butter or almond butter is easy to make, and is a nice change of pace: simply process roasted cashews or almonds in a food processor until the spread is the desired consistency. If the spread seems too dry, add a small amount of peanut oil while you're processing. Pack all nut butters in tightly sealing plastic containers (screw-top containers are safer than pop-top containers), then put that container into a trusty zipper bag.

Fresh milk doesn't travel well at all, so unless you're car camping or have access to a big cooler with lots of ice you'll have to resort to powdered milk, or canned milk if cans are not a problem. Soy milk and rice milk are now widely available in aseptic "bricK" packaging, and you can sometimes find and ultra-pasteurized shelf-stable cow's milk (like Parmalat), especially at Italian grocery stores and co-ops. Keep in mind that once these products are opened, they need refrigeration and will spoil just like they would in your refrigerator, so don't open more than you can use.

Yogurt keeps for a few days unrefrigerated if it's not too hot, and is great on fresh fruit like apples or, if you're lucky, freshly picked wild berries.

Vacuum-packed foil pouches of tuna and salmon are great for camping. If you will be carrying cans, you can bring canned meat, tuna, seafood, smoked oysters, kippered herring, and all sorts of proteins that are great in the back country. Be sure to rinse out all your empty cans, crush them as flat as possible to reduce bulk (some people burn them first in a campfire to make them easier to flatten), and *pack them out*. Few things are more distressing than coming into a campsite and finding empty cans strewn about.

Choosing Rice, Pasta, and Other Starches

I'm not going to bother with a full list of every item you can buy; if you walk through the aisles of your regular grocery store, you'll find all sorts of foods that will work for camping, and with modern food marketing practices the list probably changes monthly. Health-food stores, co-ops and camping stores have choices you may not find at the grocery store.

However, some staples come in so many varieties that it may be confusing, especially to the novice cook. The different types all have their place, but cooking times and methods may differ. It's important to use the type specified in a recipe, or, if substituting another type, to understand the cooking differences and adjust the recipe accordingly.

For example, many recipes in this book call for **converted rice**. To produce this, the processor "polishes" rice to remove the germ, bran, and husk, then the rice is parboiled and enriched with iron and thiamine. This type of rice cooks a bit more quickly than its closest cousin, long-grain rice, uses a bit less water, and is slightly less sticky, all of which make it ideal for camping mixes. **Long-grain rice**, which is the most common rice in North America, can be substituted freely; you may need to add a bit more water. Fragrant rices, like **jasmine**, **basmati**, or **"pecan" rice**, generally cook in about the same amount of time as converted, and make a delicious but expensive substitute.

Medium-grain rice takes about the same cooking time as converted and can be used in its place; but it is softer and creamier, so the dish will have a different texture than intended. **Arborio** is a short-grain rice imported from Italy; it's a bit fussy to cook properly in camp, and unless you're familiar with its preparation at home, I wouldn't recommend substituting it in recipes.

Brown rice is unpolished rice; only the husk has been removed, leaving the germ and bran intact. It's more nutritious than white rice, but takes twice as long to cook, so can't be substituted for converted rice without significant adaptation. If you wish to use it in a mix, pack the rice separately from the other ingredients; at camp, boil the amount of water called for in the recipe, and soak the brown rice for 25 minutes before proceeding with the recipe (you may also need to add additional water to the dish before it's done cooking).

Wild rice is the seed of a native aquatic plant; it has a nutty flavor. If you use it in place of white rice, the dish will have a different flavor and texture. The most common form is paddy-grown "wild" rice, which takes a long time to cook; pack and pre-soak it like brown rice, above. Truly wild rice cooks more quickly and tastes better; see page 199 for a source for the genuine stuff.

Instant rice cooks very quickly, but it has an almost mushy texture and is nutritionally poor. Some recipes in this book use it for convenience. If you want to substitute instant rice for converted rice in a recipe, carry the rice separately, and add it only during the last 5 minutes of cooking; conversely, to use converted or long-grain rice in place of instant rice in a recipe, pre-soak the rice for 10 minutes in boiling water, cook it for a few minutes, then proceed with the recipe as directed.

At first glance, pasta may appear to be as confusing as rice; after all, there are dozens of types available at even a small grocery store. But pasta is more intuitive than rice; in general, you can tell how quickly it will cook just by looking at it (thin pasta obviously cooks more quickly than thick pasta; small shapes more quickly than large). The only significant difference to note is the actual grain or flour used to make the pasta. Italian pasta, and some quality domestic brands, are made with hard durum wheat; their texture is superior to the common American brands that are made with soft wheat flour. How can you tell? In general, if the package doesn't trumpet "durum wheat", then it's made with soft flour. Flavored pastas such as spinach, tomato, lemon-pepper and the like are in vogue these days; however, these flavorings don't affect the cooking time, and actually most have little effect on the taste. So feel free to use any of these that please you; they add visual interest to many dishes, which is important too. Another option is lupini pasta, found at health-food stores and larger grocery stores. This type contains no wheat at all, and is great for people who can't tolerate wheat. Its texture is a bit odd compared to wheat pasta, but it beats no pasta at all! Nutritionally, it's far superior to wheat pasta, and boasts complete protein. It comes in shapes ranging from spaghetti to linguini to macaroni and more. By the way, all pasta is best cooked only to the *al dente* stage; this means that when you bite a piece, there is still some firmness in the center (the phrase literally means "to the teeth" in Italian).

Bread choices need to be considered carefully. Soft bread gets mashed into a gummy ball almost immediately after being put in a pack, and even if carried in a special camper's bread box, it doesn't hold up well to the rigors of camping. Hearty, whole-grain breads and sourdough last better, and seem a more natural choice. Pita bread and tortillas are good choices, because they can stand a fair amount of abuse without falling apart. If they dry out and become stale, it's easy to refresh them. Heat a skillet and toss the pita or tortilla in with a few drops of water; cover the skillet quickly to steam the bread. Or, sprinkle the bread with a few drops of water, then wrap in foil and heat over warm (not hot) coals for a minute or two. You can also make fresh biscuits, cornbread, bannock, and other breads in camp; see recipes on pages 72-87.

Beans are commonly sold in dried forms, but most take too long to cook to be useful in camping. However, dried *cooked* beans are another matter; they rehydrate fairly quickly, and are a real boon to the camping menu. Canned beans can be dried with equally good results. You'll see recipes throughout this book that call for "dried cooked or canned beans"; you cannot substitute "raw" dried beans in these recipes. Another option is sold under the name of "instant beans," and these are basically cooked beans that have been dried, then flaked or ground coarsely. They rehydrate almost instantly, as the name suggests. Look for them at health-food stores, co-ops, and in large grocery stores.

In addition to rice, pasta, bread, and beans, there are lots of other starches you can buy. Select hearty, thick crackers like hard tack rather than buttery, delicate ones, unless you want to eat cracker crumbs. Choose sturdy breakfast cereals like granola, Grape Nuts, or hot cereal; cornflakes don't travel well. Or make your own hot cereal mix (see page 63). Potatoes come in a wide variety of forms. Fresh spuds are bulky but travel well. Freeze-dried potatoes can be pricey if bought at the camping store; a better option is to buy dried potatoes at the grocery store. You'll find them next to the instant mashed potatoes. Hash browns are readily available, as are sliced potatoes in boxed mixes like Betty Crocker's Au Gratin Potatoes. These sliced potatoes are great to use in packing your own mixes; and the sauce packets can be used too. You'll find a number of recipes in this book that use both the dried potato slices and the sauce-mix packets (usually not in the same recipe). If you want dried diced potatoes, dry them at home from frozen diced potatoes; see pages 34-35.

About Butter, Bacon Fat, and Cooking Oil

When I fry freshly caught fish, the only thing I'll use is real, unsalted butter. The taste is simply beyond compare, and is worth any hassle I go through to bring butter to camp. If we're traveling by motorboat and have a cooler, it's easy to keep butter cold; I just pack it into a plastic container that seals tightly. But when the gear has to be lighter, I carry clarified butter, which is butter with the milk solids removed. Since it's actually these solids that get rancid, clarified butter keeps without refrigeration for months. As an added bonus, clarified butter can be heated to a much higher temperature than unclarified butter without burning. It's used extensively in Indian cooking; they call it *ghee*, and you'll sometimes see it at a health-food store or co-op under that name. Unsalted butter, by the way, has a much fresher taste than salted butter, although in its unclarified form it spoils more quickly than salted butter.

To clarify butter: melt a stick or two in a small heavy-bottomed pan over medium heat (don't let it burn), or place it in a microwave-safe measuring cup and melt in the microwave. Spoon off the foam on top, then pour only the clear yellow liquid into a bowl or tightly sealing plastic container, leaving the milky liquid in the pan. (This residue is the milk solids; use it at home to flavor hot cereal, pasta, or other hot foods. Keep it refrigerated until used.) At this point, the yellow liquid can simply be chilled until it hardens, and it's ready to go. However, if you really want to do the job right, scrape off any foam on top of the chilled butter; re-melt it, strain through several layers of cheesecloth to remove the last remaining bits of milk solids, and pour into the plastic container. This second step is a good idea if you're going to be out in really hot weather, or for an extended trip. Place the sealed container into a plastic bag before packing it; in fact, be safe and put *that* bag into another. This stuff will really make a mess in your pack if the lid pops off.

If you want the flavor of butter without the calories or carrying problems, look for Butter Buds or other butter-flavored sprinkles in the spice aisle of your grocery store. I use it in a lot of the recipes in this book to add butter flavor. It won't fool anybody into thinking you've got real butter in the dish, but it's pretty good; and it won't go rancid. Because it has no fat, you can't use it for frying or greasing a skillet.

Bacon fat is great for frying potatoes, and some people like to fry fish in it. A little adds a nice flavor to skillet breads as well. It's certainly not practical to carry bacon fat to camp; a more likely scenario is what to do with it after you've cooked the breakfast bacon. If you have another small container that will seal tightly (like the one you used for the butter), you can drain the cooled fat into that and carry it to your next camp. I usually don't want to mess with it, though, so I'm faced with getting rid of it before I leave camp. My usual scheme is to mop it up with paper towels that I've brought along especially for the purpose, which I either burn in the campfire before leaving or pack out in a plastic bag with other garbage. Don't ever dump this stuff – or any grease, for that matter – in the woods; it will attract every critter in the county.

Cooking oil is another thing that will destroy everything in your pack if it gets out of its bottle. I use a Nalgene bottle (available at camping stores), and I place the bottle into doubled plastic zipper bags to add extra security. I don't take very much along; usually, a bottle that holds a cup is enough. I shudder every time I see a book of "camping recipes" that calls for actual deep-frying in a quart or more of oil. To me, unless you're car-camping or living in a camper-trailer, this is a bad idea; and even then, a quart of oil that's been heated to boiling seems like an accident waiting to happen, given the primitive nature of most outdoor cooking situations. It's also very messy, with the splattering grease and spills that are sure to occur when you pour the oil back into its bottle after cooking. I used to work with a fellow who went to Canada every year for a fishing trip with "the guys," and I know they deep-fried their fish; but I never did ask him how they managed it, as they had to carry all their gear, including boats and motors, for a quarter-mile over rough terrain.

You'll notice I haven't said anything about margarine yet. Personally, I don't like the stuff. But it works well as a spread and for lower-heat cooking, and it won't go rancid like unclarified butter. Carry sticks in the same way as butter, or buy the handy squeeze margarine (be sure to double-bag it in plastic).

Water and Other Wet Stuff

You'll need more liquid during a day of active hiking, canoeing, or biking than during a sedentary day at the office. Water requirements also increase in hot weather; and if your menu relies primarily on dried foods, you'll need additional water for reconstituting. You can conserve water in the back country by using only the minimum needed to boil pasta and rice; instead of draining the cooking water away, use it to reconstitute the sauce, vegetables, or whatever is being served with the rice or pasta. Moisture in fresh or rehydrated fruits and vegetables counts toward your daily water requirement; so does the liquid in soups and sauces.

Developed campsites have fresh water available; but at back-country sites you're on your own. If you're camping in arid country, you'll have to carry all your water, unless you're *absolutely certain* there's an uncontaminated source where you'll be going. If you're camping near lakes or streams and plan on drawing water from them, you need some sort of water purification system to protect yourself from microorganisms that can make you very, very sick. There is some disagreement as to the effectiveness of the old standby – boiling water for 5 minutes to purify it. I still trust it if the water was drawn from a good source, but others say that it doesn't get rid of certain microscopic cysts that can cause problems. You'll also need to carry extra fuel if you rely on the boiling method, and this can be a major drawback.

Portable equipment for purifying water is changing and improving every year, so you should check with your camping-supply store or a reputable outfitter to get the filtering unit that's best for you. Top-ranked systems combine mechanical filtration with a chemical treatment, and are said to be 100% effective. Katadyn, MSR and First Need are commonly available.

Purification tablets are another option, but they aren't recommended for long-term use and add an unpleasant taste to the water (although some kits use a two-step system that neutralizes the taste). Many people mask the taste by dousing treated water with powdered sweet drink mixes, which doesn't appeal to me. Purification tablets have a short life once the bottle is opened, so you'll need fresh tablets for your next trip if you use this method. Even if you're not relying on these tablets, it makes sense to carry a fresh, unopened bottle in case your purification equipment breaks down or you are suddenly not willing to trust boiling (you might run into some sick campers out in the boonies, which could quickly change your mind about drinking untreated water!).

Some campers – and I've done it, too – still dip water out of the lake and drink it with no further treatment. Do this at your own risk! The only lakes I've done it on are remote Boundary Waters lakes, and even then, I've taken water only from the deeper parts of large lakes, away from campsites. Never drink water that you've taken near shore. If you choose to dip water from the deeps of a large lake, play it safe and treat it or boil it for 5 minutes. To restore some of the fresh taste to boiled water, pour it back and forth between two clean pots to aerate it; this helps remove the flat taste caused by boiling.

The Daily Menu Plan

Even if you're the type of person – like me – who routinely skips breakfast in favor of a pot of coffee, you need to begin your camping day with a good meal. You'll be expending more energy than usual, and a decent breakfast will provide your body with the fuel it needs.

Many campers, especially backpackers and canoeists, eat a light lunch or mid-day snack, and then have a big meal in the evening. We generally take our largest meal at mid-day, however, and go for a lighter meal in the evening. There are a few good reasons for this, and you may want to try this plan also. For one thing, we're generally fishing or hunting on our camping trips, and the middle of the day isn't usually a good time for either activity; the beginning and end of the day are better. We don't feel like we're missing out on anything if we take a lunch break that's several hours long; in fact, we enjoy just hanging around during the mid-day, watching birds, swimming, foraging for wild berries, or sometimes even napping. Our evening meal is usually lighter and easier to prepare than the mid-day meal; that way, we can fish during the prime sunset hours and still get to bed at a fairly reasonable hour. Plus, I sometimes enjoy preparing dishes that are a bit complicated for special camping days, and that's a lot easier to do by daylight than by lantern light.

I carry a list of each day's meals, and note whether a campfire is part of the plan for each meal or not. If the day is rainy and wet, it's easy to choose a meal from the list that can be cooked entirely on the campstove. I can also quickly scan the list to see what sounds good at the moment. If we're day-tripping and will be stopping for shore lunch away from base camp, I know by looking at the list what pots, pans and other equipment I'll need so I don't have to bring the entire kitchen along.

Here are some menu ideas that have worked for us in the past. All starred recipes are in this book; check the index for the page number. For these plans, the cook kit for 2 or 3 people includes a standard-sized skillet, medium pot, and a small pot. For 4 or 5 people, an additional frying pan or a griddle is included; a large pot is carried instead of the small pot. Beverages should be based on personal taste, and are not included in the list.

QUICK BREAKFAST MENUS

1. *For 2 to 4 people:* Cereal with Fruit* (make a double batch for 4 people), pan-fried Canadian bacon, optional fresh eggs or Southwestern Omelette* in same skillet

2. *For any number of people, per serving:* Hot Breakfast Nuggets*, Egg-in-a-Basket*, fresh orange

3. *For 2 to 5 people:* French Toast* (make a double batch for 4 or 5 people), Maple-Stewed Apples*, optional bacon

BREAKFASTS THAT TAKE A LITTLE MORE TIME TO PREPARE

4. *For 2 to 4 people:* Banana-Buttermilk Pancakes*, Apple-Flavored Syrup Mix*, Canadian bacon pan-fried in skillet before pancakes and kept warm

5. *For 2 to 4 people:* Breakfast Tortilla Roll-Ups* (make a double batch for 3 or 4 people), sliced apple topped with yogurt and granola, optional Creamy Breakfast Rice* or Frijoles Refritos*

BREAKFASTS FOR A LEISURELY DAY

6. *For 2 to 4 people:* Blueberry Scones*, fresh eggs or Southwestern Omelette*, fresh-caught pan-fried fish or ham slice

7. *For 4 people:* Birds' Nests*, Maple-Stewed Apples *, pan-fried Canadian bacon or ham slice, Spicy Tomato Juice/Bloody Mary Mix*

QUICK LUNCHES OR LIGHT DINNERS

1. *For 2 or 3 people:* Pasta Carbonara*, fresh carrot sticks, salami, crackers

2. *For 4 or 5 people:* Turkey Tetrazzini with Spring Vegetables*, Carrot-Apple-Raisin Salad with Blue Cheese Dressing*

3. *For 2 or 3 people:* Chili Mac*, Cheddar cheese, crackers or pita bread
   For 4 or 5 people: Same as above, but add Northwoods Guide's Shore Lunch*

4. *For 2 or 3 people:* Clam Chowder*, fresh carrot sticks, Skillet-Baked Biscuits*

5. *For 2 or 3 people:* Ramen-Cabbage Salad*, Gouda cheese, crackers
   For 4 or 5 people: Also prepare Salmon Patties* or pan-fried fish

LUNCHES OR LIGHT DINNERS THAT TAKE LONGER TO PREPARE

6. *For 2 or 3 people:* Upside-Down Sloppy Joes*, fresh cucumber

7. *For 4 or 5 people:* Barbecued Beef Sandwiches*, Corn Fritters*, pickles

QUICK DINNER MENUS

1. *For 2 or 3 people:* Chicken with Stuffing and Gravy*, carrot sticks

2. *For 4 or 5 people:* Borscht*, Northwoods Guide's Shore Lunch*, crackers

DINNERS THAT TAKE JUST A LITTLE MORE TIME TO PREPARE

3. *For 2 to 4 people:* Garlic Chicken with Curry Spices*, Skillet-Baked Biscuits*, rehydrated dried julienned carrots with butter and herbs

4. *For 4 to 5 people:* Minestrone Soup with Pesto*, Blue Cornmeal Bannock*, Cheddar cheese

LEISURELY DINNERS

5. *For 2 or 3 people:* Bacon-Mushroom-Tomato Quiche*, Stir-Fried Vegetables*

6. *For 3 to 5 people:* Corn Chowder*, Tamale Pie*, warm flour tortillas, Monterey Jack cheese

7. *For 4 or 5 people:* Blackened Steak*, Nutty Rice*, Minnesota Green Bean Casserole*

Chapter Two
Dried Foods: Homemade and Store-Bought

Many recipes in this book use dried ingredients. Dried food has a lot to offer the back-country cook: it's lightweight, doesn't bruise like fresh fruits and vegetables, and keeps for your entire trip without refrigeration. You can dry almost anything, so your camping menu isn't limited to commercial freeze-dried dinners or boxed supermarket concoctions. A dried mix won't go bad if you don't use it; if fishing was better than you dared hope and you didn't use all your mixes, bring them home and they'll be ready for your next trip. And if you prefer, you can pack meals that are free of the additives, extra salt and sugar, or preservatives commonly found in most supermarket pre-packaged dinners.

Lots of freeze-dried meals are available at camping stores. Some are decent, but many are lacking in flavor, bulk and nutrition, and they aren't really cheaper. Compare a typical entrée like Turkey Tetrazzini. You'll pay about $7.25 (2012) for a foil pouch that's supposed to feed two; in reality, a *single camper* could eat the whole thing and still feel unsatisfied, from both a fullness and taste standpoint. The Turkey Tetrazzini on page 129 adds up like this:

3 tablespoons Parmesan cheese (from an 8-ounce can)	=	$ .28
2 tablespoons all-purpose flour (from a 5-pound bag)	=	.01
2 tablespoons powdered milk (from a 25.6-ounce box)	=	.11
1 tablespoon Butter Buds (from a 2.5-ounce jar)	=	.21
¾ teaspoon chicken bouillon (from a 3.75-ounce jar)	=	.07
⅛ teaspoon white pepper (from a 1-ounce can)	=	.01
1 ounce freeze-dried turkey (one package)	=	5.00
¼ cup dried mushroom slices (from a 3.5-ounce bag)	=	.35
¼ cup dried carrot slices (from 5 ounces fresh)	=	.23
3 tablespoons dried sliced green onion (two onions)	=	.15
2 tablespoons dried celery slices (one rib)	=	.15
2 cups thin noodles (from a 16-ounce bag)	=	.50
TOTAL		**$ 7.07**

This costs about the same as the freeze-dried dinner, yet serves *three or four campers* adequately (and if you used "imitation chicken" as described on page 14, total cost drops to about half that of the freeze-dried dinner). I think the flavor and texture are better in the home-packed version. Plus, you won't have to pack out that bulky foil pouch; the plastic bags used to pack the homemade mix are re-usable, easy to pack out, and recyclable.

When I first read about drying foods at home for camping, I was cautiously enthusiastic. I wasn't sure it would be worth the trouble; and how much work was it, anyway? In fact, I was quite surprised how easy it really is. And the dishes I've been able to concoct are beyond anything I could have imagined.

Not all the dried ingredients I use are things I dry myself. I also buy dried foods at the supermarket: dried fruits, seasoning and sauce mixes (although if you're a purist about additives and preservatives, stay away from these), grains, potato flakes and slices, bouillon, fruit leathers, milk powder, herbs… you see, there are lots of dried foods you use already in your daily cooking. Co-ops have a wide variety of dried foods untouched by preservatives, including sun-dried fruits without sulfur, textured vegetable protein (TVP), and more grains than you ever heard of. Ethnic markets are another source; check out an Asian store for dried mushrooms, imitation chicken or beef, dried tofu, and a variety of soups and seasoning mixes (watch out for MSG, though, if you're sensitive to this chemical; it's common in Asian seasonings and mixes). Specialty shops carry items of interest, including sun-dried tomatoes, dried fruits, and seasoning mixtures (as well as hard-to-find items like quality olive oil). Health-food stores offer granola, grains, dried buttermilk powder, additive-free dried fruits, nuts, and dried vegetable mixes. If you can't find what you're looking for or don't live near any of these specialty places, there are mail-order sources that sell dried foods, spice mixes, and other items of interest; many of these can be easily found on the internet (see page 199 for addresses, phone numbers and website URLs of some useful mail-order companies).

When purchasing dried foods, it pays to shop around a bit. For example, many supermarkets carry small boxes of dried Chinese black mushrooms; a ¾-ounce box costs $4.50 (*$95.99 per pound*). Local Asian grocers sell dried Chinese black mushrooms for $4.00 for 3½ ounces (*$18.28 per pound*); and I think they're nicer mushrooms than those in the little supermarket boxes. You'll find similar bargains at other ethnic markets, as well as co-ops.

I still use some freeze-dried foods when I package trail mixes. Home-dried meat like jerky takes a long time to dry, and a *really* long time to reconstitute on the trail. Some vegetables also take a surprisingly long time to reconstitute (corn being the one that pops to mind first); so sometimes I specify freeze-dried vegetables in the recipes. However, generally, I'll give instructions for using home-dried vegetables as well as the freeze-dried version, in case your camping schedule is leisurely enough to allow for a longer soak.

Even if you don't want to get into drying foods at home, you can still save money by packaging your own foods with readily available ingredients. At the camping store, you can buy a 3-ounce foil package of hash browns with green peppers and onions for $1.95; it serves two. Or, you can buy a 5.2-ounce box of dehydrated hash browns at the grocery store for $1.75, add some dehydrated green bell pepper and onion from the spice aisle at the supermarket, and make two batches of hash browns for less than half the cost per batch. And as far as I can tell, the potatoes are about the same in the two versions.

One last option for obtaining dried foods is to find someone to dry it "to order." A sign posted at your local co-op might put you in touch with someone who would dry foods for a nominal charge (or perhaps if you supply the raw produce, they'll dry it in exchange for part of the dried yield). Check to be sure that proper sanitary procedures will be followed. You should have an idea of the dried yield to expect; for example, if you provide them with 3 pounds of carrots, you can expect approximately 2¼ cups of dried carrot slices. The information on the following pages will help you calculate yields.

The Basics of Home Drying

Home drying works on a simple principle: warm air is circulated over prepared foods to remove the moisture. Key elements are:

- **Preliminary food preparation.** This includes steps like washing and slicing zucchini; chopping and blanching cabbage; or cooking and puréeing apples for fruit leather.

- **Proper drying racks.** Slices or chunks of food, or whole small foods like beans and peas, are placed on grids to allow air flow and drying on both top and bottom. Slurries or foods with a lot of liquid, like puréed fruit, salsa, or spaghetti sauce need to be spread out thinly on solid sheets; they will dry only from the top.

- **Warm, circulating air.** Drying temperature is generally between 90°F and 150°F; the 125°F–145°F range is considered ideal for most foods. Warm air carries away more moisture than cool air. Air circulation speeds drying by pulling moist air away from the food, and bathing it in fresh, dry air.

When I first started experimenting with home drying, I simply put prepared foods on racks or sheet pans, and dried them in the oven. This works pretty well, and is probably the way that most camper/cooks will get started. After all, almost everyone has, or has access to, an oven, so there's really no investment. And if your needs are minimal, you may very well be happy with the oven as a permanent solution. (You could also try sun-drying, if you live in an area that is consistently warm, arid, and sunny. I have no personal experience with this method of drying, since I live in Minnesota; here, summers are hot, humid and unpredictable, and winters are long and cold. I have read that sun-drying is suitable mainly for sugary foods like fruit, that it takes days instead of hours, and that it is more work than other drying methods. If this still appeals to you, contact your local Extension Service for more information, or look for books that go into more depth on the subject.)

If you do quite a bit of camping and want to prepare more than just an occasional dried meal, you are wise to purchase or build a food dryer. I use an American Harvest (Nesco) Snackmaster. A thermostat controls drying temperature, and a fan in the base circulates air from the bottom out through a hole in the top. Each round tray has a capacity of .86 square foot. The unit came with four trays, and I have bought additional trays to increase its drying capacity; it can operate with up to 12 trays. My total investment, including additional screen inserts and solid inserts, was about $125. There are lots of other brands and styles available; shop around to see what looks best to you.

Homemade food dryers are less of an investment than commercial food dryers, but may not last as long because the heat may cause the wood to dry out and split. It's been suggested that homemade wooden dryers are a bit of a fire hazard after the wood gets dry; so use them with caution. If you want to make your own dryer, check out the plans in Gretchen McHugh's wonderful book, *The Hungry Hiker's Book of Good Cooking*. You could also check with your County Agricultural Extension agent for information and plans, or look through back issues of back-to-the-land magazines. To get started, buy a half-dozen metal cake-cooling racks, and base the size of your dryer on them. (Hi-Mountain Jerky also sells excellent racks with heavy metal screens, designed for drying jerky. These racks are expensive, but they're heavy-duty and last forever; they're fantastic for jerky. See page 199 for Hi Mountain's address, phone number and URL.) Build an open-front wooden box out of sturdy, unpainted plywood to enclose the racks; nail strips of wood along the sides to create sliders for the racks, leaving several inches between them. Allow about 18" from the bottom of the box to the first rack, then attach a porcelain light bulb holder to the bottom. Leave openings for ventilation at both the top and bottom of the enclosure. Use a 150- to 200-watt bulb (check the temperature with an oven thermometer, and adjust the wattage to reach the desired temperature). Use hinges or whatever method your carpentry skills allow to put a front door on the unit; it should be an inch or two short at the bottom to allow air to enter. The door should swing away or come off completely, so you can remove and add racks. If you want to get fancy, add a small fan at the bottom for circulation; if you don't have a fan, rotate the racks frequently, as the dryer won't be an even temperature from top to bottom.

Convection ovens also work for drying foods, although I've never used one for this purpose. If you have one, your instruction manual will give you information on settings, timetables, and accessories for drying.

Cold smokers are great for drying jerky and smoking fish, but they don't work well for general drying (unless you enjoy smoke-flavored fruit leather!). The most common commercially available type is an aluminum enclosure with a pull-out rack assembly or slide-out shelves; there's a hot plate on the bottom for heat, and you place a pan of wood chips over it to provide smoke. See the jerky recipes on pages 190-191 for cold-smoking information.

No matter what type of dryer you use, you'll often need to use mesh or a screen insert to prevent the dried food from falling through the racks. Drying causes foods to shrink as they lose moisture; and the chopped cabbage that sits so nicely on the rack going into the dryer will probably end up falling through onto whatever is on the rack below it. The best material I've found for lining racks for oven-drying (or for a homemade dryer) is the white netting material sold at fabric stores for bridal veils. It's cheap (I spent 69¢ on a hunk of it that was big enough to line six full-size racks, with leftovers), it stands up to the heat of the dryer, it's easy to wash, and doesn't come unravelled or get tangled up. I attach it to the racks with wire twist-ties from a box of plastic sandwich bags. Cheesecloth is another mesh option, although it *does* come unravelled, wads up into a hopeless ball when you wash it, and gets tangled in everything, including the dried foods. Commercial dryers have special plastic mesh inserts to place over the plastic tray grid, and these work very well.

If you're drying a semi-liquid food in the oven or home-made dryer, spread it out on a cookie sheet. Line the cookie sheet with plastic wrap to prevent the dried food from sticking; secure the edges of the plastic wrap with freezer tape to keep it in place during filling and drying. (Don't use waxed paper or foil; you'll never get the dried food off of them.) Alternately, spray the cookie sheet with a light coating of non-stick spray such as Pam. Some foods are best dried on plastic wrap rather than on oiled sheets; the oily residue left on the dried food isn't very appealing on fruit leather and the like. Commercial dryers have solid liner sheets that work well, although even these need to be sprayed with non-stick spray for some foods.

Selecting and Preparing Foods for the Dryer

In general, foods to be preserved by any method – drying, canning, or freezing – should be as fresh as possible, and at the peak of ripeness. If you have your own garden or orchard, it's easy to pick vegetables or fruits, then process them the same day. However, most of us don't have that luxury; we buy the best produce we can find, and go from there.

Almost all fresh, raw foods need preparation before drying, whether it's simply peeling and slicing, or a more involved treatment like steam-blanching. You can save some work by using frozen vegetables and fruits where appropriate; some canned foods also produce good results. Any necessary pre-treatment was done before the food was frozen or canned, so all you need do is empty the foods onto the trays and start drying. As a general rule, if a food is available in both frozen and canned forms (like corn or green beans), the frozen form will dry better. However, in most cases, properly prepared fresh foods will produce the best results. One notable exception to this is potatoes; I've found that frozen diced potatoes dry better and are much less work than fresh potatoes, although if you've got a bumper crop of spuds, go to it.

Wash fresh fruits and vegetables well before drying, even if they're going to be peeled; pesticide sprays are common on store-bought produce. Lightweight waxy coatings are often applied to produce (especially cucumbers, eggplants, and apples) to keep them fresh; you need to remove all this junk as well. A scrub with soapy water will do the job; rinse well after scrubbing, because soap is dangerous if it gets into food. (A friend of ours was taken to the hospital a few years ago, with what appeared to be a heart attack; the actual diagnosis was that his problem was caused by dish soap residue in a plastic container he'd used to bring some leftover food to the office.) Rutabagas, and sometimes turnips, are often treated to a heavier wax coating; the best solution for this is to peel the vegetable, and wash it after peeling to remove any traces of wax or soil that remain. Most co-ops sell fruits and vegetables that are untreated; they don't look as pretty in the displays and don't keep as long, but many people feel they are superior in taste and nutrition. Also wash your hands with hot, soapy water before handling foods to be dried; proper hygiene is important in any food preservation method. Some of the really dangerous germs and bacteria, like botulism, can't live on dried food (that's why we can safely keep properly dried foods at room temperature); however, you don't want to introduce any nasties into your foods before drying.

Pages 28-41 provide instructions for specific vegetables, fruits, and meats. Here are some general techniques that are used in those instructions.

BLANCHING

This means to partially cook a vegetable or fruit before drying. Blanching softens the fibers, making rehydration quicker. It also helps preserve color and taste by destroying enzymes that adversely affect dried foods. *Steam-blanching* is preferable to blanching in boiling water because fewer nutrients are lost. I prefer the microwave for steam-blanching; it's quicker and easier than stovetop steam-blanching. To steam-blanch in the microwave: peel, chop, or slice food as desired. Place into a microwave-safe bowl; sprinkle with a little water. Cover and microwave on HIGH for about half the time it would take to fully cook the food, stirring occasionally. To steam-blanch on the stovetop, place prepared food in a metal or bamboo steaming basket, then place the basket over a pot containing several inches of boiling water. Cover the basket, and cook for about half the time it would take to cook the food fully.

SYRUP-BLANCHING

Used strictly for fruits, the syrup-blanching method requires that you partially cook fruits in syrup before drying. Fruits prepared in this manner are softer and stickier than untreated fruits, but have better color. The syrup, which I've borrowed from Deanna DeLong's *How To Dry Foods*, is made by combining 1 cup sugar and 1 cup white corn syrup with 2 cups water. Bring to a boil before adding prepared fruit (this amount of syrup is adequate for about 1½ pounds fruit); simmer 5 minutes. Drain and rinse fruit in cold water before drying.

SULFURING

This treatment provides attractive, commercial-looking dried fruits. However, I don't use sulfuring; I prefer my dried fruits less attractive but more natural, and there are health concerns with sulfuring. Sulfuring is quite a production, and is messy as well as smelly. If this technique appeals to you, consult your Extension Service for more information; you'll also find complete instructions in the aforementioned *How To Dry Foods*. Most commercial dried fruits are sulfured, by the way. Again, turn to a co-op or one of the whole-foods markets that are cropping up in and around urban areas for unsulfured fruits.

Loading Trays, Determining Doneness, and Storing

Arrange prepared foods in even layers on the drying racks, using mesh or solid liners as appropriate. Air circulation is important; there should be spaces between the pieces, and none should overlap. Sliced peaches may take 5 hours to dry on a given day, but if the pieces overlap, they'll take 10 hours to become fully dry. Total volume in the dryer also affects drying time. Drying times will be longer in a heavily loaded dryer than one with just a small amount of food in it. Don't dry strong vegetables like cabbage or onions in the same batch with fruits or mild vegetables; the flavors may transfer. Mild vegetables can be dried in the same batch with fruits, meats or other mild vegetables.

I've read conflicting information on proper drying temperatures. One well-respected manual says to start drying at a lower temperature, then raise the temperature as the foods become drier. Others recommend the opposite: start higher, and reduce temperature after a while. I've tried both methods, and my admittedly unscientific experiments were inconclusive. So I start drying at a higher temperature, because I figure the food could use some extra heat to warm to dryer temperature; then I reduce the heat by 10°F after an hour. The books that recommend this high-to-low method claim the actual temperature of the food is as much as 30°F less than the dryer temperature, especially at the beginning when full moisture in the food causes cooling by evaporation.

I load all the trays and stack them on the dryer or in the oven before I start drying. This way, I know what time drying started for the entire batch, and I don't lose heat by constantly opening the dryer. If you prefer to start drying while you prepare additional trays, don't add fresh food after the first hour. Fresh food added to a partially dry load adds moisture to the system, and could actually re-moisturize the partially dried foods.

Rotate the trays occasionally during drying. Rearrange or stir the food periodically; that way, if food pieces are touching, you'll expose overlapping areas to encourage even drying. I've also noticed that food near the edges of the trays dries more quickly, so rearranging exposes all pieces to the heat and air more evenly. I set a kitchen timer to ring every hour, to remind me to rotate and rearrange; however, you don't have to tend the dryer that frequently if you don't want to. If you're drying in your gas oven, in fact, you'll probably end up leaving food in the oven overnight, unattended, with the pilot light on.

To check food for dryness, remove a piece or two from the dryer, and cool to room temperature before checking. If you're drying a liquid or semi-solid like a fruit leather, remove the entire tray and let it cool slightly before checking. The individual directions for vegetables, fruits, and meats give guidelines to help determine when a food is sufficiently dry.

If you dry a load that contains trays with different foods on them, some of the foods will probably be dry before others. Simply remove the trays that contain the dry foods, and continue drying the rest. If you're drying large pieces of moisture-laden foods like pineapple, individual pieces may dry at different rates; you may need to remove individual pieces as they become dry.

I generally let dried food stand on the trays at room temperature overnight before transferring it to storage containers, to evaporate any trace moisture. However, if the weather is humid, food may absorb moisture from the air. In this case, transfer the cooled food to a sealed container, and let it "equalize" for a day or two, stirring or shaking occasionally, before storage. Trace moisture will be evenly distributed among the food pieces. If you notice condensation or moisture build-up, return the entire batch to the dryer for another hour or two.

Commercially dried foods are prepared with sophisticated equipment, and keep for a long time at room temperature. However, it's difficult to be certain the optimum amount of moisture has been removed during home drying, so take extra precautions when storing home-dried foods. Place in sealed plastic bags or moisture-proof containers, or vacuum-pack them (page 55). A dry root cellar is a good storage spot; the refrigerator or freezer is even better. Home-dried foods stored should be OK for a year if frozen, although nutrients will be lost during storage. Six months is about as long as I store home-dried food in the refrigerator or root cellar; if I store food at room temperature, I use it within two months. Check your dried food occasionally. If a batch shows signs of mold or if it looks or smells funky, *throw it away* rather than take a chance.

Drying Vegetables

Dried vegetables weigh one-quarter to one-tenth their fresh weight, and also lose volume, making them easy to pack and carry into the back country. Some rehydrate in just a few minutes, while others take an hour or more. When you're planning dried-food menus, be sure to take this into account; if you try to rehydrate dried zucchini, mushrooms, and corn all together, the zucchini and mushrooms will be falling apart while the corn is still tough.

Some vegetables, like beets, turnips, and rutabagas need to be peeled before drying. Carrots and potatoes are more tender after rehydrating if they're peeled before drying, but you can leave the peels on if you prefer, to retain the vitamins and fiber in the peel. Wash all fresh vegetables thoroughly, and trim away any bruises or damaged spots.

Slice, chop, julienne, or shred vegetables into their final form before blanching and drying. Thinner, smaller pieces dry and rehydrate more quickly than thicker, larger pieces. All pieces in a batch should be the same approximate size and thickness, so both drying and rehydrating are even. Julienne or matchstick pieces (page 31) dry evenly and are attractive when reconstituted; shredded vegetables often dry into wisps that are almost too fine. A food processor is great for making even slices of carrots, zucchini, potatoes, and firm vegetables, and also makes quick work of julienning and chopping.

The individual listings below give approximate yields of fresh-to-dried vegetables, as well as approximate drying times. Remember, though, that yields and times are approximate, and can vary depending on your specific cutting techniques and equipment. Unless otherwise noted in the individual listings, start drying at 145°F, then lower the temperature to 135°F after one hour.

ARTICHOKE HEARTS
1 cup sliced canned artichoke hearts packed in water (¼" slices) = ½ cup dried
Canned artichoke hearts work very well, and are easier to prepare than fresh artichokes. Drain them, and cut out any brown spots or tough leaves. Slice ¼" thick, cutting down through the heart rather than across. *Doneness test:* light and crispy. *Total drying time:* 4 to 6 hours. Quick to rehydrate.

BEANS, GARBANZO (chickpeas)
1 cup cooked or canned garbanzos = ¾ cup dried
Canned garbanzos are easy to dry; simply drain and rinse. If you're starting with dried garbanzos, cook as usual, then drain and rinse before drying. *Doneness test:* hard, completely dry; some beans may "pop" like popcorn. *Total drying time:* 5 to 6 hours. Dried cooked or canned garbanzo beans take a moderate amount of time to rehydrate. Garbanzos can also be mashed before drying; see the recipe for **Hummus** (page 189) for an example.

BEANS, GREEN OR STRING
1 cup green beans, cut into 2" lengths ("straight-cut") = scant ¼ cup dried
1 cup green beans, cut French-style = a heaping ¼ cup dried (loosely packed)
Frozen green beans dry more quickly and rehydrate better than fresh beans; canned green beans have poor color and taste, and are not recommended. Steam-blanch fresh beans before drying; use the freshest beans you can get, as older beans are tough when rehydrated. French-cut green beans dry and rehydrate more quickly than straight-cut beans. Place French-cut beans on a solid sheet for drying rather than a mesh insert; the dried beans shrivel up into brittle, curly pieces that are really a pain to disentangle from the mesh. *Doneness test:* straight-cut beans will be hard and somewhat shriveled, while French-cut beans will be brittle, curly, and very shriveled up. *Total drying time:* 4 to 6 hours for straight-cut beans, 3 to 4 hours for French-cut. Straight-cut beans are slow to rehydrate; French-cut beans rehydrate fairly quickly.

BEANS, SHELL (Cannelini, great northern, kidney, lima, navy, pinto, etc.)
1 cup canned or cooked = generally about ¾ cup dried, depending on variety
Canned shell beans dry well; drain and rinse before spreading on dryer trays. Some shell beans are available frozen, and are ready for the dryer when you buy them. If you're starting with uncooked dried shell beans, boil them until tender before drying; dried pre-cooked shell beans rehydrate and cook at camp much more quickly than plain dried beans. (Lentils are an exception, and cook so quickly from their original dried state that they don't need to be pre-cooked and dried.) *Doneness test:* lightweight, hard; some may "pop" like popcorn. *Total drying time:* 4 to 7 hours. Smaller shell beans rehydrate fairly quickly (10 to 15 minutes), but larger beans like limas can take 30 minutes to rehydrate.

BEETS
1 cup diced beets (⅜" dice) = scant ¼ cup dried
1 cup julienned beets (⅛" julienne) = ½ cup dried (loosely packed)
1 cup sliced beets (⅛" slices) = scant ½ cup dried
Fresh or frozen beets are the best, but canned beets are acceptable. If using fresh beets, steam or boil whole beets in the skins until just tender, then hold under cold running water and slip skins off; slice, dice or julienne. Canned or frozen beets need no pretreatment if they're pre-cut; whole beets need to be sliced, diced or julienned before drying. In my experience, julienned canned beets are thinner than the julienne cut I use, and can be wispy when dry (but they're perfect for **Borscht**, page 88). *Doneness test:* dark in color, leathery, somewhat curled up. *Total drying time:* 3 to 6 hours. Julienned beets rehydrate very quickly; sliced or diced beets take a little longer.

CABBAGE (Green, red, Chinese)
1 cup chopped or shredded cabbage (tightly packed) = ⅓ cup dried (loosely packed)
Cabbage smells very strong while it's drying, and shouldn't be dried in the same load with fruits or delicate vegetables. Steam-blanch chopped or shredded cabbage until bright-colored and tender-crisp; add a sprinkling of vinegar to red cabbage before blanching to preserve color. A 1½-pound cabbage will yield 6 to 8 cups before drying. Dry cabbage at 150°F for an hour, then at 140°F until dry. Because cabbage leaves vary so much in thickness from the core to the outer part, you will need to sort through the cabbage as it's drying, and remove the thin, dried pieces first while the other pieces continue drying. *Doneness test:* dried green or Chinese cabbage is fairly bright in color if it has been steam-blanched; if dried without blanching, it will be pale. Red cabbage is deep purple when dry. All varieties will be lightweight and crisp; if the cabbage seems rubbery and pliable, it isn't dry enough. *Total drying time:* 5 to 7 hours. Dried cabbage rehydrates fairly quickly.

CARROTS
1 cup julienned carrots(⅛" julienne) = ½ cup dried
1 cup shredded carrots = ⅓ cup dried
1 cup sliced carrots (⅛" slices) = ¼ cup dried
Fresh carrots are the best choice, followed closely by frozen carrots. Canned carrots yield poor results, and should be used as a last resort. Fresh carrots will be more tender when rehydrated if you peel them before cutting, but this isn't essential. Steam-blanch fresh carrots before drying; frozen carrots need

How to Julienne Vegetables by Hand

Cut firm vegetables (peeled if appropriate) into 2" or 3" lengths. Slice evenly, usually about ⅛" thick.

Stack 4 or 5 slices, with a flat slice (not a rounded outside slice) on the bottom for stability. (Stack shown from the side for clarity; lay the stack flat for cutting.)

Slice across the stack into matchstick pieces; the slices should be as wide as they are thick (⅛" x ⅛").

How to Julienne Vegetables with a Food Processor

Cut firm vegetables (peeled if appropriate) into 2" or 3" lengths; arrange in the feed tube. Slice with the standard slicing blade, using firm, steady pressure (pictured). Continue until all vegetables are sliced. Remove all the slices from the work bowl.

Assemble the top of the food processor. Hold it upside down; arrange the slices in a layer as shown. Pack slices firmly; you'll have to flip the top right-side up onto the processor, and if the layer of slices is loosely packed, the slices will fall out.

Make layers of slices until the feed tube is firmly filled. Carefully turn the feed tube over and place it onto the work bowl (pictured). Slice with firm, steady pressure. Re-load the feed tube and continue until all the vegetables are julienned.

Julienned Vegetables, Dried and Reconstituted

Julienned carrots before rehydrating

Julienned carrots after rehydrating

no pretreatment. To save prep time, buy already-julienned carrots (typically available in bags, next to the baby-cut carrots at supermarkets). *Doneness test:* leathery, deep orange. *Total drying time:* shredded or julienned carrots take 3½ to 6 hours, sliced carrots 5 to 6½ hours. Sliced carrots are very slow to rehydrate; shredded carrots rehydrate fairly quickly.

CELERY
1 cup sliced or diced celery (⅛" slices or ¼" dice) = scant 2 tablespoons dried
Two average ribs yield a cup of sliced or diced celery. It shrinks to a fraction of its original volume and its flavor intensifies after drying, so a little dried celery goes a long way. Steam-blanch until bright green before drying to preserve color and speed rehydration. If using in combination with foods that don't require lengthy soaking or cooking, de-string celery before cutting; it will rehydrate in half the time of regular celery. To de-string before dehydrating it, snap a rib until it is just held together by the strings. Peel strings back from one half of the rib, then the other. De-stringing reduces yield per rib. *Doneness test:* shriveled, tough, fairly dark. *Total drying time:* 3½ to 5 hours if de-stringed, 4½ to 6 hours if not de-stringed. Celery takes a fairly long time to rehydrate if not de-stringed.

CORN
1 cup kernels = ⅓-½ cup dried
Frozen corn is ideal for drying and needs no pretreatment. Fresh corn should be cut off the cobs and steam-blanched before drying. Canned corn takes longer to dry and is less attractive when dried, but does yield acceptable results and requires only draining before drying. *Doneness test:* hard, wrinkled, deep golden brown. *Total drying time:* 4 to 5½ hours. Dried corn takes a long time to rehydrate; plan on soaking for an hour or more before cooking.

CUCUMBER
1 cup sliced cucumber (¼" slices) = ¼ cup dried
I don't really care for dried cucumbers, but some people enjoy using them like chips or crackers. To each her own! Wash firm, fresh cucumbers to remove any wax on the skin; slice ¼" thick. *Doneness test:* very lightweight, crispy. *Total drying time:* 4½ to 5½ hours. Eat in dry form; they are mushy if reconstituted.

EGGPLANT
1 cup sliced or diced eggplant (½" slices or dice) = ½ cup dried
Wash, peel, quarter lengthwise, and slice or dice. Steam-blanch until just tender. A medium eggplant will yield about 2½ cups before drying. *Doneness test:* lightweight, no soft spots; cream-to-brown color. *Total drying time:* 4½ to 5½ hours. Dried eggplant rehydrates fairly quickly, but is somewhat mushy; it is best cooked with other vegetables, or in a sauce.

GREENS (Beet, collard, kale, mustard, spinach)
1 cup coarsely chopped greens (tightly packed) = ¾ cup dried (loosely packed)
Thick-leaved raw greens like kale dry better than thin-leaved raw greens like spinach; frozen greens don't dry well. Wash well, then chop into 1-1½" pieces. Greens need no other pretreatment. *Doneness test:* brittle, crumbly. *Total drying time:* 2 to 3 hours. Dried greens rehydrate quickly. Best used in soups or stews, or as an "accent" in other vegetable or potato dishes.

LEEKS
1 cup sliced leeks (¼" slices) = ½ cup dried
Leeks make a delicious addition to soups, stews, and vegetable dishes. Trim off and discard the root fibers, and the leaves where they become spread open (keep a little of the green part, where it is still tightly bunched). Wash very well; the leaves collect a lot of grit. Cut in half lengthwise, then slice ¼" thick. One leek yields about 2 cups sliced (before drying). *Doneness test:* crisp, lightweight. *Total drying time:* 3½ to 4½ hours. Dried leeks rehydrate quickly.

MUSHROOMS
1 cup sliced mushrooms (⅛" slices) = about ⅓ cup dried, depending on variety
1 cup halved morels or quartered button mushrooms = about ⅓ cup dried
Wash mushrooms to remove any grit; morels need particular attention. Solid-capped mushrooms like button mushrooms commonly sold at supermarkets, shiitake, Crimini, and Portobello can be sliced; or cut button mushrooms into quarters. Morels are hollow; simply cut in half. *Doneness test:* slices and morel halves are crispy and lightweight; quarters are lightweight, spongy, somewhat shrivelled. *Total drying time:* 2¾ to 4 hours. Mushrooms rehydrate quickly.

ONION, GREEN (also called scallions or spring onions)
1 cup sliced green onion (½" slices) = scant ½ cup dried
Wash well, and remove root fibers. Slice white and green parts; no blanching is necessary. Four green onions yield a cup of fresh sliced onion. *Doneness test:* somewhat shriveled, lightweight, crispy. *Total drying time:* 3 to 5 hours. Green onions rehydrate quickly, and are nice added to soups, stir-fry dishes, or omelets.

ONION (Red, white, yellow)
1 cup diced onion (¼" dice) = ⅓ cup dried
Generally, I don't fool around drying onions; they're readily available at the grocery store. But red onions aren't available dried; and if you have a bumper crop of any type of onion, here's how to dry them. Peel, then cut into ¼" dice. One large onion yields about 2 cups diced fresh onion. Spread on a solid liner to make removal easier (dried onions get caught in mesh liners). *Doneness test:* brittle, hard. *Total drying time:* 5 to 6 hours. Onions rehydrate fairly quickly.

PARSNIPS
1 cup sliced parsnips (⅛" slices) = ½ cup dried
Peel raw parsnips, and slice into circles ⅛" thick. Cut the larger circles from the top of the parsnip into halves or quarters so all pieces are somewhat uniform in overall size. One large parsnip will yield about 2 cups sliced parsnips (before drying). Steam-blanch until tender-crisp. *Doneness test:* lightweight, hard. *Total drying time:* 3 to 4 hours. Parsnips are somewhat slow to rehydrate.

PEAS, BLACK-EYED
1 cup cooked or canned black-eyed peas = ½ cup dried
Like shell beans, black-eyed peas need to be cooked, then dried, to make camp preparation quick and easy. Canned black-eyed peas work well; simply drain and rinse. *Doneness test:* dry, light, hard. *Total drying time:* 3½ to 5 hours. Dried cooked or canned black-eyed peas rehydrate fairly quickly.

PEAPODS (thin Oriental-type)
1 cup peapods = generous 1 cup dried
Thin peapods, like those used in salads or stir-fried dishes, dry fairly well and add visual interest to trail food. Thick edible peapods like sugar-snap peas aren't suitable for drying. Snip ends and steam-blanch fresh peapods; frozen peapods dry well and need no further pretreatment. *Doneness test:* crispy. *Total drying time:* 4 to 5¼ hours. Peapods rehydrate fairly quickly.

PEAS, GREEN (SWEET OR ENGLISH)
1 cup shelled peas = scant ⅓ cup dried
If you grow fresh peas, they will dry nicely if you first remove and discard the pods, then steam-blanch the peas until they're bright green. Otherwise, frozen peas are the logical choice; they're ready to go right from the freezer bag to the dryer tray. Canned peas aren't satisfactory; use them only if you have no other choice. *Doneness test:* small, shriveled, hard. *Total drying time:* 4 to 6 hours. Dried fresh or frozen peas take a moderate amount of time to rehydrate.

PEPPERS, BELL (Green, orange, red, or yellow)
1 cup diced fresh peppers (½" dice) = ¼ cup dried
1 cup sliced fresh peppers (½" x 2" strips) = scant ⅓ cup dried
You can buy dehydrated diced green bell peppers at most grocery stores; they're with the spices, and are expensive. If you dry your own, you aren't limited to diced green peppers. Red, orange, or yellow peppers add great color to many dishes, and strips of pepper are great for stir-fry dishes. A whole pepper generally yields about 1½ cups diced or sliced pepper (before drying). Wash fresh peppers, then remove stem, seeds, and soft inner ribs; slice into strips, or dice into ½" squares (don't dice too small, as they shrink during drying). Frozen diced or sliced peppers also work well, and are convenient. *Doneness test:* dry, shriveled, leathery. *Total drying time:* 5 to 7 hours. Dried bell peppers take a moderate amount of time to rehydrate.

PEPPERS, HOT
Yield is not really a factor with dried hot peppers; generally, you'll use a certain number of peppers in a recipe, or will crumble them and measure the flakes. Thin-fleshed peppers like cayenne can be dried by simply laying them in an airy spot and turning them over occasionally; you can also use a needle and thread to string them through the stem end, then hang this as a decoration while they're drying. Large, thick-fleshed hot peppers like Hungarian wax should be treated like bell peppers, above; fresh jalapeño peppers are best sliced into ⅛"-thick rings, seeds and all, before drying. Pickled jalapeño rings (sold in cans or jars by the salsa and refried beans in most grocery stores) dry very well; the vinegar adds a nice flavor to many dishes. Doneness test for fresh or pickled jalapeños: firm, leathery. Total drying time for fresh or pickled jalapeños: 2¾ to 3¾ hours. Dried jalapeño slices reconstitute fairly quickly.

POTATOES
1 cup diced frozen potatoes (¼" dice) = ⅓ cup dried
I generally buy boxed dried potatoes, like Betty Crocker Au Gratin Potatoes,

rather than mess around drying potato slices; dried hash browns are readily available also. Diced potatoes aren't as easy to find (you can buy freeze-dried diced potato mixes at camping stores, but they're a bit pricey), so I dry those myself. I use frozen, diced potatoes because they're so easy; simply dump them onto the dryer trays with no pretreatment. If you want to dry fresh potatoes, scrub them well, then peel or not as you prefer (the peels add a bit more nutrition and fiber, but are tough when rehydrated); cut up as desired. Steam-blanch until not quite tender. *Doneness test:* hard, white, no soft spots. *Total drying time:* 3 to 5 hours. Diced or sliced potatoes take a moderate amount of time to rehydrate; boxed hash browns rehydrate more quickly.

POTATOES, SWEET (including yams)
1 cup sliced cooked or canned sweet potatoes (⅛" slices) = ½ cup dried
Sweet potatoes or yams should be peeled, sliced and steam-blanched until just tender, just like white potatoes. One large sweet potato yields about 2½ cups sliced (before drying). Canned sweet potatoes work fine; rinse well and slice before drying. *Doneness test:* hard, darkened. *Total drying time:* 9 to 12 hours. Dried sweet potatoes and yams take a moderate amount of time to rehydrate.

RUTABAGA
1 cup diced rutabaga (¼" dice) = ½ cup dried
Rutabagas are often are coated with a thick wax to preserve freshness. Peel waxed or unwaxed rutabagas and rinse in cold water before cutting, then steam-blanch until just tender. One medium rutabaga yields 2 cups sliced or diced (before drying). *Doneness test:* hard, somewhat shriveled. *Total drying time:* 4 to 7 hours. Dried rutabagas take a moderate amount of time to rehydrate.

SQUASH, SUMMER (Crookneck, yellow, zucchini)
1 cup diced squash (½" to ⅜" dice) = generous ⅛ cup dried
1 cup julienned squash (⅛" x ⅛" x 2" strips) = generous ¼ cup dried
1 cup sliced squash (⅛" thick slices) = ¼ cup dried
Summer squash needs no blanching before drying; simply wash, discard stem end, and cut up as desired. If the squash is large, cut into halves or quarters lengthwise before slicing. Blanched or frozen squash dry and rehydrate more quickly, but are mushier when reconstituted than fresh squash that has been dried without blanching. *Doneness test:* crisp, lightweight, somewhat shriveled. *Total drying time:* 4 to 5 hours. Summer squash is quick to rehydrate.

SQUASH, WINTER (Acorn, buttercup, butternut, Hubbard; also pumpkin)
1 cup puréed cooked squash = scant ¾ cup dried (broken in pieces to measure)
1 cup sliced squash pieces (¼" x 1" x 1½") = scant ⅔ cup dried
For sliced squash: peel squash and remove seeds and stringy pulp. Cut into lengths no wider than 1½"; slice ¼" thick. Steam-blanch until not quite tender. For puréed squash: cut in half, and scoop out seeds and stringy pulp. Cook squash by baking, boiling, microwaving, or steaming until tender. Scoop cooked flesh away from shell, and purée in food processor or potato ricer, or mash well with potato masher. Spread evenly on dryer trays lined with plastic wrap or solid liner sheets. *Doneness test:* slices will be leathery and firm; purée will be leathery to brittle, with no sticky spots. *Total drying time:* 8 to 10 hours. Puréed squash reconstitutes very quickly; slices are a bit slow to rehydrate.

TOMATOES

1 cup diced tomato (½" dice) = scant ¼ cup dried
1 cup halved plum tomatoes = ⅓ cup dried
1 cup sliced tomato (½" slices) = ¼ cup dried

Wash tomatoes and cut away blossom core. Cut into quarters before slicing or dicing. Plum and other small tomatoes can simply be halved or quartered. Place diced tomatoes on a solid liner sheet or plastic-lined trays. One medium tomato yields a cup of diced or sliced tomato (before drying). *Doneness test:* leathery, shrunken. *Total drying time:* 8 to 12 hours. Dried diced or sliced tomatoes rehydrate fairly quickly; halves take longer.

TOMATO SAUCE, TOMATO PASTE

Tomato sauce or paste dries into a leather (like a fruit leather), and it's hard to describe an accurate way to measure these leathers. Recipes in this book give measurements based on a specific amount of tomato paste or sauce; for example, a recipe will call for "one-half of the leather from an 8-ounce can of tomato sauce." Line dryer trays with plastic wrap, or use a solid liner. Pour sauce onto lined tray, and gently tilt the tray to distribute evenly, ⅛" deep or less. Spread paste with a spatula to an even thickness, ¼" or less. After a few hours of drying, peel leather from the liner and turn it over to speed drying. *Doneness test:* leathery, pliable, no sticky spots. *Total drying time:* 4 to 6 hours.

TURNIPS: Yields and techniques are the same as parsnips, page 33.

YAMS, see: Potatoes, Sweet

ZUCCHINI, see Squash, Summer

Drying Fruits

The variety of dried fruits that is readily available far outstrips the variety of dried vegetables; I usually buy dried fruits at the grocery store, health-food store, or co-op rather than dry them myself (plus, Minnesota doesn't have a great fruit-growing climate; most fruits are shipped here from warm climates, making them less economical for me). I've provided information on drying a number of fruits in the pages following, in case you live in a fruit-growing area. Also, there are a few fruits like cantaloupe and watermelon that aren't available commercially dried, yet make interesting additions to the trail cook's pantry.

Commercially dried fruits are often sulfured for better appearance and texture. There are some health concerns with sulfur, and it's a messy, smelly operation; I don't recommend it. Most fruits simply need washing and cutting before going into the dryer. A few can be syrup-blanched (page 27) to give them an almost candied texture and color. Home-dried fruits tend to be harder and drier than commercially dried fruits, but taste as good or better.

As with vegetables, many fruits are available frozen, and these work fairly well. Frozen fruits are easy to dry because any necessary pre-treatment has already been done before they were frozen. Some fruits, especially frozen strawberries and blueberries, release a lot of juice while they're drying, so you may want to put a solid sheet underneath the tray of fruit to catch the juices.

I usually dry fruits at 145°F, which is a higher setting than I use for most vegetables. If you're drying a mixed batch of foods that should be dried at different temperatures, use the lower setting; it will take longer, but less nutrients will be lost. Individual listings below give approximate yields of fresh-to-dried fruits, as well as approximate drying times. Yields and times can vary depending on your specific cutting techniques and equipment.

Dried fruits are often eaten out-of-hand as a snack. During cooking, dried fruit rehydrates quickly, so rehydration ranges aren't given below.

APPLES
1 cup sliced apples (¼" slices) = ½ cup dried
Peel and core apples before slicing. One medium apple yields 1¼ cups (before drying). *Doneness test:* leathery-to-hard. *Total drying time:* 4½ to 5½ hours.

BANANAS
1 cup sliced bananas (⅜" slices) = ½ cup dried
Bananas with brown-flecked skins are nicer when dried than bananas that are just barely ripe. Wash banana before peeling to remove residual pesticide on the skin. One medium banana produces a cup of fresh banana slices. *Doneness test:* leathery-to-hard; fully ripe bananas have a deeper color when dried than just-ripe bananas. *Total drying time:* 7½ to 9 hours.

BLUEBERRIES
1 cup fresh or frozen blueberries = ¼ cup dried
Frozen or fresh blueberries both dry well, and require no pretreatment; fresh blueberries can be dipped briefly into boiling water to "checK" (break) the skin, which reduces drying time. *Doneness test:* hard, dark, wrinkled; frozen and "checked" blueberries are slightly flattened. *Total drying time:* 7½ to 9½ hours.

CANTALOUPE, HONEYDEW
1 cup sliced melon pieces (¼" x 1" x 1") = ¼ cup dried
Dried cantaloupe or honeydew pieces are a delightfully different snack. Peel melons and remove seeds before slicing. Half a medium-sized melon yields about 2½ cups of pieces (before drying). *Doneness test:* thin, leathery. *Total drying time:* 7 to 10 hours; cantaloupe dry more quickly than honeydews.

CHERRIES
1 cup pitted, halved cherries = ¼ cup dried
Wash fresh cherries before pitting (check at a housewares stores for a plunger-style cherry pitter); cut pitted cherries in half. Canned cherries (packed in water, not in syrup) also work well; simply drain and cut in half. Place cherries cut-side up on mesh liners. *Doneness test:* leathery, dark, shrivelled, somewhat sticky. *Total drying time:* 8 to 12 hours.

CITRUS FRUITS (Grapefruit, lemon, lime, oranges)
1 cup sliced citrus fruit (½" slices) = scant ⅔ cup dried
I don't care for dried citrus slices, but some people enjoy eating them as a snack, rinds and all! Scrub fruit well with a brush to remove any pesticide traces or peel treatment. Cut into quarters or eighths, slice, and pick out seeds. *Doneness test:* lightweight, crispy. *Total drying time:* 7½ to 9 hours.

KIWI FRUIT
1 cup kiwi slices (¼" slices) = scant ⅓ cup dried
Kiwi make a nice snack or addition to trail mix, and are good in mixed-fruit dishes. Peel kiwi, then quarter and slice. One kiwi yields about ¾ cup before drying. *Doneness test:* leathery, shrunken. *Total drying time:* 5½ to 6½ hours.

LEATHERS
Almost any fruit can be dried into a leather; simply purée in a blender or food processor and spread on solid sheets to dry. Applesauce can be dried with no additional preparation. Citrus fruits are too watery, but can be combined with other fruits to make a mixed leather. Other mixes are interesting; try canned pineapple with banana and apples, or fresh raspberries and canned apricots. If the purée isn't sweet enough, add honey or corn syrup to taste. You can also add spices like cinnamon to the purée. For additional interest, sprinkle the purée with finely chopped nuts, granola, or shredded coconut before drying.

If drying in the oven or a home-made dryer, line cookie sheets with plastic wrap, then tape the wrap to the edges of the cookie sheets to keep it in place during filling and drying. Commercial dryers come with solid liner sheets that work well, but you may want to spray them with non-stick spray; experiment with a small batch to see how your liner sheets perform. The purée should be fairly thick; applesauce has an ideal consistency, but other purées may be a little thinner. If the purée is too watery, it will take too long to dry, and may be brittle when dry. Pour purée onto prepared sheets or dryer trays. Tilt the sheets to evenly distribute purée; it should be about ¼" deep. Dry at 130°F–140°F until leathery with no sticky spots; peel from the sheets and flip once during drying if the bottom is not drying properly. *Total drying time:* 4 to 10 hours. If you've used sheets lined with plastic wrap, the leather can be peeled off any time; if you've used solid liner sheets, peel off the leather while it is still warm. Roll up all leathers, and wrap in plastic wrap.

PEACHES
1 cup thin-sliced peaches (¼" slices) = ½ cup dried
1 cup peach wedges = scant ⅓ cup dried
Fresh peaches work best, although canned or frozen peaches also produce acceptable results. For fresh peaches: dip briefly in boiling water, then place under cold running water for a minute or so; skins will slip off easily. Slice into halves up to the pit; pull halves apart, and remove pit. Cut each half into halves or quarters; these are referred to above as wedges and can be dried as is. Or, slice each wedge into ¼" slices; these are referred to above as thin-sliced peaches. Peaches can be syrup-blanched first if a candied product is desired; I prefer them unblanched. Canned and frozen peaches are sold as "sliced peaches" but are actually wedges. Frozen peach wedges can be dried as is, or sliced like fresh peach wedges; canned peaches should be rinsed, then dried as wedges, as they are too soft to slice. Place canned peaches on dryer trays that are lined with plastic wrap or liner sheets. One fresh peach yields about ¾ cup slices or wedges. *Doneness test:* leathery; canned peaches have a candied appearance, and will stick to the liner sheets. *Total drying time:* 8 to 10 hours.

PEARS
1 cup sliced pears (⅛" slices) = ¼ cup dried
Peel pears, then slice into quarters and remove the core before slicing. Pears can be dried with no further pretreatment to produce dry, leathery slices; syrup blanching produces dried pears that are moister and slightly candied. (I prefer pears that haven't been syrup-blanched.) One average pear yields 1½ cups slices (before drying). *Doneness test:* leathery if not syrup-blanched; candied in appearance if syrup-blanched. *Total drying time:* 5 to 6½ hours.

PINEAPPLE
1 cup pineapple chunks (½" chunks) = generous ⅓ cup dried
Fresh pineapple is the best choice, although canned pineapple also works. To prepare fresh pineapple: cut off and discard top, bottom, and rind; remove eyes. Cut sides away from core; discard core. Slice sides into ½" chunks. If you prefer chewier, sweeter dried pineapple, syrup-blanch fresh pineapple before drying. Canned pineapple should be drained and rinsed; cut slices into ½" chunks. *Doneness test:* dried fresh untreated pineapple is leathery, lightweight, and straw-colored; syrup-blanched fresh pineapple is moister, almost candied in appearance, and deeper in color. Dried canned pineapple is leathery, slightly sticky, and deep golden in color. *Total drying time:* 8 to 9 hours.

PUMPKIN, see Squash, Winter (with vegetable listings)

STRAWBERRIES
1 cup strawberry halves = generous ¼ cup dried
Wash fresh strawberries and remove cap, then cut in half; larger berries may need to be cut into quarters. Frozen strawberries can also be used. Place strawberries cut-side up on dryer trays to prevent juice loss; they may still drip while drying, especially frozen strawberries, so it's a good idea to put an empty solid sheet under the tray to catch juices. *Doneness test:* leathery, spongy in thick spots; frozen berries flatten during drying. *Total drying time:* 7 to 9 hours.

WATERMELON
1 cup watermelon chunks (½" x 1" x 2") = scant ¼ cup dried
Dried watermelon makes an interesting snack; it resembles taffy in texture and is very sweet and flavorful. Wash melon, then cut away rind, including white inner area. Slice ½" thick, then into strips approximately 1" x 2". Pick out large seeds. *Doneness test:* thin, shrivelled, flat, pliable, with no soft spots; looks like dried salmon. *Total drying time:* 7 to 9 hours.

Drying Meats

Ground beef and other ground meats are easy to dry, and work well in many recipes. Larger pieces of meat, like those normally used in stir-fry dishes, stroganoff, or stews, take a long time to dry and a long time to rehydrate at camp; generally, I use freeze-dried meats for these dishes when I'm camping.

Look in the pre-packaged lunch meat section at the grocery store and you'll find pouches of sliced, pressed luncheon meats (Carl Buddig is a brand that seems to be common); many varieties are available, from beef to ham to chicken to corned beef. These dry and rehydrate quickly, and are a nice addition to the lightweight camper's menu.

Home-dried cooked bacon tastes better than the bottled bacon pieces from the grocery store (Hormel now markets actual bacon in both "bits" and "pieces"; both are a vast improvement over imitation bacon bits). Keep in mind, however, that real bacon that's been dried, whether it's your own or store-bought, doesn't keep as long as the imitation bacon bits, which never need refrigeration. Canadian bacon dries well, but needs a good bit of pre-soaking in camp before cooking.

Jerky keeps well on the trail. It is a traditional out-of-hand snack for hikers, and can be used in stir-fry dishes, stews, and soups if it is pre-soaked for an hour or two before cooking. Even after pre-soaking, the meat will not be very tender when cooked, but the chewiness is good in certain dishes. Jerky that's been made from ground meat is less chewy when cooked than the regular whole-muscle type. Jerky can be dried in the oven or dehydrator, but a cold smoker gives a better flavor. See pages 190-191 for jerky-making instructions.

Meat (with the exception of cold-smoked jerky, page 190) should be dried at higher temperatures than most fruits and vegetables. 140°F is acceptable if you're combining meat in a load with fruits or vegetables; if you're drying a load that contains nothing but meat, dry at 150°F-160°F. As stated previously, home drying isn't as sophisticated as commercial drying. It's hard to know if the correct amount of moisture has been removed from home-dried foods; and in the case of meats, small amounts of fat left in the dried product will turn rancid if left unrefrigerated. Play it safe: keep all home-dried meats in the refrigerator or freezer until you're packing for your trip.

BACON
1 pound sliced, cut-up bacon = scant 1½ cups dried
Buy the leanest bacon you can find. Cut into ½" pieces. Fry over medium heat until crisp and browned, stirring occasionally. With a slotted spoon, transfer cooked bacon to a mesh colander set in the sink; rinse the bacon quickly with very hot water, shaking the colander to expose more of the bacon to the hot water. Let drain for a few minutes, then transfer to dryer trays that are lined with paper towels. After the bacon is dry, place a fresh paper towel in the storage container before transferring the bacon into it; the towel will absorb additional grease during storage. *Doneness test:* crumbly, brittle. *Total drying time:* 3 to 6 hours. Dried bacon doesn't need rehydrating; simply use in recipes.

CANADIAN BACON
1 pound Canadian bacon strips (⅛" x ¼" x 2"; 2 cups fresh) = ¾ cup dried
Canadian bacon is very lean, and usually requires no trimming; however, if there are fat chunks on the outside, remove and discard them before drying. Slice ⅛" thick, then cut the slices into ¼" strips, no longer than 2". Because it is fully cured like ham, it needs no cooking before drying. After the meat is dry, blot it with paper towels to remove surface grease. Place a fresh paper towel in the storage container before transferring the dried Canadian bacon into it; the towel will absorb additional grease during storage. *Doneness test:*

stiff, dry, oily, dark rose color. *Total drying time:* 4 to 7 hours. Dried Canadian bacon needs a fair amount of soaking time to soften it before cooking.

GROUND BEEF, GROUND TURKEY, GROUND VENISON
1 pound extra-lean ground meat = 1⅓ cups dried
Buy the leanest ground meat possible. Fry in a large skillet, stirring frequently to break up chunks, until completely cooked and evenly crumbled. Transfer cooked meat to a mesh colander set in the sink; rinse the meat quickly with very hot water, shaking the colander to expose more of the meat to the hot water. (The rinsing removes fat which can turn rancid while the dried meat is in storage.) Let drain for a few minutes, then spread evenly on dryer trays that are lined with paper towels. Stir occasionally during drying. *Doneness test:* hard, crumbly, darker in color than before drying. *Total drying time:* 4 to 8 hours. Dried ground meat rehydrates fairly quickly.

SAUSAGE, BULK
1 pound bulk sausage = ⅔ to 1 cup dried
Buy bulk (ground uncased) sausage, or remove and discard the casings from Italian sausage, breakfast links, or other uncooked sausages. Fry, drain, and rinse the meat as directed for ground beef, above. Spread evenly on dryer trays that are lined with paper towels. Stir occasionally during drying. After the sausage is dry, spread it on newspaper that has been covered with clean paper towels, and let stand an hour or two to absorb grease. Place a fresh paper towel in the storage container before transferring the dried sausage into it; the towel will absorb additional grease during storage. *Doneness test:* hard, crumbly, darker in color than before drying. *Total drying time:* 6 to 8 hours. Dried bulk sausage meat rehydrates fairly quickly.

SLICED, PRESSED LUNCHEON MEAT (also known as "chipped")
One 2.5-ounce package sliced meat = 1 cup dried (crumbled, loosely packed)
Separate the slices, and arrange in a single layer on dryer trays (if the pieces overlap slightly at the beginning, don't worry; they shrink very quickly during drying and can easily be rearranged to eliminate the overlap after an hour of drying). After the meat is dry, place on paper towels and blot to remove surface grease; the slices will crumble during blotting. *Doneness test:* brittle, crumbly; darker in color than before drying. *Total drying time:* 2 to 4½ hours. Dried pressed meat rehydrates quickly.

Chapter Three

Equipment and Techniques for the Back-Country Kitchen

The amount of gear you'll be able to pack depends on your mode of transportation and the size of your group. Car campers can carry a lot more than canoeists; hikers and cross-country bikers will carry less than canoeists. Large groups need more pots and pans than a solo camper.

Cooking techniques will also vary, depending on your specific trip plan. For example, in some camping areas, open fires are completely prohibited, making camp stoves essential. Even in areas where campfires are permitted, many campers also carry a stove; they're especially useful for a quick meal, or in wet weather where lighting a campfire may be difficult.

Cookware and Utensils

Each camper will need a drinking cup, fork and/or spoon, and a plate and/or bowl (the solo camper may, of course, forego this luxury and eat directly from the cooking pot). Depending on the size of the group and the packing arrangements, these items could be carried with the rest of the kitchen gear; or, in a large group, each camper might carry this gear in their own pack.

For two campers, a minimum cookware set includes one or two small- to medium-sized nesting pots, and a skillet. I also consider a coffeepot a necessity, as I don't like instant coffee; one of the great pleasures of camping is brewing a fresh pot of coffee in the crisp morning. Minimum cooking utensils include a spoon for stirring, a small spatula, a fork for blending sauces, and a small knife.

For a group of four or more people, a set of larger nesting pots is a good idea; one pot should be at least 4 quarts. It's great for cooking pasta, rice, or soup for a crowd, and also doubles as a sink (an 8-quart pot is the ultimate back-country sink and pasta cooker, but is too large to cook something like soup unless you're serving six or more people). A full-size skillet or griddle is essential, especially if you expect to be cooking fish.

Pots designed for camping have bail handles (like a bucket), fold-back wire handles, or removable handles, making them easier to pack than everyday pots with straight handles. Most camping pots are lightweight stainless steel or spun aluminum; because the metal is thin, scorching is a problem, especially over an uneven campfire or blazing-hot camp stove (a diffuser helps with this problem; see page 46). I prefer stainless steel to aluminum because it dents less easily and stands up to the scorch-and-scour cycle better. Aluminum pots have also been linked to various ailments, including eczema and Alzheimer's disease. They shouldn't be used to cook acid foods (for example, tomato sauces, or dishes with lemon juice or vinegar) because the acid chemically reacts with the aluminum, causing pitting and discoloration as well as a metallic taste in the food. With all these cautions, you may still choose to buy aluminum pots, especially after you check the price on stainless pots. Most people feel the short-term exposure during a camping trip isn't that great a problem.

Another option is enameled steel, the traditional "speckleware" that is so picturesque. It holds and spreads heat slightly better than thin stainless steel or aluminum. Well-made brands feature a rounded stainless-steel rim to prevent chipping. With care, this cookware lasts for years. My camping coffeepot and coffeecups are speckleware, and have great aesthetic value to me.

Non-stick cookware is becoming more common at camping stores. Many camp cooks swear by it because cleanup is so easy. I don't use any non-stick cookware, either at camp or at home. I keep pet birds at my home, and know that overheated Teflon and other non-stick finishes emit fumes that are deadly to birds. I figure if it's toxic to them, it isn't doing me – or the wildlife – any favors, either. If it does scorch, the surface will be damaged by scouring.

You may want to purchase a set of nesting pots, rather than trying to assemble your own. Camping stores have lots of sets priced from $30 to $100 depending on material and number of pots; many come with stuff-sacks. Often, the lids are supposed to double as frying pans. One note about that: because the material on these lid/frying pans is generally thin, food scorches easily in them; the serious cook will carry a cast-iron or cast-aluminum skillet or griddle.

The old-time scout's cookset, which you can often find for a few dollars at an Army surplus store, can be useful for one- or two-person parties. Camping stores have an aluminum version that doesn't take the heat as well as the original; it sells for about $15. These cooksets includes a cup (useful as a measuring device), which nests in a small pot with a bail handle; a lid fits on the pot, and that, in turn, fits into a small skillet with a pivoting handle. A wing nut tightens the handle into its extended position for cooking. A lid that's like a small pie tin is secured over the skillet-and-pot with the pivoting handle; the lid doubles as a plate, and is great for breading fish.

For a skillet, I swear by my trusty, well-seasoned 9" cast-iron skillet. Yes, it's heavy; but the results are worth the weight, especially with all the fish I cook on camping trips. As shown on page 50, I nest the scout cookset into the skillet, along with forks, spoons, salt-and-pepper dispenser, soap, and cooking utensils. My speckleware plates sit upside-down on top of the cookset (cushioned by a dish towel and potholder), and the whole thing slides into a sturdy canvas drawstring bag that I sewed. For most camping trips, the only cookware I bring is this skillet set, a small set of nesting stainless pots, and of course, my speckleware coffeepot and mugs.

Another excellent choice is the square cast-aluminum skillet available through many camping stores and outfitters for around $45. It's much heavier than spun aluminum, and holds heat evenly; it features a removable clamp-on wooden handle that stows away easily. Canoe outfitters often send this skillet out with their parties because it's sturdy and durable as well as effective. If you can't find this skillet at your local camping store, contact Voyageur Trading Post (see page 199 for address).

Check the housewares area at a department store for a small, short-handled spatula. There really isn't a substitute for flipping pancakes (although the old-time woodsman reportedly used a piece of bark, or a sliver of fresh-cut log, as a spatula), and they're perfect for pan-frying fish, potatoes, or stir-fry dishes. You can also use the spatula to scrape burned food from the bottom of a pan.

Small wooden implements are handy. Although wood burns if left near a campfire, it doesn't conduct heat, so the handles are always grippable. My Italian grandfather gave me several "meatball turners" that he carved from olive wood; they're small spatulas, and work great in the back country. You may be able to find a similar tool at a housewares shop or camping store. A small wooden spoon is also useful. Look for one made of olive wood rather than the more common pine; olive wood is less porous, so it lasts longer and doesn't absorb flavors. If the handle is too long to fit inside your cook kit, shorten it with a saw.

The pocket knife carried by most campers gets dull (not to mention dirty) from whittling marshmallow sticks, cutting rope, and other camp chores, so a small, sharp kitchen knife earns its keep. Buy a knife with a blade protector to help keep the knife sharp. Or, wrap the knife in a dishtowel or potholder for packing. Stow the knife inside a pot or other rigid container; otherwise, it may cut your pack, gear, or even *you* if you fall during a climb or portage.

Many recipes in this book, as well as commercially packaged meals, require that you add a measured amount of water to a dry mix at camp. Most camp cookware isn't marked with measurement lines, so you'll need to figure out how much water is held by the cups and pots you'll be carrying. Camp cups usually hold 8 ounces; check yours at home so you can measure with it at camp. Some Sierra-type cups are marked with handy measurements. If you use aluminum pots, pour a measured amount of water into the pot at home and scratch the surface at 1-cup intervals. When in doubt about a measured amount of water at camp, use less rather than more. It's easy to add additional water if the food is sticking or a sauce is too thick, but you can't take it out once it's in the dish.

Selecting Camp Stoves

There's no substitute for a crackling campfire. The ambience it provides is, for many people, an irreplaceable part of camping. However, it can take an hour or more before a campfire is ready for cooking, and cooking over open fire can be tricky. In some camping areas, campfires aren't allowed any more; you need a portable camp stove or grill for cooking. And even in areas that do permit campfires, the weather or other conditions may make a campfire inadvisable or illegal. (As an example, the summer of 1995 was exceptionally dry in the upper Midwest. A forest fire that destroyed close to 75,000 acres in Minnesota and Ontario was traced to an improperly extinguished campfire. Open fires were banned after that for the rest of the summer.)

The majority of camp stoves used in the back country burn white gas. It's readily available in the United States and Canada (Coleman fuel is a common brand), and provides high heat output. Several of these stoves, like the Coleman Dual Fuel models, can burn automobile gas as well; the Peak 1 Apex Triple Fuel also burns kerosene, in addition to white gas and automobile gas.

Some models have built-in fuel tanks that you refill with a funnel; others hook up to a separate fuel bottle by means of a flexible hose and special connector.

Kerosene stoves are another option. This fuel is available worldwide, while white gas can be hard to find in Europe. Kerosene provides high heat, and more cooking time than an equal amount of white gas. Unlike white gas, though, it doesn't evaporate readily when spilled, and leaves an oily residue behind. The Primus Multi-Fuel stove can burn LP (propane) gas, kerosene, white gas or unleaded automobile fuel, making it a versatile choice.

Some stoves use butane or butane/propane cartridges. Unlike white gas or kerosene stoves, butane stoves require no priming; simply turn the knob and light. Cartridges can be tricky to install, depending on stove design. Some can't be removed until the fuel is exhausted; if your cartridge is running low at the start of meal preparation, you'll have to cook until it runs out, then allow the stove to cool before changing the cartridge. Cartridge stoves don't perform well in cold weather, and non-refillable cartridges are an ecological nightmare.

Like butane stoves, propane stoves require no priming. Unlike disposable butane cartridges, the large "bulK" propane cylinders are refillable. Many hardware stores and gas stations operate bulk-cylinder exchange programs. Bring in an empty bulk cylinder and exchange it for one that has been re-filled; you just pay for the fuel and run rather than waiting to have your cylinder re-filled. Propane cylinders are bulky and heavy, so propane stoves are used mainly for base camp or car camping.

Single-burner stoves are lighter than double-burner stoves, and are the backpacker's choice. When shopping for a single-burner stove, consider stove stability and the support system for the pot. Some stoves, notably the Svea 123, are notoriously "tippy" even before you put a pot on them, although the Svea is easy to tuck away in a pack because of its streamlined design. Also consider the size of the flame ring; a large ring provides more even heat and is less likely to scorch food than a focused, torch-like flame. My Peak 1 Feather 400 has fold-out feet for stability and a wide flame ring, and weighs about 2 pounds when filled with fuel; this amount is enough for a weekend trip. The MSR single-burner stoves are even lighter; most hold a bit more fuel, but cost more.

Canoeists, especially a group of four or more, often carry a two-burner stove; the weight and bulk are worth the additional cooking capacity. These suitcase-style stoves are extremely stable, and have built-in windscreens. My Coleman 424 Dual Fuel double-burner stove weighs just under 10 pounds. Three-burner stoves are a luxury in base camp, and are good for car camping; these stoves are generally powered by bulk propane cylinders.

Avoid carrying fuel containers or stoves with built-in fuel tanks in the same pack as the food; if you have no choice, pack the food *above* the fuel in the pack. Double-bag fuel containers in plastic zipper bags to contain any fuel leaks. If your single-burner stove is fairly narrow, make a transport case by cutting off the bottoms of two 2-liter plastic pop bottles. Put the stove in one, then slip the other over the top. A padded stuff sack is another option to keep the stove from getting beat up in your pack. Two- and three-burner suitcase-style stoves need no additional protection. As shown in the photos on page 51, I tuck a cutting board, fuel bottle, and a few other items inside my two-burner stove, so there's no fuel and less gear rattling around loose in the food pack.

Practice with a new stove at home. At camp, make sure your stove is resting solidly on a stable surface before you light it; place your largest pot on it and if the stove seems tippy, set up in another spot. Clear flammable debris from the area around the stove. Never leave a burning stove unattended; don't use a camp stove inside a tent or in any poorly ventilated location. Don't re-fuel a hot stove; let it cool first. If your stove is acting funny, or making noises it usually doesn't make, turn it off and let it cool down, then check carefully to determine if there's a problem. If it is spitting fuel, shut it off immediately and don't use it until the problem can be solved. Some seasoned campers carry a few spare parts for their stoves so they can effect emergency back-country repairs.

Camp Ovens, Grills, and Other Accessories

In the old cowboy days, the camp "cookie" baked biscuits, pies, pot roasts, and cakes in a cast-iron Dutch oven; coals piled on the flat lid provided heat from the top in addition to the heat coming from the coals that the pot was sitting on. If you're not travelling with a Dutch oven, however, you can still do some real baking at camp if you use a special camp oven.

The best of these I've found is the Outback Oven. It's lightweight (about ½ pound) and portable, and comes in several sizes; it works with camp stoves that have an offset fuel tank, and can be used with care on a campfire. (The manufacturer recommends that these not be used on a stove that has a fuel tank right below the burner; trapped heat can cause the fuel tank to explode.) Baking is done in your regular camp cooking pots, or in the special pan provided with the larger model. The oven consists of a diffuser plate with riser bars, a folding "metalized" convection dome, a thermometer, and a reflector shield. It heats quickly to baking temperature, and maintains that level easily. The diffuser plate, which is set on the riser bars to elevate it off the direct heat, helps prevent scorching, and can be used without the convection dome for cooking rice, sauces, and other dishes that are prone to scorching. The convection dome isn't just for baking, either; in cold weather, it holds the heat to speed any cooking chore. Because it's so efficient, it reduces fuel consumption by a third or more. See the photos of the Outback Oven on page 52. If your local camping store doesn't have one in stock, you can find a source for these by typing "Outback Oven" into an internet search engine.

The Coleman Camp Oven shown on page 53 is an alternative when weight and bulk aren't a concern (it folds to 12" x 12" x 2", and weighs a bit over 7 pounds). Its box design allows the use of pie pans, muffin pans, and standard baking dishes, but it can only be used with a full-size camp stove. Pre-heating takes a long time, especially in cold weather. I have some friends who turn out amazing back-country multi-course meals, including homemade bread and fresh-baked desserts, with the aid of a Coleman oven.

Most campfire grates are too sooty and dirty to use like a charcoal grill for grilling steak, sausage, or fish. If you're car camping or travelling in a mobile camper, you can carry a small charcoal or propane grill. Portable, folding grill grates can be used to cook steaks and other foods over a campfire (and also work fairly well to support pots over an open fire), but these can be bulky and messy to pack along. Hanging tripod-style grates look good in theory, but tend to swing around wildly; it's very easy to accidentally dump your pot of food into the fire, ruining both your dinner *and* the fire.

You can buy expensive specialty grilling racks for fish at camping stores and gourmet shops, but these are limited to whole fish of a specific size; plus, they're bulky to tote along. **Easy Rack-Grilled Fish** (page 163) demonstrates how to use inexpensive cake-cooling racks for the same purpose. This technique works over a campfire as well as over a charcoal grill.

A folding campstove stand is a handy item if space and weight aren't at a premium. Most stands are designed to hold a two- or three-burner stove, and also provide an additional shelf for various odds and ends. As shown in the top photo on page 54, stands are great in grasslands and other areas lacking natural places to set your stove, and have the added benefit of keeping flames away from dry grass. They take up little room when folded.

Other Back-Country Kitchen Necessities

Your dishwashing kit can be as simple as a bottle of camp soap, an old dishrag, and a towel. Carry a small piece of steel wool for scorched pots if you wish, but don't use pre-soaped pads; they make too many suds for the wilderness. Detergent is bad news in lakes and streams, so even if your camp soap says it's biodegradable, you still should empty the dish water into the woods at least 150 yards from any lake or stream. Sand makes a great natural scouring agent, by the way, as does snow or pine needles. I rarely wash my cast-iron skillet during a trip; I simply wipe the inside with a paper towel while it's still warm, scratching with a spatula to remove any crusty spots, then burn the paper towel or pack it out with the garbage. The light coating of grease remaining in the skillet helps prevent rust, and I don't have any greasy water to dispose of.

Carry a tarp to rig as a kitchen fly during rainy weather. The fly also makes a good windbreak. The best plastic tarps are reinforced with fiber strands, and feature doubled edges with metal grommets for tying the tarp off. Nylon or canvas tarps are also available, and are better in cold weather because they don't become brittle like a plastic tarp (for a line of exceptional lightweight nylon tarps, check out Cooke Custom Sewing; see page 199 for contact information). Rig your tarp at an angle, so the rain will run off the back side rather than pool in an ominous well above you.

An 18" square of bridal-veil netting (see page 25) makes a fine back-country strainer. Stretch it over the top of your cooking pot and pour through it, or get someone to hold the net over a bowl. If you need to rinse freshly foraged greens or berries, put them into the netting and gather it into a bundle for rinsing; after rinsing, swing the bundle in an arc to dry the greens by centrifugal force. The net dries quickly after rinsing, and can be wadded up for storage.

A small jar of a seasoning blend comes in handy for spicing up all sorts of foods. Supermarkets carry a wide variety of seasoned salts, as well as salt-free seasoning blends. I also love Hi Mountain Jerky's Wild River Trout Seasoning for potatoes and vegetables as well as fish, and their Western Sizzle seasonings are great for all sorts of grilled meats (see page 199 for mail-order address, phone number and website URL).

Building a Campfire

At Girl Scout camp when I was a kid, we'd sit around the campfire every night telling spooky stories. We *had* to build the fire as large as possible, to keep the ghosts away! When the coals were burned down to glowing embers, we'd scuttle off to our sleeping bags; the counselors stayed up until the embers died, enjoying the peace and solitude that can only come after putting 30 squirming girls to bed. And if the counselors had been in the mood for a midnight snack, the fire would have been at the perfect stage.

The proper cooking fire is a small one, based on a bed of coals. The coals provide even, steady heat, and help ignite fuel that you add to the fire. Before putting flame to tinder, have all your wood gathered and cut or broken to the proper size. You'll need *tinder* to get the fire started: fallen bark chips, tiny twigs, and dead evergreen sprays work well. Dry leaves and dead grass also work, but burn up quickly. (We usually carry a few pieces of Georgia fatwood, available from L.L. Bean; this amazing wood will get even wet fuel burning.) *Kindling* is the next size, and consists of twigs as thick as a pencil, up to the thickness of your thumb. *Fuel* is anything larger; for cooking, gather a good supply of smaller fuel, ranging from carrot-sized up to wrist-sized. Save the logs that are the size of your arm for a true campfire after you're done cooking.

Gather only dead, dry wood. Never cut boughs from a standing tree or bush, even if the wood appears dead; never peel bark from a tree. Dry wood obviously burns a whole lot better than wet wood; head into the thickest part of the forest and scout around under dense overhead canopy to find dry wood after a rainstorm. Modern ethics dictate that you gather wood away from your campsite, and in the woods a distance from the shoreline of a lake or river, to keep the campsite and shoreline as natural looking as possible.

Federal or state campgrounds have fire grates at designated campsites; see the photo of a typical U.S. Forest Service grate on the facing page (taken in Minnesota's Boundary Waters Canoe Area). These supply a place to set your cooking pots, and some provide a degree of fire containment. If camping in an area that has no grates, you'll need to rig up some rocks to act as a fire ring, and use the rocks or a portable grate to support your pots. Some wilderness enthusiasts recommend that you turn over the fire-blackened rocks as you're breaking camp, or throw them into the woods so they won't be seen by the next people to pass through. Use your judgement on this; it makes little sense to do this if the area is likely to be used by additional campers, because they'll end up blackening yet more rocks if they don't happen to come across yours.

Don't take rocks from a stream or lake for your fire ring. Not only will this cause erosion in the streambed or lakeshore, but internal moisture may cause the rock to explode from the heat of the fire. Dry rocks from the forest are a safer choice. Those blackened rocks around the fire pit have already withstood the test; there's another reason for leaving them in place around the fire ring.

The safest fire is one built on a base of solid rock or gravel. Clear away all burnable debris around the fire site, and set up a ring of rocks as a fire barrier and windscreen. Have piles of tinder, kindling, and fuel nearby, but not so close to the fire that they'll ignite accidentally. Make a small pile of tinder, and lay a few pieces of small kindling across it. Light the tinder; when the fire catches, begin adding kindling, a piece at a time. If the flame threatens to go

A pleasant back-country scene: a skillet of
Potatoes with Bacon and Onions *(page 104) shares the*
fire with a pot of coffee, while a foil-wrapped packet of Herbed
Fish and Carrots in Foil *(page 161) cooks directly on the coals.*

49

A home-assembled cookware kit. **Top photo:** *(A) Scout cookset consisting of cup, small pot with lid, frying pan with folding handle, lid that doubles as a plate or bowl. (B) Dish towel and dishrag. (C) Cast-iron skillet, with forks, stirring spoon, knife, vegetable peeler. (D) Pot holder. (E) Hand lotion, salt-and-pepper shaker, camp soap. (F) Speckleware plates. (G) Drawstring stuff sack (triple layers: plastic sandwiched between two layers of canvas, sized to fit assembled cook kit).* **Middle photo:** *Assembled scout cookset inside skillet, nestled next to utensils and plastic bottles.* **Bottom left photo:** *Plates upside-down over cookset, cushioned by dish towel and potholder.* **Bottom right photo:** *The assembled cookware kit in the drawstring sack; string wrapped around handle and tied off to secure.*

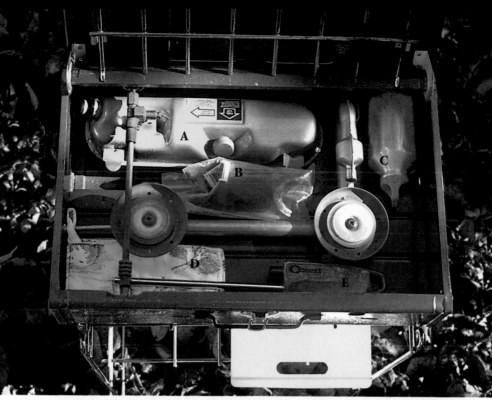

Above: Piezoelectric lighters are great; you don't have to worry about wet matches. And if the stove is already warm, your hand doesn't have to go near the hot grate.

Tuck miscellaneous items into the odd spaces of your box-type stove, to stay organized and also conserve packing space. **Top photo:** Coleman 2-burner stove with (A) fuel tank, (B) fuel filter funnel in plastic bag to keep it clean, (C) spare fuel canister made of spun aluminum, (D) potholder, and (E) piezoelectric lighter (see small photo at bottom right). Other items might include a small kitchen knife in a sheath, some matches in a waterproof container, or perhaps a small spatula. **Bottom left photo:** A small cutting board fits neatly over the other items, and the grate folds down over the cutting board. The cutting board is really handy at camp, and prevents you from dulling your knife by using a metal plate or pot lid as a cutting board. You may have to buy a larger cutting board and cut it to fit your stove; it can be hard to find really small ones like this.

Photos at left:
Outback Oven
(shown with Peak 1 camping cookset, on two-burner stove; also works well on a single-burner stove)

The Outback Oven's diffuser plate (A) helps spread heat evenly. An essential part of this back-country oven system, the diffuser also works well as a stand-alone unit to eliminate hot spots, a common cause of scorching and burned food.

A special flame-resistant convection dome (B) traps hot air; its special "metalized" interior reflects heat back into the cooking pot. The provided thermometer (C) monitors cooking temperature.

Left: The Outback Oven in use.

Below: Close-up of thermometer.

Other Camp Baking Techniques

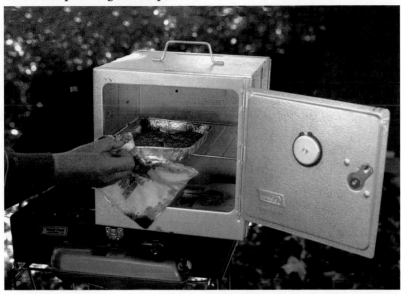

The Coleman Camp Oven is suitable for use on two- or three-burner stoves. With it, you can use standard baking pans, muffin tins, and pie plates. It is too bulky and heavy for lightweight camping. Pictured: **Blueberry Scones in a Camp Oven** *(page 63).*

A cast-iron frying pan can be used as an oven to bake over open coals. Place the food to be baked (in this case, **Campfire-Baked Yeast Bread**, *page 76-77) in a pan that fits inside the skillet. Scatter a half dozen black roofer's nails* or small, dry pebbles inside the skillet; this creates an air space to prevent the bottom of the food from burning. Place the smaller pan on top of the nails, then cover the skillet with a lid, allowing room for expansion of the baked goods if appropriate. Place the skillet over the coals; in these photos, the skillet is resting on some larger logs, but a grate works just as well. Bake, rotating the pan occasionally, until done.*

*Don't use galvanized nails, as they emit toxic fumes when heated.

Many campsites are primitive, and lack picnic tables or other convenient places to place the stove, pots, and other back-country kitchen items. A folding stove stand, like the one shown in the top photo, can be a great help. This model, for a two-burner cookstove, has two shelves: one for the stove, and another below for other items. It folds flat for storage and transport. This photo was taken on the high desert plains of western Wyoming; as you can see, the stove should be used above ground level to prevent starting a grassfire. Sometimes you can adapt a campsite feature to suit your needs. In the bottom photo, the author is shown cooking on a two-burner stove that is resting on a Forest Service campfire grate. When this photo was taken, there were forest fires burning in Minnesota's Boundary Waters Canoe Area (where the photo was taken), making open fires dangerous; all cooking was done on campstoves, and the fire grates became useful as places to set up the stove.

A vacuum sealer, like the FoodSaver shown here, seals ingredients in a waterproof plastic bag. Because all the air is removed during vacuum-sealing, the finished package takes up less room than the same ingredients packed into a zipper-style plastic bag. The plastic bags used in vacuum-packing are fairly heavy and also heat-resistant, so you can use them to rehydrate dried foods in boiling water (see page 155). Shown are the ingredients for **Minnesota Green Bean Casserole** *(page 109). The sliced almonds (A), powdered milk (B) and purchased sauce mix (C) will be packed into the small plastic bag (D) and sealed with the shown twist-tie. This small bag will then be sealed in a vacuum bag with the dried onions (E), dried French-cut green beans (F) and dried mushroom pieces (G). The finished pack is shown in the inset photo.*

Vacuum-packing is also a good way to carry small items such as emergency medical supplies (photo below, at right). Don't put everyday supplies in a vacuum bag, though; once the bag is opened, it will be harder to close up than a zipper-style bag.

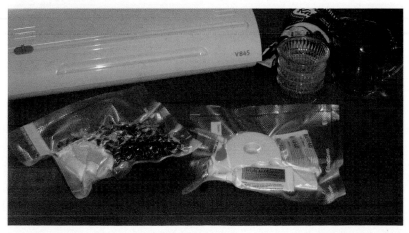

Campfire Cooking Techniques

As shown in the photo at left, you can cook some foods over a campfire with no special utensils. Here, the author is baking **Italian Stick Bread** *(page 72-73), while a side of lake trout cooks on a split log (***Planked Fish,** *page 165).*

Below: *To make cleanup easier, rub liquid camp soap or dish soap on the outside of your cooking pots (left) before cooking over an open fire. The soot will wipe off easily afterward (right).*

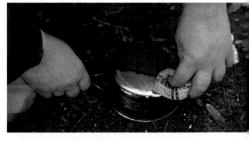

How to Wrap Food in Foil for Campfire Cooking (The "Drugstore Wrap")

Place the food in the center of the foil, then bring the long edges together on top. Fold the long edge over once, then continue roll-folding until it's snug against the food. There should be several inches at each open end that are clear of food.

Roll the ends in tightly, compressing the food and making sure that each end has at least three complete rolls. This prevents the juices from escaping during cooking, and also gives you something to hold onto when turning the packet.

out, blow gently on it, then toss on a bit more tinder. Once the kindling is burning, begin adding small fuel; continue in this manner, working up to the largest pieces, until you have a bed of coals with an active but small fire. Keep the fire burning as long as you need it by adding thumb- to carrot-sized fuel.

For simple tasks like boiling water, this is all the fire you'll need. For longer cooking methods like frying fish or potatoes, roasting whole vegetables, or making stew, a bed of very hot coals works better than an active flame, and requires less tending. To build a campfire for sustained cooking, add larger pieces of wood, up to the thickness of your wrist, to your small fire; a campfire in an oblong shape works best. When the fire has burned down to a bed of large coals, begin cooking over one half; keep an active fire going in the other half, and shovel more coals into the cooking half as needed. If the fire area is too small for such a scheme, you'll have to tend your smaller bed of coals more frequently, adding additional carrot-sized fuel as needed to keep the fire going.

Portable grates from camping-supply stores range from the 12½" x 6½" model favored by backpackers because of its size and light weight (13 ounces), to the 23" x 12" heavy-duty model weighing about 6 pounds. Most have fold-in legs. Choose one with longer legs; short legs put your pot too close to the heat and make it difficult to tend the fire without upsetting the grate. Cake-cooling racks, sold at department stores, can be used to support pots over a fire, although these are sometimes flimsier than camping grates and must be propped on rocks over the fire because they have no legs. E-Z Camping makes a portable 12" x 16" *camp grill,* which could serve as a grate to hold pots, or as an actual grill to cook steaks or fish; it's a nice idea, although the grate is very heavy.

General Camp Cooking Techniques

Cooking at home is fairly predictable: the stove won't suddenly "go out" in the middle of meal preparation, you can vary the heat intensity with precision, and you've got four burners to use at one time. Camp-stove cookery isn't so straightforward, but there are a few things you can do to improve your results.

Heat loss due to wind or cold weather may be the number one problem in camp cooking. Cover your pot when boiling or simmering to retain heat. The Outback Oven (page 46) can be used to help retain heat in everyday camp cooking. A windscreen helps prevent heat loss by convection, and also prevents the stove or campfire from being blown out. Some stoves feature a built-in windscreen; separate windscreens are available at camping stores. Use natural features of the campsite as a windbreak; for example, set up your stove or fire pit on the lee side of a boulder pile. Your kitchen fly also serves as a windbreak, although strong winds have a way of curling around the fly. Don't place your stove too close to your fly, or to anything else that's flammable for that matter.

Scorching is another common problem in camp cooking. Rice, stews or thick sauces, and dishes with milk or cheese in them scorch easily. Quality cookware for home use has a thick bottom, which spreads heat evenly; most camping cookware is made of thin metal, for lighter weight. As mentioned in the stove discussion on pages 44-46, a large flame ring on your stove helps distribute the heat evenly, but even with this type of stove, you'll still have hot spots. The best solution is to move the pots around on the burner or campfire grate frequently; stirring also helps prevent sticking and burning. A diffuser plate, like the one that comes with the Outback Oven (page 52), spreads the heat evenly, reducing the need for frequent rotating and stirring.

Another challenge in camp cooking is making the best use of a single-burner stove. The best advice is to prepare the longest-cooking food first, then set it aside in a warm place while you prepare the quicker-cooking food. Many recipes in this book call for bringing a mix to the boil, then removing it from the heat to stand for a time before final cooking. This technique frees up the stove to prepare another dish, and also saves fuel. In cold or windy weather, place the covered pot in your sleeping bag during the standing time to preserve the heat. See page 156 for single-burner meal management tips.

Cooking Over an Open Fire

The heat provided by a campfire is somewhat uneven, so be sure to move your pots around occasionally to prevent scorching and ensure even cooking. Sometimes, you'll want to "turn up the heat" on a campfire (perhaps to crisp up some fried fish, or get a new pot of water boiling). Simply add a dry pine spray, cluster of small twigs, or a few pieces of dry bark to the coals right under the pan; it will be the same as turning a stove burner to high.

The exterior of your cookware will become blackened with soot from cooking over a campfire. In spite of the fact that water boils faster in a black pot, I prefer to keep my pots clean. A coating of camp soap or dish soap on the outsides of the pot (see photos on page 56) makes the soot easy to remove, saving some arduous scrubbing. If you prefer to avoid soaping, carry your pots in a plastic bag to avoid fouling everything in your pack with soot.

Whole vegetables roasted directly on or over the coals develop a wonderful, nutty flavor. Roast hard-skinned squash like acorn and buttercup with no pretreatment. Soak corn-on-the-cob in water before putting on or over coals; don't follow any advice you may see about peeling back the husks to remove the silk prior to roasting (see full instructions on page 113). Unpeeled potatoes can be roasted unwrapped, although the skins may be charred beyond the edible stage; wrap potatoes in foil before roasting if you want to eat the skins.

Some camper's cookbooks tell how to concoct all sorts of utensils with foil, from skillets to cake pans to build-on-the-spot ovens. To me, this is a bit silly, and seems like a bad idea from an ecological perspective. The sooty, messy foil needs to be packed out with the garbage; it doesn't burn well in the campfire. (If you do burn your foil, sift through the ashes to pick out any foil pieces that remain unburned.) I occasionally roast foil-wrapped packets of foods directly in the coals or on the grate; this makes more sense to me than constructing flimsy single-use implements that don't work very well. See pages 112, 135, 140, 161, 162, 181, 182 and 186 for foil-packet recipes.

There are two keys to successful foil roasting. The foil must be thick enough to resist puncturing by coals, rocks, and rough grates; and the packet must be folded properly to seal in juices (see photos on page 56). Heavy-duty foil works best; if you're using regular-weight foil, use twice the length needed and double it over. Width is important, too; 18" wide foil works better than the more common 12" wide foil. The extra width provides enough working area to make the proper folds. Rather than carrying a whole roll of foil, I tear off pieces of the proper size for the cooking I'll be doing, then fold them into squares that tuck into the food pack. If the dish requires dry herbs, I'll sprinkle them into the foil before folding so I don't have to carry them separately.

Place the foil packet on a grate above the campfire, or directly on the coals. If the packet is on the coals, flip and rotate it frequently to avoid burning, but be careful not to puncture the foil as you turn it. Use tongs or a long stick to move the packet around. It's better to let a foil-wrapped packet cook a little too long than to unwrap it too soon, as it's hard to re-wrap the packet properly.

About Bears: A Final Word

It's a fact: bears are attracted to food (and also to suntan lotion, motor oil, bait, toothpaste … anything that smells). They will swim from shore to an island, or from island to island, in search of food; they've been known to hang around trails waiting for hikers or hunters to come by. Once a bear finds food at a campsite, it will come back to the same site again. Bear problems are worse in some years than others, and vary from region to region. Black bears are generally less dangerous than grizzlies, but still need to be taken seriously.

Common wisdom is to suspend your food packs and anything else that smells between trees so the bear can't get at them. Many campers feel this is not as effective as it used to be; especially at well-used campsites, bears learn which trees campers use, and also learn that a few swipes sever the rope, bringing the packs down. Some seasoned campers place the packs underneath an overturned canoe with the cookware piled on top to act as a "bear alarm;" others claim that a bear won't hesitate to chew a hole through your Kevlar canoe, and then you're "up the creek without a paddle" (or worse, with a punctured canoe). I've read of veteran campers who simply place the food packs in the forest, well off any paths; they believe the bears won't look for food in such an unaccustomed spot, and claim great success with the method.

I think the best course of action is to talk with local outfitters, the Forest Service, or natural-resources agencies for an update on bear activity and effective prevention measures in your camping area. Sometimes, a campsite where bear activity has been a problem will be posted as closed; respect that closing! Keep a clean camp, so bears have no reason to return should they stop by. Avoid a campsite that has obviously been the site of a bear visit. Some campsites in known bear areas are equipped with bear lockers, and these are great. If a bear does come into camp while you're there, make noise to scare it away, but don't throw anything directly at it. If worse comes to worst, give up

your packs rather than fight a bear; we're simply not equipped for battle as well as they are.

A steel bear locker in Minnesota's Voyageurs National Park

Chapter Four

Breakfast

Nutritional studies tell us that breakfast is the most important meal of the day, and nowhere is that more true than in the back country. The energy boost provided by a good breakfast will keep you going throughout the morning without fatigue, cramps, or loss of energy.

Some traditional breakfast classics, as well as some new dishes sure to become favorites, appear on the next few pages. In addition, you may want to consider **Miniature Cinnamon-Nut Rolls** (page 87), **Bacon-Mushroom-Tomato Quiche** (page 133), **Paradell** (page 180), or **English Muffin Pies** (page 182). **Hash Browns** (page 98) or **Potato Pancakes** (page 99) also make a great accompaniment to a breakfast of fresh-caught fish or simple bacon and eggs.

 ## Southwestern Omelette

2 or 3 servings

A flavor-filled all-in-one breakfast that's sure to get you going.

 Place in a small plastic bag and seal with a twist-tie:
 ½ cup powdered egg
 1½ teaspoons chili powder blend
 ¼ teaspoon salt

Combine in quart plastic zipper bag:
 ¼ cup crumbled dried pressed beef slices
 4 teaspoons dried diced green bell pepper
 1 tablespoon dried onion flakes
 2 teaspoons dried celery slices
  The small sealed bag with the powdered egg

Carry separately:
  Clarified butter, oil or bacon drippings for frying

At camp:

Remove the small bag with the powdered egg and set aside. In medium bowl, combine ¾ cup water with meat/vegetable mixture; let stand 15 to 20 minutes. Blend powdered egg into meat/vegetable mixture. Fry over medium heat in lightly greased skillet, stirring and turning occasionally, until eggs are set, about 5 minutes.

French Toast Mix

Carry this mix in your pack until you have some sliced bread that is going stale, then make this easy breakfast. It's great served with warm **Maple-Stewed Apples** *(see recipe below), syrup or jam.*

Combine in gallon plastic zipper bag:

⅓ cup powdered egg
2 tablespoons nonfat dry milk powder
1 teaspoon Butter Buds
½ teaspoon sugar
⅛ teaspoon cinnamon
⅛ teaspoon nutmeg
⅛ teaspoon salt

Carry separately:

4 regular-sized slices of whole wheat or other firm bread
Clarified butter or oil for frying

At camp:

Add ½ cup cold water to egg mixture in bag. Seal bag, leaving about half-full of air. Bunch up the top of the bag, and shake vigorously to blend the egg mixture with the water; if there are lumps, knead the bag to smooth out.

Place two slices of bread in the bag side-by-side. Place two more slices on top of the first two. Re-seal the bag, and gently rotate the bag, separating the bread pieces to allow the egg mixture to get between the slices, until all pieces have been coated with egg mixture. Let the bag stand, turning occasionally, until the bread slices have absorbed all of the egg mixture, about 5 minutes.

Heat frying pan or griddle over medium heat; grease with clarified butter. Cook the French toast slices until golden brown; turn and cook second side.

Maple-Stewed Apples

Variable servings

This simple recipe can be adapted to any number of campers. Serve over hot cereal, pancakes, or French toast, or alongside eggs, bacon, and toast.

Carry separately:

Dried apple slices, whole or cut up (1 cup for 3 servings)
Maple syrup (1 tablespoon for 3 servings)
Butter Buds or butter (½ teaspoon Butter Buds or 1½ teaspoons butter for 3 servings)

At camp:

Measure the amount of apples you want to prepare, then bring half that measure of water to a boil (for example, use ½ cup water for 1 cup dried apple slices). Add the apples. Stir in maple syrup in the ratio of 1 tablespoon syrup per cup of dried apples. Return to boiling. Reduce heat; simmer, stirring occasionally, for about 3 minutes. Cover and remove from heat. Let stand 5 or 10 minutes. Stir in Butter Buds or a pat of butter, using the ratio of ½ teaspoon Butter Buds or 1½ teaspoons butter per cup of dried apples.

Blueberry Scones on a Campstove

3 or 4 servings

It's pretty hard to turn out a proper scone at a primitive campsite. But these come close! Fair warning: these require about 15 minutes of undivided attention from the cook, or perhaps from a hungry helper.

Make the scone mix:

1	cup all-purpose flour
¼	cup room-temperature shortening
3	tablespoons sugar
2	tablespoons nonfat dry milk powder
2	teaspoons baking powder
2	teaspoons Butter Buds
¼	teaspoon salt

Follow the mixing instructions for biscuit mix on page 78 to cut together the mix. This recipe makes about 1¾ cups mix, enough for two batches of scones.

Place in a small plastic bag and seal with a twist-tie:

4	teaspoons sugar
½	teaspoon cinnamon

Combine in pint plastic zipper bag:

⅓ cup dried blueberries (about 2 ounces)
Half of the scone mix recipe (about ⅞ cup)
The small sealed bag with the cinnamon-sugar

Carry separately:

Clarified butter for greasing the pan
A little flour for dusting skillet and forming scones

At camp:

Butter the inside of a small skillet. Sprinkle 1 teaspoon flour inside the skillet; shake to distribute. If the skillet has a fire-proof lid that can be clamped on tightly (see scout cookset, page 43), butter and flour the inside of the lid.

In a medium bowl, combine 3 tablespoons cold water with the blueberry-scone mix; stir with fork just until mix is moistened. (If it seems too dry, add a few drops of cold water to the mix. Don't use too much water or stir longer than necessary; the scones will be tough.) Flour your hands, and form dough into flat, round biscuits, shaped to fit snugly in a single layer in your skillet. Place the scones in the prepared skillet. Cover with the lid or a piece of foil.

Place the skillet over a low flame. Cook for about 2 minutes, then begin rotating the pan frequently so the heat doesn't concentrate in one spot. If the scones seem to be burning, remove the pan from the heat for a minute, then return to the heat and continue rotating frequently. After about 8 minutes total, flip the entire skillet over if it has a clamp-on lid; otherwise, remove the foil, turn the scones over, re-cover the pan and return to the heat. Cook for another 5 minutes, rotating frequently. Check the scones for doneness; when properly cooked, they will be browned and slightly springy to the touch. If they are not quite done, flip if necessary and return to the heat for another 2 to 5 minutes. Cool slightly and sprinkle with the cinnamon-sugar mixture before serving.

Blueberry Scones in a Campfire

3 or 4 servings

If you have a campfire, it's easier to cook the scones in the fire than on your campstove. Wrap the entire skillet/lid in foil; the foil will hold the skillet and lid together, and will also make skillet clean-up easier. Or, use two small baking pans that are the same size as each other; wrap in foil as described, or clamp together with four metal "binder clips" sold at office-supply stores (used to clamp many sheets of paper together; they're black, with silver handles that fold back). Smaller "disposable" foil pans work for this also; clamp together or cover with more foil.

Follow the mixing and forming instructions for Blueberry Scones on a Campstove (facing page). If your pan is going directly into the fire with no foil over-wrap, rub the outside with liquid soap after you clamp it together; the soap coating will make it easy to wash off the soot.

Cook the scones over a bed of coals, not a blazing fire. Push a fairly thin bed of coals off to the side of the fire (this will cool the coals down slightly, so you won't be as likely to burn the scones). Place the clamped-together or wrapped pan on top of the small bed of coals. Shovel some more coals on top of the pan. Let it cook for about 15 minutes, then remove the pan from the coals. Open the pan carefully to prevent ashes from getting into the pan. If the scones aren't done, re-seal and return the pan to the fire for a few minutes. Cool slightly and sprinkle with the cinnamon-sugar mixture before serving.

Blueberry Scones in a Camp Oven *(photo page 53)*   3 or 4 servings

This recipe works well with any camp oven (page 46). Butter and flour a medium pot; follow the mixing and forming instructions for Blueberry Scones on a Campstove (facing page). Pre-heat camp oven if necessary.* You don't need to cover the pan when you're baking scones in a camp oven. Bake until golden brown, 15 to 25 minutes. Cool slightly and sprinkle with the cinnamon-sugar mixture before serving.

*The Outback Oven requires no pre-heating. Box-style camp ovens should be pre-heated to 300°F-350°F before mixing and baking.

Hot Cereal with Fruit

2 or 3 servings

This hearty mix already has the milk and sugar in it.

Combine in pint plastic zipper bag:
- ½   cup granola
- ⅓   cup quick-cooking oatmeal or multi-grain cereal
- ⅓   cup chopped dried fruit
- ¼   cup nonfat dry milk powder
- 2   tablespoons brown sugar
- ½   teaspoon salt

At camp:

In medium pot, boil 1 cup water. Add mix. Cook for 5 minutes or until oatmeal is done, stirring frequently to prevent sticking.

Creamy Breakfast Rice

2 or 3 servings

When we were kids, my mom used to pour warm milk over leftover cooked rice; we'd sprinkle it with cinnamon-sugar and raisins, and enjoy a different kind of hot cereal. This recipe brings back those memories to me, and is great on a cold morning in camp. Use any kind of dried fruit you like; it's especially good with a mix of dried peaches and apples.

Combine in pint plastic zipper bag:
- ½ cup medium-grain rice (you can use regular converted or long-grain rice if you prefer; it cooks more quickly, but isn't as creamy)
- 2 tablespoons diced dried fruit, or raisins, or currants
- 2 tablespoons chopped pecans, walnuts, or almonds
- 2 tablespoons nonfat dry milk powder
- 1 tablespoon brown sugar
  A good pinch of each: cinnamon, nutmeg and salt

Carry separately:
  Butter or margarine for serving, optional

At camp:

In medium pot, boil 1¼ cups water. Add mix; stir thoroughly. Cover and remove from heat; let stand 10 minutes. Return to boiling. Reduce heat and simmer, stirring frequently, for about 10 minutes; if mixture becomes dry before rice is cooked, add a little additional water. When rice is almost tender, cover and remove from heat; let stand, covered, 5 minutes or longer. Top each serving with a pat of butter for extra flavor.

Grits with Egg and Cheese

Per serving

*An easy breakfast that's surprisingly hearty and filling. Pack individually bagged portions in a larger plastic bag as directed in **Hot Breakfast Nuggets,** opposite, or combine two or more portions in a single bag.*

Place in a small plastic bag and seal with a twist-tie:
- 3 tablespoons quick-cooking grits (not instant grits)
- 1 teaspoon shelf-stable grated Parmesan cheese
- ⅛ teaspoon Butter Buds
- ⅛ teaspoon salt
  Dash cayenne pepper, optional

Carry separately:
- 1 whole raw egg

At camp:

For 1 or 2 servings, use a small pot; for 3 or more servings, a medium to large pot works best. A diffuser plate (page 58) helps prevent scorching. Boil 1 cup water per serving. Add mix. Cook, stirring frequently, for 3 minutes; mixture will be somewhat thickened. Add one egg per serving. Cover pot and reduce heat to simmer. Cook for 2 minutes. Remove from heat and let stand another minute; yolks should still be runny.

Hot Breakfast Nuggets

1 serving per bag

For a delightful change-of-pace from traditional hot cereals, try this easy recipe. Simply stir boiling water into the mix, and it's ready to eat. For just a few servings, it's easiest to measure individual portions into light plastic bags. If your group is large, or you want to carry a number of servings, try the bulk recipe below.

Place in a small plastic bag and seal with a twist-tie:

½	cup Grape Nuts or other wheat-barley nugget cereal
1	tablespoon plus 1 teaspoon nonfat dry milk powder
1	heaping tablespoon diced dried fruit (I use Sunmaid Fruit Bits)
½	teaspoon sugar
⅛	teaspoon Butter Buds

Combine ingredients for one serving in a lightweight plastic bag; seal with a twist tie.

Place sealed bags into a heavier plastic bag or other container for transport.

At camp:
Empty contents of one bag into a serving bowl or large cup. Add ½ cup boiling water; stir well.

Hot Breakfast Nuggets – Bulk Recipe

10 servings

To carry this recipe in bulk, pack it in two parts: the cereal and fruit in one bag, and the powdered ingredients in another. Otherwise, the powdered ingredients sink to the bottom of the bag with the cereal and fruit, and can't be portioned out correctly.

In heavyweight plastic bag or doubled bread bags, combine:

5	cups Grape Nuts or other wheat-barley nugget cereal
¾	cup diced dried fruit (I use Sunmaid Fruit Bits)

In smaller plastic bag, combine, shake well and seal with a twist-tie:

⅞	cup nonfat dry milk powder
5	tablespoons sugar
1¼	teaspoons Butter Buds

At camp:
Place a heaping ½ cup of cereal/fruit mix into a serving bowl or large cup; add a scant 2 tablespoons of the powdered mix. Add ½ cup boiling water; stir well.

Banana-Buttermilk Pancakes

About 8 pancakes

A nice change-of-pace from regular pancakes that's sure to be a favorite with banana lovers. Bacon is particularly suited as a side dish.

½ cup dried banana slices

In food processor or blender, chop banana slices until the largest chunks are no larger than corn kernels. Place in a small plastic bag and seal with a twist-tie.

Combine in quart plastic zipper bag:
- ¾ cup all-purpose flour
- ¼ cup powdered egg
- 2 tablespoons dry buttermilk powder
- 2 teaspoons sugar
- ½ teaspoon baking powder
- ¼ teaspoon nutmeg
- The small sealed bag with the chopped banana

Carry separately:
- Oil for frying
- Syrup, jam, or **Brown Sugar Syrup Mix** (page 68), optional

At camp:

In small pan, combine chopped banana with ¾ cup water. Bring to a boil. Cook, stirring frequently, until mixture thickens to the consistency of oatmeal, about 5 minutes. Remove from heat; let cool 5 or 10 minutes. Stir in ½ cup cold water. Combine banana mixture with dry ingredients in a bowl; stir just until moist. If batter is too thick, add a little additional water. Pour batter by scant ¼ cupfuls onto hot, lightly oiled griddle or frying pan; when surface begins to bubble, flip and cook second side. Serve with syrup or jam.

How to Pack Commercial Pancake Mix for Camping

There are so many interesting pancake mixes available that it seems unnecessary to concoct your own mix for standard pancakes. Re-package any mix with nonfat dry milk powder and powdered egg to replace the fresh milk and fresh eggs that are called for on the package directions. Here's how to figure out the additional dry ingredients.

Measure the amount of mix that you will want to prepare at one meal into a quart plastic zipper bag. Next, look at the chart on the package. For each egg called for in the chart, add ¼ cup powdered egg; you'll need to increase the water by just under ¼ cup per ¼ cup of egg powder added. For each cup of milk called for in the chart, add ¼ cup of nonfat dry milk powder; you'll need to increase the water by about ¾ cup per ¼ cup of dry milk powder added. Calculate the new amount of water needed, and write this on the bag.

At camp:

Measure water as calculated. Add most, but not all, of the water to the bag with the mix. Seal the bag, and shake well to mix. If the mixture is too thick, add the additional water as necessary until the desired consistency is reached.

Egg-in-a-Basket

When I was a little girl, my Uncle Joe came to live with us briefly after serving in the Korean war. He used to fix these for my sister and me as a special treat. They're still one of my favorite breakfasts, and adapt easily to the camper's menu.

Carry separately (per serving):

   1   slice bread
   1   teaspoon clarified butter or margarine
   1   whole raw egg
       Salt and pepper to taste

At camp:

Cut a hole, about 1½" in diameter, in the center of the bread slice (my uncle used to cut the hole by using a small juice glass as a "cookie cutter"). In skillet, melt half the butter; fry the bread slice until one side is golden brown. With spatula, temporarily remove the bread from the skillet, then melt the remaining butter. Return the bread to the skillet, browned side up; at the same time, add the cut-out circle of bread to the skillet so it will brown also. Carefully break the egg into the hole in the center of the bread. Salt and pepper to taste. Cook over medium heat until the bottom is firmly set. Use a spatula to flip the bread and egg; then, flip the small circle to brown the other side. Cook until the second side is set; the yolk should still be runny. When serving, place the browned circle on top of the egg in the hole.

The egg added to the already-browned side of the bread

The finished Egg-in-a-Basket, with some bacon and a few orange quarters

Apple-Flavored Syrup Mix   Enough mix for about 3½ cups syrup

If you don't want to carry real maple syrup for your pancakes, French toast or hot cereal, you can make "imitation" syrup from dry mixes. I've heard of such a mix that supposedly produces a maple-flavored syrup substitute, but I've never seen it at the camping stores. I came up with two make-at-home mixes that taste pretty good in the back country.

    1   cup brown sugar
    ⅓   cup white sugar
    2   tablespoons Butter Buds
    1   package (3.5 ounces) instant applesauce mix (I use Richmoor)
Combine all ingredients in a food processor or blender; process until well blended and free of lumps. (If you don't have a food processor or blender, you can place the ingredients in a quart jar, cover, and shake well; it's not quite as thorough, but gets the job done.) Store the mix in a glass jar. When you're packing for a trip, measure ¼ cup per batch into a plastic bag or small container; you may need to break up clumps of sugar before measuring.

At camp:

In a small pot, boil ⅓ cup water. Add ¼ cup mix; return to boiling, stirring constantly to blend. Cook for about a minute. Cool slightly before serving. This will make just under ½ cup of syrup.

Brown Sugar Syrup Mix   Enough mix for about 2½ cups syrup

This makes a syrup substitute that is more watery and thin than the Apple-Flavored Syrup *above.*

    ⅔   cup brown sugar
    ⅓   cup white sugar
    1   tablespoon Butter Buds
Combine all ingredients in a food processor or blender; process until well blended and free of lumps. (If you don't have a food processor or blender, you can place the ingredients in a quart jar, cover, and shake well.) Store the mix in a glass jar. When you're packing for a trip, measure ¼ cup per batch into a plastic bag or small container; you may need to break up clumps of sugar before measuring.

At camp:

In a small pot, boil ⅓ cup water. Add ¼ cup mix; return to boiling, stirring constantly to blend. Cook for about a minute. Cool slightly before serving. This will make just under ½ cup of syrup.

Birds' Nests

This is a "social-camping" recipe, suited to a relaxed day with friends or family. If you've been up early fishing, these make a great brunch served with fried fish and fresh fruit. Or, accompany these with bacon or breakfast sausages. Note: this recipe requires a box-style camp oven.

Place in a small plastic bag and seal with a twist-tie:
  ¾   cup Italian-style bread crumbs* (I use Progresso brand)

Carry separately:
  2   tablespoons butter or margarine
  5   whole raw eggs

Special utensils needed:
  4   individual foil cupcake cups, or small cupcake pan

At camp:

Pre-heat box-style camp oven to 300°F-325°F. While oven is heating, prepare the Birds' Nests. Place crumbs in medium bowl. In small saucepan, melt butter. Drizzle butter over the crumbs while tossing with a fork to mix. Make a small "well" in the middle of the crumb mixture; add one egg to the well. Beat with fork, incorporating as few crumbs as possible. When egg is reasonably well-beaten, use fork to mix well with crumbs. Reserving about 4 teaspoons crumb mixture for garnish, divide mixture evenly among foil cups. Press firmly into bottom and up sides of cups, making a crust that is about ⅛" thick along the sides. Set aside until oven is ready.

When oven is pre-heated, carefully drop one room-temperature egg** into each prepared cup. Divide remaining crumbs evenly to top each of the eggs. Place cups into pre-heated oven. Bake until whites are just set; yolks should still be runny. Check for doneness by quickly removing a cup from the oven; re-close oven immediately. When done, the white will no longer be clear, and will be moderately firm; if the white jiggles when the cup is tapped, the egg isn't done. Total cooking time will vary, depending on camp oven, but should be 10 to 20 minutes.

Birds' Nests can be unmolded onto individual plates to serve, or can be eaten directly out of individual foil cups.

*If you prefer, use any seasoned bread crumb mix in place of the Italian bread crumbs.

**Eggs will cook more quickly if they're at room temperature. To bring cold eggs to room temperature, place them for about 10 minutes in a bowl of water that feels warm to the touch, and let them stand while you prepare the crumb crust.

Breakfast Tortilla Roll-Ups

2 servings; easily doubled

Whether you're car-camping and have access to all fresh ingredients, or are backpacking and using only lightweight, mostly dried foods, you can fix these tasty Mexican-inspired roll-ups with the directions below. Fresh fruit is a natural accompaniment. If you are planning on a strenuous day, or if it will be a long time until lunch, a side dish of **Frijoles Refritos** *(page 141) provides extra starch and protein.*

Place in a small plastic bag and seal with a twist-tie:

- ½ teaspoon chili powder blend
- ⅛ teaspoon salt
  A pinch of crumbled dried oregano leaves

Combine in freezer-weight pint plastic zipper bag:

- ⅓ cup dried mixed red, yellow and green bell pepper strips
- 3 tablespoons dried cooked, crumbled bulk Italian or chorizo* sausage
- 1 tablespoon dried celery slices (preferably de-stringed; see page 32)
- 1 teaspoon dried onion flakes
  The small bag with the spices

Carry separately:

- 2 flour tortillas, 8" diameter
- 2 teaspoons clarified butter or margarine
- 2 whole raw eggs, or ⅔ cup dried powdered egg
- 1 ounce co-jack or other cheese, or ¼ cup grated
- 2 tablespoons salsa, or 2 packets of salsa from a fast-food restaurant, or a portion of **Camper's Salsa** (page 184)

At camp:

Remove small bag of spices and set aside. Add enough boiling water to zipper bag to just cover vegetables, about ¾ cup (see page 155). If using dried salsa, mix it in a small bowl or cup with a few tablespoons of boiling water. Let vegetables and sausage stand until tender, 15 to 20 minutes. Drain off soaking liquid (note: the liquid is now a tasty broth that can be enjoyed by the cook as a pre-meal warmup). Shred or coarsely chop the cheese; set aside.

To steam the tortillas:** Heat a medium skillet over medium-high heat. Add tortillas. Lift the edge of the tortillas slightly, and add about ½ teaspoon water to the bottom of the skillet. Cover skillet immediately; let tortillas steam for one minute. Turn tortillas; add another ½ teaspoon water, cover and steam for one minute. Fold tortillas in half and wrap in a clean towel or paper towel; place in a sleeping bag or in a larger towel to keep warm.

Melt 1 teaspoon of the butter in the skillet. Add the drained vegetables and sausage, and the seasoning mix. Cook, stirring occasionally, for two or three minutes. If using powdered eggs: while the vegetables are cooking, blend the egg powder with ⅔ cup cold water in a small bowl.

Add the remaining teaspoon of butter to the skillet. Add the two eggs, or the reconstituted powdered egg; stir well with a fork to break up the eggs and mix them with the vegetables and sausage.

Cook the egg mixture over medium heat, stirring occasionally, until the eggs are set. Sprinkle the cheese over the eggs. Cover and remove from heat; let stand for a minute or two to melt the cheese.

While the eggs are standing, spread each tortilla with a tablespoon of the salsa. Divide the eggs evenly between the two tortillas, piling them in a line along the center of the tortilla. Fold the bottom of the tortilla up over the eggs (this makes it easier to eat: you can hold the rolled up tortilla with the folded end on the bottom and the filling won't fall out). Fold in one side, and roll up to completely enclose the egg filling.

*Chorizo is a spicy Mexican sausage. It can be found at Mexican markets, and also at some supermarkets or butcher shops.

**If you have a campfire, you can heat the tortillas over the fire instead of steaming them. Sprinkle them with a few drops water and wrap in foil (it's OK to fold them in half to make a smaller packet to use less foil). Place on a grate at the edge of the fire; you don't want them to get very much heat, just a little. Turn and rotate occasionally so they don't burn or dry out in one spot.

Breakfast Tortilla Roll-Ups with Fresh Veggies

If you'll be car camping and will have fresh vegetables, you can make this dish with fresh vegetables instead of the more labor-intensive dried vegetables.

Place in a small plastic bag and seal with a twist-tie:
- ½ teaspoon chili powder blend
- ⅛ teaspoon salt
- A pinch of crumbled dried oregano leaves

Carry separately:
- About ¼ of a small green bell pepper
- About ¼ of a small red or yellow bell pepper
- About ¼ of a small onion
- 1 rib celery
- 1 uncooked Italian or chorizo link sausage
- 2 flour tortillas, 8" diameter
- 1 teaspoon clarified butter or margarine
- 2 whole raw eggs
- ¼ cup shredded co-jack or other cheese
- 2 tablespoons salsa, or 2 packets of salsa from a fast-food restaurant

At camp:

Dice the vegetables; set aside. Steam tortillas as directed. Remove and discard the casing from the sausage; crumble the sausage meat into the skillet. Cook over medium heat, stirring frequently to break up, until the meat just loses its pink color. Add the peppers, onion, celery, and seasoning mix. Cook until vegetables are tender, about five minutes, stirring frequently. Add butter if the skillet seems too dry to cook the eggs. Add eggs and proceed as directed.

Chapter Five

Camp Breads

Few things are as satisfying as biting into a freshly baked biscuit at camp. Bread is difficult to transport into the back country; it's bulky, and gets crushed or smashed easily. With the recipes in this section, you can make a variety of camp breads, biscuits, and dumplings to get the carbohydrate boost you need, and the fresh-baked flavor you crave.

Most camp bread is made without yeast; baking powder usually provides the leavening. Yeast breads are lighter in texture but take longer to make, because the yeast needs time to grow. **Campfire-Baked Yeast Bread** (page 76) and **Yeast Rolls Baked on a Stick** (page 83) use frozen bread dough to make some lazy-day yeast breads in camp. **Bread-Machine Mix and Variations** on pages 86-87 take advantage of a commercially boxed mix to produce relatively quick yeast rolls in camp.

Italian Stick Bread
2 batches; 2 stick breads per batch

Adults and kids alike will love this bread. It's a delightful change-of-pace bread that's flavorful and fun to cook. You'll need a campfire to cook this bread-on-a-stick; be sure to use only quality wood for your fire (no railroad ties or painted wood!). This recipe makes two batches.

- 1 cup all-purpose flour
- 3 tablespoons nonfat dry milk powder
- 2 tablespoons cornmeal
- 1 teaspoon baking powder
- ½ teaspoon salt
- ½ teaspoon crumbled dried basil leaves
- ¼ teaspoon crumbled dried oregano leaves
- ¼ teaspoon garlic powder
- ¼ teaspoon cream of tartar
- ¼ teaspoon baking soda
- ¼ cup room-temperature shortening

In food processor or mixing bowl, combine flour, powdered milk, cornmeal, baking powder, salt, basil, oregano, garlic powder, cream of tartar and baking soda. Pulse to combine, or mix well with a fork or pastry blender (see detailed instructions for making biscuit mix on page 78; use the same technique for this recipe). Cut the shortening into the flour until the mixture is crumbly. Divide mix into two 1-cup batches; place each batch into a large plastic bag, and seal with a twist-tie. Store mix in the refrigerator until you're packing for your trip.

At camp:

Find two downed hardwood sticks (not softwoods like pine or fir), at least one-half inch in diameter and at least 3 feet long. The sticks should be as straight as possible, with few side branches. Strip the bark from about 8 inches of one end of each stick (a pocket knife works well for this; strip the bark with a carving motion away from yourself). You'll need a campfire, with the coals burned down and ready for cooking.

In medium bowl, combine one batch mix with ¼ cup cold water. Stir with fork until the dough forms a ball; don't overmix, or the bread will be tough. Divide the dough into two equal portions. Form one portion into a "rope" as thick as your finger; flatten slightly with your hands. Wrap the flattened dough around the stick in a spiral, pressing the spiral together at the beginning and end to seal it onto the stick. Toast over prepared coals as though toasting a marshmallow, rotating frequently, until puffy and golden brown on the outside; bread should feel springy when pressed lightly, not soggy. To eat, peel the bread off the stick in large chunks.

Italian-Flavored Biscuits

4 to 6 biscuits

If you aren't going to have a campfire, you can still cook a batch of these tasty Italian-flavored biscuits. They won't be as crusty as the bread sticks on the previous page, but are still very tasty.

Follow at-home mixing and packing instructions for **Italian Stick Bread** on page 72.

Carry separately:

      A batch of the **Italian Stick Bread** mix
      Clarified butter or oil for greasing skillet
      Medium skillet with lid, or foil for cover

At camp:

Lightly grease the skillet; set aside. In medium bowl, combine mix with ¼ cup cold water. Stir with fork until the dough forms a ball; don't overmix, or the biscuits will be tough. Form into 4 to 6 slightly flat biscuits; arrange side-by-side in greased skillet. Cover skillet. Cook over medium heat, rotating skillet frequently to prevent burning, until the bottoms of the biscuits are golden brown. Turn and cook, rotating skillet frequently, until the second side is golden brown and biscuits are cooked through.

Note: These could also be baked in a camp oven; follow baking directions for **Biscuits in a Camp Oven** on page 81.

Chinese Scallion Bread

Although I've made this recipe at home a number of times, I wouldn't have thought to make it at camp until I saw a similar recipe in The L.L.Bean Game & Fish Cookbook. *I've adapted my recipe for camp use. It's a nice change-of-pace camp bread that goes well with almost anything. A slight word of caution: this recipe is a bit more work to prepare than some of the other pan breads (don't try to prepare it when you pull into camp after dark, in the middle of a thunderstorm!).*

1	cup all-purpose flour
1	tablespoon nonfat dry milk powder
1½	teaspoons baking powder
1	teaspoon sugar
¼	teaspoon salt
¼	teaspoon white pepper
1	tablespoon sesame oil
3	tablespoons room-temperature shortening

In food processor or mixing bowl, combine flour, powdered milk, baking powder, sugar, salt and white pepper. Pulse to combine, or mix well with a fork or pastry blender (see detailed instructions for making biscuit mix on page 78; use the same technique for this recipe). In a small bowl or measuring cup, blend the sesame oil into the shortening. Cut the shortening mixture into the flour until the mixture is crumbly. Place mix in a large plastic bag, and seal with a twist-tie. Store mix in the refrigerator until you're packing for your trip.

Carry separately:
3	whole fresh green onions, or ¼ cup dried sliced green onions
2	tablespoons oil or clarified butter*
1	teaspoon sugar
	The bag with the flour mix

At camp:

Remove the root ends of the green onions, and slice both the green and white parts into thin rings (if using dried green onions, reconstitute for about 15 minutes in cold water; drain well and squeeze out excess water). Set aside.

In medium bowl, combine mix with ¼ cup cold water. Stir with fork until the dough forms a ball; don't overmix, or the bread will be tough. Set aside.

In medium skillet, heat half the oil over medium heat (or melt half the clarified butter). Sprinkle half the green onions evenly into the skillet. Sprinkle with half the sugar. Proceed as directed in photos on next page.

*Don't use regular butter or margarine for this recipe, because it will burn. Clarified butter doesn't burn as easily because the milk solids have been removed.

Form the bread dough into a rough patty with your hands. Place into the skillet, on top of the green onions.

Press the bread out carefully with your fingertips to flatten; finish flattening with a spatula to avoid burning yourself. The bread should fill the skillet when you're done pressing. Cook for about 5 minutes over medium heat, rotating the pan frequently over the flame to avoid burning one spot.

Using a spatula, carefully slide the bread onto a large plate, cooked-side down. Return the skillet to the heat. Add the remaining oil and green onions; sprinkle with the remaining sugar.

Working quickly but carefully, flip the bread from the plate into the skillet with the uncooked side down. Cook over medium heat until the bottom is golden brown and the bread is done, about 5 minutes; rotate the pan frequently over the flame to avoid burning one spot.

Campfire-Baked Yeast Bread *(photo page 53)*   1 loaf bread

This is definitely a "convenience-camping" recipe, suitable for car camping or for the first night of an easy trip. Store-bought frozen bread dough is baked over an open campfire in a "skillet oven" formed from a covered cast-iron skillet and a smaller cake pan, which is placed inside the skillet on top of some nails. The nails create an air space, preventing the bread from burning. Note: this will remove most of the seasoning from your cast-iron skillet, so you'll have to season it again. One more note: these instructions look complicated, but really are very simple.

- 1 loaf (1 pound) frozen uncooked yeast bread dough
    (I prefer Rhodes Honey-Wheat)
    Lightweight 8" round pan
    Small amount of shortening or non-stick spray
- 1 teaspoon cornmeal
- 12 small black roofing nails or large-headed black tacks (do *not* use
    galvanized nails; they emit toxic fumes when heated)
    Medium cast-iron skillet with lid, or foil for cover

If the drive to your campsite is 2 to 4 hours: Thaw the frozen bread dough the night before you leave for your trip. Place the frozen dough in a lightly greased loaf pan; cover with plastic wrap. Place in the refrigerator overnight to thaw. Just before you leave for your drive to the campsite, lightly grease the 8" round pan; sprinkle with cornmeal. Shake out excess cornmeal. Form the thawed dough into a ball; flatten into a circle. Place the circle of dough in the prepared round pan; cover with plastic wrap. Place the pan of bread in the car in a warm, steady, upright location; it will rise while you drive to the campsite.

If your drive to the campsite is 4 to 8 hours: The bread dough will both thaw *and* rise on your drive to the campsite. Lightly grease the 8" round pan; sprinkle with cornmeal. Shake out excess cornmeal. Place the frozen dough into the prepared pan; cover with plastic wrap. Place the pan of bread in the car in a warm, steady, upright location. When you get to camp, form the thawed dough into a ball; flatten into a circle. Return to the round pan; re-cover with the plastic wrap and allow to rise again for another hour or so, while you build the campfire.

At camp:

Don't panic if it takes a bit of time to get the campfire ready. Bread dough is quite resilient, and can handle several risings if necessary. Check the dough by poking your finger into it. If the dent made by your finger springs back, the bread can continue rising. If the dent remains, the bread has risen and needs to be "punched down" and re-formed if the campfire coals aren't ready. Simply punch your fist firmly into the bread dough to deflate it; then re-shape into a circle and put back into the pan. Re-cover and let the bread rise again until it has almost doubled. The second rising will take approximately half the time of the first rising (rising time at the campsite will depend on the air temperature; bread rises slowly on a cool day, and more quickly in warm weather).

When the bread has risen properly, it should have almost doubled in volume; as explained on the previous page, if you poke your finger into the dough, the dent will remain. Don't get too hung up on this, though; the bread will probably come out fine no matter what you do!

When campfire coals are ready and the bread has risen, rub the outside of the cast-iron skillet with dish soap to make cleanup easier (see page 56); be careful not to get any soap inside the skillet! Scatter the roofing nails into the bottom of the skillet; place the round pan with the risen bread on top of the nails. Proceed as directed in photos below.

The photo at left shows the risen bread in the small round pan, placed in the skillet. To the left is a flame-spreader ring that came with a wok; I've covered it with foil to use as a lid over the skillet while the bread bakes. Any type of lid will work, as long as it can stand the heat of the campfire; if you cover the skillet simply with foil, make a slight dome in the center to allow the bread to rise during cooking.

Place the skillet on a grate over the campfire coals. The coals should be hot enough that you can hold your hand about 2 inches above the grate for two or three seconds without pain. If the coals are too hot, the bread will burn; if they're too cold, the bread will take a long time to cook.

Place the cover over the skillet. Cook the bread, rotating the pan frequently to prevent hot spots, until the crust is browned and firm; the bread should sound hollow when you rap it with your knuckles. This should take from 45 minutes to 1¼ hours. You will need to push fresh coals under the grate occasionally to keep the baking temperature correct.

Biscuit Mixes

The next three pages present five basic biscuit mixes. Each can be used in any of the recipes in this book that call for biscuit mix; simply choose the mix that suits your fancy. For instructions on baking biscuits, see **Skillet-Baked Biscuits** (page 81), **Biscuits in a Camp Oven** (page 81), or **Campfire Biscuits** (page 82). The five basic recipes can also be used to make dumplings; specific dishes featuring dumplings can be found in later chapters.

Light and Fluffy Biscuit Mix   2 cups mix

After experimenting with a number of biscuit mixes, I've settled on this as my favorite all-purpose mix. The combination of cream of tartar, baking powder, and baking soda provides a high-rising, light biscuit.

- 1¼   cups all-purpose flour
- 3   tablespoons nonfat dry milk powder
- 1   teaspoon baking powder
- ¼   teaspoon cream of tartar
- ¼   teaspoon baking soda
- ¼   teaspoon salt
- ¼   cup room-temperature shortening

Food processor method: Fit food processor with steel blade. Add flour, dry milk, baking powder, cream of tartar, baking soda and salt to work bowl. Pulse on-and-off quickly, three or four times, to blend ingredients. Add shortening. Pulse on-and-off quickly, five or six times, until shortening is "cut in" to dry ingredients; mixture will resemble cornmeal in consistency. Divide mixture into two 1-cup batches (unless you plan to make a lot of biscuits at one time), and store in plastic bags in the refrigerator until you're packing for your trip.

Hand-mixing method: Sift flour, dry milk, baking powder, cream of tartar, baking soda and salt together into a large mixing bowl. Divide shortening into four pieces and add to flour mixture. "Cut" shortening into flour mixture by working the mixture with a pastry blender; or use two forks, working both forks together to break up the shortening and cut it into the flour. With either the pastry blender or the fork method, the mixture will resemble cornmeal in consistency when it is cut together properly. Divide mixture into two 1-cup batches (unless you plan to make a lot of biscuits at one time), and store in plastic bags in the refrigerator until you're packing for your trip.

Slightly Sweet Biscuit Mix

2 cups mix

This recipe is a little sweeter and denser than the Light and Fluffy Biscuit Mix above. It also uses no cream of tartar, which is something you may not have in your spice cabinet. Try both mixes to see which suits your personal taste.

1¼   cups all-purpose flour
4   teaspoons nonfat dry milk powder
1½   teaspoons baking powder
1½   teaspoons sugar
¼   teaspoon salt
¼   cup room-temperature shortening

Follow mixing and packing instructions for **Light and Fluffy Biscuit Mix**, page 78.

Whole-Wheat Biscuit Mix

2 cups mix

Hearty whole wheat adds flavor and texture to this biscuit mix.

¾   cup whole wheat flour
½   cup all-purpose flour
3   tablespoons nonfat dry milk powder
1   teaspoon baking powder
1   teaspoon sugar
¼   teaspoon cream of tartar
¼   teaspoon baking soda
¼   teaspoon salt
¼   cup room-temperature shortening

Follow mixing and packing instructions for **Light and Fluffy Biscuit Mix**, page 78.

Bisquick Plus

1 cup mix

This isn't really a recipe; it's more like packing instructions. If you don't want to make your own biscuit mix from any of the recipes on these pages, you can use Bisquick or any other commercial buttermilk baking mix; just add dry powdered milk when you're packing. At camp, all you need to add is water; you don't have to carry milk. Like many commercial products, this mix has more salt than any of the homemade mixes.

1   cup Bisquick or other buttermilk baking mix
2   tablespoons nonfat dry milk powder

Shake ingredients together in a jar or plastic bag until well mixed.

Potato Biscuit Mix

2 cups mix

Potato flakes and a bit of bacon grease give this mix an earthy flavor. It makes particularly good dumplings.

1	cup all-purpose flour
½	cup instant mashed potato flakes
3	tablespoons nonfat dry milk powder
1	teaspoon baking powder
¼	teaspoon cream of tartar
¼	teaspoon baking soda
¼	teaspoon salt
3	tablespoons room-temperature shortening
2	teaspoons room-temperature bacon drippings

Food processor method: Fit food processor with steel blade. Add flour, potato flakes, dry milk, baking powder, cream of tartar, baking soda and salt to work bowl. Pulse on-and-off quickly, three or four times, to blend ingredients. Add shortening and bacon drippings. Pulse on-and-off quickly, five or six times, until shortening is "cut in" to dry ingredients; mixture will resemble cornmeal in consistency. Divide mixture into two 1-cup batches (unless you plan to make a lot of biscuits at one time), and store in plastic bags in the refrigerator until you're packing for your trip.

Hand-mixing method: Sift flour, dry milk, baking powder, cream of tartar, baking soda and salt together into a large mixing bowl. Crush potato flakes to the consistency of coarse meal in a blender or mortar-and-pestle, or run through a food mill. Add crushed potato flakes to flour mixture; stir well to mix. Divide shortening into three pieces and add to flour mixture. Add bacon drippings. "Cut" shortening into flour mixture by working the mixture with a pastry blender; or use two forks, working both forks together to break up the shortening and cut the it into the flour. With either the pastry blender or the fork method, the mixture will resemble cornmeal in consistency when it is cut together properly. Divide mixture into two 1-cup batches (unless you plan to make a lot of biscuits at one time), and store in plastic bags in the refrigerator until you're packing for your trip.

Skillet-Baked Biscuits

4 to 6 biscuits

Use this technique to bake biscuits on a camp stove. It can also be used to bake biscuits on a grate above a campfire, although the technique in **Campfire Biscuits** *on page 82 produces lighter, fluffier biscuits.*

Carry separately:

A 1-cup batch of any of the biscuit mixes on pages 78-80
Clarified butter or oil for greasing skillet
Medium skillet with lid (or carry foil to use as a lid)

At camp:

Lightly grease the skillet; set aside. In medium bowl, combine mix with ¼ cup cold water. Stir with fork until the dough forms a ball; don't overmix, or the biscuits will be tough. Form into 4 to 6 slightly flat biscuits; arrange side-by-side in greased skillet. Cover skillet. Cook over medium heat, rotating skillet frequently to prevent burning, until the bottoms of the biscuits are golden brown. Turn and cook, rotating skillet frequently, until the second side is golden brown and biscuits are cooked through.

Biscuits in a Camp Oven

4 to 6 biscuits

Biscuits made by this method are generally lighter and fluffier than those that are baked in a skillet as described above.

Carry separately:

A 1-cup batch of any of the biscuit mixes on pages 78-80
Clarified butter or oil for greasing skillet
Medium pot or baking dish for use with camp oven

At camp:

If baking in a box-type camp oven (like the Coleman Campstove Oven, page 46), pre-heat the oven to 300°F-350°F before mixing biscuit dough.

In medium bowl, combine mix with ¼ cup cold water. Stir with fork until the dough forms a ball; don't overmix, or the biscuits will be tough.

If baking in the Outback Oven (page 46), lightly grease a medium (6" to 7" diameter) cooking pot. Drop dough by rounded tablespoons into greased pot, or form into 4 to 6 slightly flat biscuits and arrange side-by-side in greased pot. Cover pot and place on diffuser plate; position thermometer and cover with convection dome. Heat until thermometer reads BAKE, then begin timing. Bake for 10 to 15 minutes, or until biscuits are firm to the touch. For browner, firmer biscuits: when thermometer reaches BAKE, remove the convection dome, thermometer, and pot lid, then quickly replace convection dome and continue baking. Begin timing as soon as you replace the convection dome.

If baking in a box-type camp oven, lightly grease a baking pan or medium cooking pot. Drop dough by rounded tablespoons into greased pan, or form into 4 to 6 slightly flat biscuits and arrange side-by-side in greased pan. Place uncovered pan in preheated camp oven; bake for 8 to 12 minutes, or until biscuits are lightly browned.

Campfire Biscuits

4 to 6 biscuits

If you will have a campfire, you can bake wonderful biscuits with just a little work. For best results, you'll need a pan with a lid that can withstand the heat of direct coals. The photos below show a clamp-together skillet from an old scout's cookset, which works very well. You can also use two clamped-together disposable aluminum pie or cake pans, a cast-iron skillet covered with foil, or anything else you can rig up; see **Blueberry Scones in a Campfire** *(page 63) for more details.*

Carry separately:

> A 1-cup batch of any of the biscuit mixes on pages 78-80
> Clarified butter or oil for greasing skillet
> Medium skillet with lid (or carry foil to use as a lid)

At camp:

You'll need a campfire, with the coals burned down and ready for cooking.

Lightly grease the baking pan; set aside. In medium bowl, combine mix with ¼ cup cold water. Stir with fork until the dough forms a ball; don't overmix, or the biscuits will be tough. For baking, follow photo instructions below.

How to Bake Biscuits in a Campfire

Drop dough by rounded tablespoons into lightly greased pan. Cover with lid, or with several layers of heavy-duty foil.

Unless your pan is disposable or is covered with foil, lightly soap the entire outside with dish soap to make clean-up easier.

Place the pan directly on the coals; scoop some coals on top of the pan as well. A pan of fish and some corn are also cooking here.

Cook 10 to 15 minutes, rotating the pan occasionally, until biscuits are browned and cooked throughout.

Yeast Rolls Baked on a Stick

Another recipe to try with frozen bread dough (similar to the recipe on pages 76-77). Halve the loaf of frozen dough with a meat saw or cleaver.

½ loaf (1-pound loaf) frozen uncooked yeast bread dough

Before you leave for the campsite: Thaw the frozen bread dough as described in **Campfire-Baked Yeast Bread**, pages 76-77, except leave the dough in the loaf pan rather than transferring it to the round pan.

At camp:

Prepare a campfire; let the coals burn down for cooking. Find six downed hardwood sticks that are fairly straight, at least one-half inch in diameter and at least 3 feet long. Strip the bark from about 4 inches of one end of each stick. Divide dough into six portions; roll each into a ball. Push each ball onto the peeled end of a stick, but don't push the stick all the way through. Press the dough into an oblong shape. Set aside to rest for 15 minutes or longer.

Each camper prepares their own roll. Cook as though toasting a marshmallow, rotating frequently, until puffy and golden brown; bread should feel springy when pressed. It will probably take 15 to 20 minutes to cook the rolls. To make cooking easier, rest the cooking stick on a forked stick driven into the ground at the edge of the campfire, rotating occasionally. When the rolls are cooked, pull off the stick and fill the hole with butter, jam, cheese, spaghetti sauce, or stew.

Blue Cornmeal Bannock

This is my adaptation of a traditional Native American recipe. The blue cornmeal provides a different taste than yellow cornmeal. Serve hot with soup and cheese as a main course, or as a side to chili, fried fish, or stew.

Combine in quart plastic zipper bag:

1 cup stone-ground blue cornmeal
⅓ cup all-purpose flour
⅓ cup nonfat dry milk powder
1 tablespoon sugar
1 teaspoon baking soda
¾ teaspoon salt

Carry separately:

1 whole raw egg
Bacon drippings or peanut oil for frying

At camp:

In medium bowl, beat egg with fork. Add mix and 1 cup cold water. Mix with fork just until there are no lumps; do not overmix. Let stand 10 minutes.

Lightly grease a 10" skillet. Heat over medium heat until warm. Pour batter into skillet; cover. Cook over medium heat until the top is bubbly and no longer liquid, 5 to 10 minutes, moving the pan around frequently to prevent scorching. Transfer the bannock to a plate with a spatula. Re-grease skillet lightly. Flip the bannock, uncooked side down, into the skillet. Cook for another 3 to 5 minutes, until the bottom is browned and done.

Beer-Rye Campfire Bannock

This makes a hearty, flavorful camp bread. The beer acts as leavening to make a lighter loaf. This bread is best when cooked with an open fire, as shown in the photos on the next page; but it can also be baked in a camp oven (see page 46). The open fire gives a wonderful smoky flavor to the bread. Be sure to use only "clean" wood for your campfire when making this recipe; don't use moldy wood, or wood that has been painted.

¾	cup rye flour
¾	cup all-purpose flour
2	tablespoons nonfat dry milk powder
1½	teaspoons baking powder
1½	teaspoons celery salt
1	teaspoon sugar
¾	teaspoon onion powder
5	tablespoons room-temperature shortening

In food processor or mixing bowl, combine rye and white flour, powdered milk, baking powder, sugar, celery salt and onion powder. Pulse to combine, or mix well with a fork or pastry blender (see detailed instructions for making biscuit mix on page 78; use the same technique for this recipe). Cut the shortening into the flour until the mixture is crumbly. Place mix in a large plastic bag, and seal with a twist-tie. Store mix in the refrigerator until you're packing for your trip.

Carry separately:

A little bacon drippings or oil to grease the skillet
The bag with the flour mix
¼ cup beer (dark beer gives a fuller flavor, but any beer will work)
A little flour to dust your hands, optional
Heavy medium skillet (cast iron works best)

At camp:

You'll need a campfire, with the coals burned down and ready for cooking.

When campfire coals are ready, rub the outside of the cast-iron skillet with camper's dish soap to make cleanup easier (see page 56); be careful not to get any soap inside the skillet! Grease the inside of the skillet lightly with bacon grease. In medium bowl, combine mix with the room-temperature beer. Stir with fork until the dough forms a ball; don't overmix, or the bread will be tough. If the dough seems too dry, add a little more beer; it's better to use too little than use too much. Proceed as directed in photos on next page.

Pat the mixture evenly into the greased skillet. The bread dough should extend to the edges of the skillet as shown. If the dough is sticking to your hands, dust your hands with a little flour.

Place the skillet on a grate over the prepared campfire coals. Cook until the bottom is golden brown (check by lifting the edge with a spatula or fork); this will take from 5 to 15 minutes, depending on your fire. Rotate the pan occasionally to prevent burning in case your fire isn't evenly hot.

When the bottom is done, prop the skillet up on its side with the top of the bread facing the fire (this campfire is in a shallow pit, and the skillet is propped against the bank; on a flat campsite, use rocks or a stick driven into the ground to prop the skillet up from behind). Cook until the top is browned and the bread is done, usually 10 to 15 minutes; rotate the skillet occasionally to cook the bread evenly.

Bread-Machine Mix and Variations

This store-bought mix works surprisingly well in a camp oven. These yeast rolls require a little more work and a lot more time to make than biscuits, but the technique is still easy enough for an adventurous back-country cook with a camp oven. At camp, the dough is mixed and kneaded in its plastic zipper bag to save mess.

1	box bread-machine bread mix (for a 1½-pound loaf)*
2	teaspoons Butter Buds

Measure the contents of the yeast packet and the dry bread mix, and divide equally between 4 quart plastic zipper bags (for most brands of bread-machine mix, each bag will get just a bit more than ½ teaspoon of yeast, and about ¾ cup of the dry mix). To each bag, add ½ teaspoon Butter Buds. Seal the bags and store them in the refrigerator until you're packing for your trip.

Carry separately:
1	batch Bread-Machine Mix blend as described above
1¾	teaspoons oil, divided

At camp:

Mixing, rising, and general baking instructions are the same for each variation. Heat ¼ cup water until it is hot to the touch; the water temperature should be like a very hot, but still tolerable, bath. Add the hot water and 1½ teaspoons oil to the bag with the bread mix. Seal the bag, and mix the dough by squeezing and kneading the bag with your hands. The dough will form a mass that pulls away from the plastic bag; if it seems too dry, add a few drops water. Knead for 5 minutes (unlike biscuit dough which gets tough with a lot of mixing, yeast dough needs to be kneaded to develop the gluten, which makes a lighter and more tender bread). Let the dough rest in the bag for 5 minutes.

While the dough rests, lightly oil the baking pan you'll be using with your camp oven. After the dough has rested 5 minutes, shape as directed in the individual Variations, and arrange in the oiled pan. Cover the pan, and set aside in a warm place to rise for 30-45 minutes (longer if the weather is cool). Normally, bread should rise until double in size; if you have the time, let it rise until doubled (this could take an hour or longer). For most camp recipes, however, the mix will still work fine even if it doesn't rise until doubled.

If baking in a box-type camp oven (like the Coleman Campstove Oven, page 46), pre-heat the oven to 300°F-350°F near the end of the rising time. At the end of the rising time, uncover the pan (unless directed to leave it covered in the Variation) and bake as directed.

If baking in the Outback Oven (page 46), no pre-heating is necessary. After rising, place the covered pot on the diffuser plate; position thermometer and cover with convection dome. Heat until thermometer reads BAKE. Remove convection dome, thermometer, and pot lid; quickly replace convection dome and bake uncovered (unless directed to leave pan covered in the Variation). Begin timing as soon as you replace the convection dome. Bake as directed.

---

*I've used both Krusteaz and Pillsbury mixes; both measure and perform similarly. Choose whatever brand and flavor you prefer: whole wheat, sourdough etc. (unless you'll be making Cinnamon-Nut Rolls; in that case, use a white or honey bread mix).

Simple Hot Rolls

4 rolls

Mix dough as directed on page 86. After the dough has rested for 5 minutes, divide it into 4 equal portions. Roll each portion into a ball, and arrange in oiled pan. Cover and let rise as directed; rolls should be almost doubled in size. Bake as directed. Baking time will be from 25 to 45 minutes; check after 25 minutes, and continue cooking if necessary. Rolls will be lightly browned on top when done, and will feel firm and springy when pressed lightly.

Miniature Cinnamon-Nut Rolls

6 small rolls

 1   batch Bread-Machine Mix blend (page 86)
 2   teaspoons sugar

At home: add the sugar to the dry mix in the bag.

Carry separately:
 2   teaspoons butter or margarine (must be soft before using at camp)
 1   tablespoon cinnamon-sugar (2½ teaspoons sugar mixed with
        ½ teaspoon cinnamon)
 2   tablespoons chopped pecans or walnuts

At camp:

Mix the dough as directed on page 86. After the dough has rested for 5 minutes, lay the sealed bag on a flat surface. Press to flatten the dough (still inside the bag) into a flat square that is about 6" x 8"; it should fill to the edges of the quart zipper bag. Slit the bag open and peel away the top, leaving the dough on the bottom part of the bag. Spread the soft butter over the dough. Sprinkle with the cinnamon-sugar and the nuts. Roll up jelly-roll fashion, starting with the long edge. Cut into 6 equal pieces; arrange around the edge of the oiled pan. Cover and let rise as directed. Bake as directed. Baking time will be from 20 to 35 minutes; check after 20 minutes, and continue cooking if necessary. Rolls will be browned when done, and will feel firm and springy when pressed lightly. Remove rolls from pan while still warm.

Rosemary-Parmesan Focaccia

4 servings

 1   batch Bread-Machine Mix blend (page 86)
 1   tablespoon shelf-stable grated Parmesan cheese
 ¼   teaspoon crushed dried rosemary leaves

At home: add the Parmesan cheese and rosemary to the dry mix in the bag.

At camp:

Mix the dough as directed on page 86. After the dough has rested for 5 minutes, form into a flat disk with your hands. Place in the oiled pan, and press to cover the bottom of the pan. Cover and let rise as directed. Prick the bread in several places with a fork. Bake as directed, except the pan should be covered during baking. Baking time will be from 15 to 30 minutes; check after 15 minutes, and continue cooking if necessary. Bread will be puffy and light in color; it will feel springy yet soft when pressed lightly.

Chapter Six

Soups

Nothing warms weary bones quicker than a bowl of hot soup. Serve it as a first course, perhaps to take the chill off while a more time-consuming main dish is prepared. Soup also makes a great light meal if accompanied with some bread or crackers, and perhaps a chunk of cheese. If you're rehydrating vegetables for another dish, use the soaking liquid to prepare a compatible soup. You'll be adding both flavor and nutrition.

Borscht
2 to 4 servings

My dad was raised in an ethnically diverse neighborhood in Chicago. He taught me to appreciate the best of a number of cuisines, including the fantastic food to be found in that city's Jewish delis. I learned to make a wonderful, sweet-sour beet borscht when I was a kid. It took some unorthodox techniques – and ingredients! – to adapt this recipe for camping, but I think it's one of the best dishes in this book.

3 tablespoons tomato paste
1 tablespoon white vinegar
1 teaspoon all-purpose flour

Line dryer tray with plastic wrap. In small bowl, blend together tomato paste, vinegar, and flour. Spread the mixture evenly over the plastic wrap. Dry at 135°F-140°F until it is leathery, about 4 hours (peel leather off the plastic wrap after about 3 hours and turn it over to promote even drying on both sides).

Combine in quart plastic zipper bag:
1 cup loosely packed dried julienned beets (finely julienned work best)
1 package (1 ounce) freeze-dried diced beef
¼ cup loosely packed dried julienned carrots
1 tablespoon dried onion flakes
1 tablespoon beef bouillon granules
2 teaspoons regular (not sugar-free) powdered lemonade mix (I use Country Time)
2 teaspoons dried snipped chives
2 teaspoons crumbled dried parsley leaves
A pinch of black pepper
The dried tomato-paste leather

At camp:

In medium pot, boil 2½ cups water. Add mix; stir well. Cover; remove from heat and let stand about 15 minutes. Stir well, and return to boiling. Reduce heat and simmer, stirring occasionally, about 5 minutes.

Caldo Verde

The name of this Portuguese dish means "green soup." It's a hearty soup that is especially delicious in cool weather. A packing note: the dried kale crumbles into powder very easily. If possible, pack the plastic bag of soup mix into a cooking pot or some other protected location so it will retain the proper texture when it's cooked. Serve with a skillet bread and some cheese as a main course, or as a side dish with fish or grilled meat.

Combine in quart plastic zipper bag:

- 2   cups dried cut-up kale
- ½   cup instant mashed potato flakes
- ⅓   cup dried cooked, crumbled bulk Italian sausage
- 2   tablespoons nonfat dry milk powder
- 1   tablespoon dried chopped onion
- 1   tablespoon chicken bouillon granules
- ½   teaspoon garlic chips
- ½   teaspoon Butter Buds
-   A pinch of black pepper

At camp:

In medium pot, boil 2⅓ cups water. Add mix; stir well. Cover; remove from heat and let stand about 20 minutes. Stir well, and return to boiling. Reduce heat and simmer, stirring occasionally, about 5 minutes.

Clam Chowder

You can substitute canned smoked oysters for the clams in this recipe to create a tasty Smoked Oyster Chowder.

Combine in pint plastic zipper bag:

- 1   package (1.8 ounces) Knorr white cream sauce mix
- ½   cup instant mashed potato flakes
- 3   tablespoons Knorr onion soup mix (half of a 1.4-ounce package)
- 2   tablespoons broken-up dried mushroom slices, optional
- 1   tablespoon nonfat dry milk powder
- 1   tablespoon dried cooked bacon pieces or bacon-flavored bits
- 2   teaspoons Butter Buds
- ½   teaspoon crumbled dried parsley leaves
- ¼   teaspoon black pepper

Carry separately:

- 1   can (6.5 ounces) chopped clams in clam juice
-   Oyster crackers or saltines, optional

At camp:

In medium pot, boil 3 cups water. Add mix, and clams with the clam juice. Stir thoroughly. Cover and return to boiling. Reduce heat and simmer, stirring occasionally, about 10 minutes. Serve with oyster crackers.

Minestrone Soup with Pesto

3 or 4 servings

When suppertime is cold, wet and nasty, serve this hearty soup as a before-dinner heat-me-up. It also works nicely as a lunch dish, especially if you have a chunk of cheese and some hearty bread or crackers.

Combine in quart plastic zipper bag:

½	cup dried sliced zucchini
2	sun-dried tomato halves, cut into ½" pieces
3	tablespoons dried corn kernels
3	tablespoons dried diced green bell peppers
2	tablespoons dried carrot slices (thin slices work best)
2	tablespoons dried celery slices
2	tablespoons bacon-flavored bits
1	tablespoon dried chopped onion
1	tablespoon chicken bouillon granules
1	tablespoon shelf-stable grated Parmesan cheese
2	teaspoons crumbled dried basil leaves
1	teaspoon Butter Buds
¼	teaspoon garlic chips
¼	teaspoon black pepper
	Half of the leather from a 6-ounce can tomato paste

At camp:

In medium pot, boil 3 cups water. Add mix; stir well. Cover; remove from heat and let stand 25 minutes or longer, stirring occasionally. Return to boiling. Reduce heat and simmer, stirring occasionally, about 10 minutes.

Chili Soup with Macaroni

2 or 3 servings

This simple soup is hearty enough to be a meal in itself, especially if you have some sharp cheddar cheese to serve with it.

Combine in quart plastic zipper bag:

½	cup macaroni
⅓	cup dried diced tomato
¼	cup dried canned or cooked pinto or great northern beans
¼	cup dried cooked ground beef
2	tablespoons dried diced red or green bell peppers
2	teaspoons dried chopped onion
½	teaspoon crumbled dried parsley leaves
½	teaspoon beef bouillon granules
½	package (1.125-ounce package) taco seasoning mix
	Half of the leather from an 8-ounce can tomato sauce

At camp:

In medium pot, boil 2½ cups water. Add mix; stir well. Cover; remove from heat and let stand about 10 minutes. Stir well, and return to boiling. Reduce heat and simmer, stirring occasionally, until macaroni is tender, 5 to 10 minutes.

Italian Pasta Soup

2 or 3 servings

I adapted this recipe from one by Mary Carroll, who was a syndicated healthy-foods columnist at the time. This wonderful soup is thick and hearty, and makes a great first-course warmer in cold weather.

Combine in quart plastic zipper bag:

⅔	cup thin, narrow spinach noodles or egg noodles
¼	cup "instant black beans" (see page 16)
¼	cup bulgur
3	sun-dried tomato halves, cut into ½" pieces
2	tablespoons shelf-stable grated Parmesan cheese
4	teaspoons vegetable bouillon granules
1	tablespoon crumbled dried parsley leaves
2	teaspoons dried chopped green bell pepper
1	teaspoon dried chopped onion
¼	teaspoon garlic powder
¼	teaspoon crumbled dried basil leaves
¼	teaspoon crumbled dried oregano leaves

At camp:

In medium pot, boil 3 cups water. Add mix; stir well. Cover and return to boiling. Reduce heat and simmer, stirring frequently, until the pasta is tender, about 10 minutes.

Potato-Dill Chowder *(photo page 153)*

2 servings

A natural accompaniment to a lighter main course, chowder can serve as a main dish if accompanied with cheese, crackers or bread, and perhaps some carrot sticks. The dill in this chowder is an unusual, but delicious, addition. For a vegetarian chowder, eliminate the bacon bits, and substitute vegetable bouillon granules for the chicken bouillon granules.

Combine in quart plastic zipper bag:

½	cup dried diced potatoes
¼	cup instant mashed potato flakes
¼	cup nonfat dry milk powder
2	tablespoons dried cooked bacon pieces or bacon-flavored bits
1	tablespoon dried onion flakes
1	tablespoon dried diced red or green bell pepper
2	teaspoons chicken bouillon granules
½	teaspoon crumbled dried dill leaves
¼	teaspoon Butter Buds, optional
	A pinch of crumbled dried thyme leaves
	A pinch of white pepper

At camp:

In medium pot, boil 1½ cups water. Add mix; stir well. Cover; remove from heat and let stand about 15 minutes. Return to boiling. Reduce heat and simmer, stirring occasionally, until potatoes are tender, 5 to 10 minutes.

Beef-Barley Soup with Caraway Dumplings   2 or 3 servings

We first had this on a cool Wyoming night after antelope hunting.
Paired with some sharp cheddar and crackers, it made a satisfying,
warming meal. If you prefer, you can make your own biscuit mix
from the recipes on pages 78-80 instead of using the ready-made mix;
substitute 1 cup of the biscuit-mix recipe for the prepared mix and
powdered milk.

For dumpling mix, place in a small plastic bag and seal with a twist-tie:
- ⅔   cup buttermilk biscuit mix
- 2   tablespoons nonfat dry milk powder
- 1   teaspoon crumbled dried parsley leaves
- ¼   teaspoon crushed caraway seeds

Combine in quart plastic zipper bag:
- 1   package (1 ounce) freeze-dried diced beef
- ⅓   cup quick-cooking barley
- 2   tablespoons dried green peas (from fresh or frozen peas)
- 1   tablespoon beef bouillon granules
- 1   teaspoon dried onion flakes
- ¾   teaspoon paprika, preferably Hungarian
- ½   teaspoon *fines herbes* or Provençal herb mixture
       One-quarter of the leather from an 8-ounce can tomato sauce
       A pinch of black pepper
       A pinch of cayenne pepper, optional
       The small sealed bag with the dumpling mix

At camp:

Set aside small bag with dumpling mix. In medium pot, boil 4 cups water.
Add beef-barley mix. Return to gentle boil; cook 10 minutes, stirring
occasionally.

While soup cooks, make dumplings: In medium bowl, combine dumpling mix
with ¼ cup cold water; mix quickly with fork just until moistened.

When soup has cooked for 10 minutes, drop dumpling mix in 6 balls on
top of soup. Cover soup; continue cooking for another 10 minutes without
removing cover. Dumplings should be firm to the touch and dry in the center
when cooked.

Corn Chowder

Serve this handsome, hearty chowder for lunch, accompanied with crackers and salami or smoked fish; or for dinner with fresh fish, sausages, or grilled burgers. Bring the mix with you when you go fishing and add the water to the zipper bag an hour before you plan to return to camp; when you come in for a break the dish can be cooked in only a few minutes. Keep the mix in the refrigerator or freezer until your trip; it will safely keep a week or more on the trail.

Place in a small plastic bag and seal with a twist-tie:

- ½ cup instant mashed potato flakes
- 3 tablespoons nonfat dry milk powder
- 1 teaspoon cornmeal
- 1 teaspoon chicken bouillon granules
- ½ teaspoon sugar
- ½ teaspoon Butter Buds
- ½ teaspoon celery salt
- A pinch of black pepper

In quart plastic zipper bag, combine:

- ⅔ cup dried corn kernels
- ¼ cup dried diced Canadian bacon
- ¼ cup dried diced red and/or green bell peppers
- ½ teaspoon dried chopped onion
- ¼ teaspoon crumbled dried thyme leaves
- The small sealed bag with the potato flakes

At camp:

Remove small plastic bag with potato flakes; set aside. Add 1 cup cold water to zipper bag with the corn and Canadian bacon mix; seal and allow to soak until corn is almost tender, about 1 hour.

In medium pot, boil 1¾ cups water. Add the corn mixture and soaking water. Cover; return to gentle boil. Cook until corn is tender, about 15 minutes. Add potato-flake mixture; reduce heat and simmer until hot and thick, 2 or 3 minutes. If chowder is too thick, add a few teaspoons of water before serving.

Chapter Seven

Side Dishes:
Starches and Vegetables

A side dish can be as simple as plain boiled rice or rehydrated cooked vegetables, or as interesting as **Rice, Anchovy, and Olive Salad** (page 100). Many are perfect for a light lunch with no accompaniment. Vegetarians will also find lots of dishes in this section that make fine main courses, perhaps supplemented by a little cheese and bread.

Plain cooked rice is a great accompaniment to many main dishes, and provides bulk as well as needed carbohydrates. To save time and fuel, and also free the stove for other cooking chores, I've developed a special camp cooking technique that I use for rice (except the instant type, which I rarely use). I add the raw rice to boiling water, then cover the pot and remove it from the stove to stand for a time before cooking. Then, I simmer the rice for about half the time that it would normally take, until the water is absorbed and the rice is almost completely cooked. I remove the pot from the heat and let it stand, covered, for a few minutes, giving me the chance to put the finishing touches on the main course; when I'm ready to go, I simply fluff the rice and serve.

Rice and rice-based dishes scorch easily near the end of cooking time, when most of the water is absorbed. The final standing time in the above method helps avoid the problem. A diffuser plate (page 58) also helps prevent scorching, although cooking times may need to be increased slightly. Another note: although stirring rice during cooking isn't recommended for normal at-home cooking, you'll need to stir it at camp during cooking. Thin camp cookware doesn't spread heat as well as normal home cookware, and the smaller, more focused flame of many camp stoves provides uneven heat.

Most recipes in this book call for converted long-grain rice; it cooks more quickly and is less sticky than other types of rice. If you wish to substitute another type of rice, see the information about rice on pages 15-16.

Safe water is sometimes in short supply at camp, so the recipes in this book make the most of the water that is used. At home, we think nothing of using several quarts of boiling water to cook pasta; we simply pour the cooking water down the drain. At camp, not only do we often need to conserve water, but our pots aren't that large. Most pasta recipes in this book use only a small amount of water that is not drained but used to make a sauce after cooking.

One final word about cooking rice, pasta, grains, and other dishes: if the food is beginning to stick to the bottom of the pot but isn't cooked yet, simply stir in a bit more water. With all the variables of the wild kitchen, you shouldn't feel the need to follow a recipe slavishly. Use your common sense rather than burn your dinner!

Plain Cooked Rice

3 servings

The basic instructions below work for any type of raw rice. Properly cooked rice isn't mushy and "popped;" the kernels still have a slight bite in the middle, and each grain is separate. Medium-grain rice is an exception; when cooked, it is creamy in consistency.

Carry separately or measure out of your bulk supply at camp:
   ½   cup rice

At camp:

In medium pot, boil 1 cup water (except brown or wild rice, which need 1¼ cups water). Add rice; stir well. Cover and remove from heat; let stand as directed in specific instructions below. Return to boiling. Reduce heat and simmer, stirring occasionally, as directed below; almost all of the liquid will have been absorbed, and the rice will be almost completely cooked. If the water is almost all gone and the rice is still crunchy, stir in a little additional water to prevent sticking, and continue cooking until the rice is almost done. Remove from the heat. Let stand, covered, as directed below. Fluff the rice with a fork before serving.

CONVERTED RICE: Combine with 1 cup boiling water and let stand, covered, 10 minutes. Return to heat; simmer about 9 minutes. Remove from heat; let stand, covered, about 3 minutes.

LONG-GRAIN RICE: Combine with 1 cup boiling water and let stand, covered, 10 minutes. Return to heat; simmer about 10 minutes. Remove from heat; let stand, covered, about 4 minutes.

MEDIUM-GRAIN RICE: Combine with 1 cup boiling water and let stand, covered, 10 minutes. Return to heat; simmer about 7 minutes. Remove from heat; let stand, covered, about 5 minutes.

BROWN RICE: Combine with 1¼ cups boiling water and let stand, covered, about 30 minutes. Return to heat; simmer about 18 minutes. Remove from heat; let stand, covered, about 5 minutes.

WILD RICE: If you bought wild rice at the store, chances are good that it's paddy-grown (not genuine, hand-harvested wild rice that truly grows in the wild). Paddy-grown rice takes much longer to cook than truly wild rice; here's how to cook it. Combine with 1¼ cups boiling water and let stand, covered, about 40 minutes. Return to heat; simmer about 20 minutes. Remove from heat; let stand, covered, about 5 minutes. (If you've got true wild rice, cook it like long-grain rice, above; you may need slightly more water and a bit more cooking time.)

Pasta Carbonara

2 servings

In the traditional preparation of this classic Northern Italian dish, hot pasta is tossed with beaten raw egg yolks and cooked bacon, then served immediately. The heat of the just-drained pasta cooks the eggs. The camping version is equally simple, and makes a hearty side dish or light, quick main course.

Place in a small plastic bag and seal with a twist-tie:

- ¼ cup powdered egg
- 3 tablespoons dried cooked bacon pieces
- 2 tablespoons shelf-stable grated Parmesan cheese
- 1 teaspoon crumbled dried parsley leaves
- ½ teaspoon garlic powder
- ½ teaspoon Butter Buds
- ¼ teaspoon salt

Carry separately:

- 1 cup fine-cut egg noodles

At camp:

In medium pot, boil 1½ cups water. Add noodles, stirring to prevent sticking. Boil, stirring occasionally, until almost tender, about 5 minutes. Add egg mixture from small bag; stir well to blend. Cook, stirring frequently, until noodles are tender, another 2 or 3 minutes.

Spanish Rice

4 servings

Use freeze-dried corn and instant rice for a quick-cooking Spanish rice. If you have a more leisurely schedule, carry home-dried corn in a separate bag; use converted or long-grain rice instead of instant. Soak the home-dried corn for 30 minutes or longer, until almost tender; then proceed with the recipe as directed, increasing cooking time to 20 minutes.

Combine in quart plastic zipper bag:

- ¾ cup instant rice
- ⅓ cup freeze-dried corn kernels
- ⅓ cup dried diced tomato
- 2 tablespoons packaged taco seasoning mix
- 1 tablespoon dried chopped onion
- ½ teaspoon crumbled dried parsley leaves
  One-quarter of the leather from a 6-ounce can tomato paste

At camp:

In medium pot, boil 1½ cups water. Add mix; stir well. Return to boiling. Reduce heat and simmer, stirring occasionally, for 5 minutes. Cover and remove from heat; let stand 5 minutes. Fluff with fork before serving.

Hopping John

This traditional Southern recipe is easy to make at camp when you use cooked or canned black-eyed peas that you've dried at home.

Combine in pint plastic zipper bag:

- ½ cup dried canned or cooked black-eyed peas
- ¼ cup medium-grain rice
- 2 tablespoons dried cooked bacon pieces or bacon-flavored bits
- 1 teaspoon dried celery slices
- ½ teaspoon dried chopped onion
- ½ teaspoon chicken bouillon granules*
- A dash cayenne pepper

At camp:

In medium pot, boil 1¾ cups water. Add mix; stir well. Cover; remove from heat and let stand about 15 minutes. Return to boiling. Reduce heat and simmer, stirring occasionally, until rice is almost tender, about 15 minutes; add a little additional water if necessary to prevent sticking. Cover and let stand about 5 minutes. The finished dish should be somewhat creamy in consistency.

*Chicken bouillon granules are not as good as something with a smoked flavor, but are easy to find. A better option is Hi Mountain Jerky's Buckboard Bean Seasoning (see page 199 for mail-order information), or ham-flavored granules if you can find them.

Barley-Mushroom Side Dish

Quick-cooking barley makes this dish fast and easy to prepare. It's great with fresh fish or any grilled meat, but seems to be particularly suited as a side dish for venison tenderloins or loin.

Combine in pint plastic zipper bag:

- ½ cup quick-cooking barley
- ¼ cup dried mushroom pieces, any variety
- 2 tablespoons pine nuts
- 2 teaspoons dried snipped chives
- 1½ teaspoons beef bouillon granules
- ⅛ teaspoon crumbled dried marjoram leaves

Carry separately:

- 1 tablespoon clarified butter or oil

At camp:

In medium skillet or pot, melt butter over medium heat. Add mix. Cook, stirring frequently, for about 5 minutes. Add 1¼ cups water; bring to a boil. Cover; remove from heat and let stand about 10 minutes. Return to boiling. Reduce heat and simmer, stirring occasionally, until barley is tender, about 5 minutes.

Hash Browns

4 servings

Hash browns are easy to assemble with ingredients available at the grocery store. You'll save about half the cost of pre-packaged freeze-dried hash browns, and can adjust the recipe to suit your taste. For additional economy, dry the onion and green pepper at home in your oven or dehydrator. For 2 servings, simply cut quantities in half.

Combine in freezer-weight quart plastic zipper bag:

6	ounces (1 box) hash browns (from grocery store; on shelf with boxed mashed potato mixes)
¼	cup dried chopped onion
3	tablespoons dried diced green bell pepper
2	teaspoons crumbled dried parsley leaves
3	tablespoons bacon-flavored bits, optional

Carry separately:

Oil, bacon drippings or clarified butter for frying

At camp:

Boil 2 cups water. Add to ingredients in zipper bag (see page 155). Let stand 10 to 15 minutes. Drain water, squeezing out excess. Fry in greased skillet, turning occasionally, until browned.

Nutty Rice *(photo page 156)*

3 to 5 servings

This dish is equally good served hot, at room temperature, or anywhere in between. Prepare the rice first, then let it sit while you use the stove to cook fish or another main course.

Combine in quart plastic zipper bag:

¾	cup converted or long-grain rice
3	tablespoons dried currants
3	tablespoons chopped pecan pieces
2	tablespoons pine nuts or slivered almonds
1	tablespoon dried chopped onion
2	teaspoons crumbled dried parsley leaves
1½	teaspoons chicken bouillon granules
¼	teaspoon garlic chips
⅛	teaspoon saffron threads, crushed thoroughly

At camp:

In medium pot, boil 2 cups water. Add mix; stir well. Cover; remove from heat and let stand about 15 minutes. Return to boiling. Reduce heat and simmer, stirring frequently, until the rice is almost tender and most of the liquid is absorbed, about 15 minutes. Remove from heat; let stand, covered, 5 minutes or longer. Fluff with fork before serving.

Potato Pancakes

4 or 5 pancakes

Serve these as a side dish with grilled meat or fried fish. They're also great for breakfast, especially on a cold, damp morning.

Combine in quart plastic zipper bag:
- 1 cup instant mashed potato flakes
- 2 tablespoons nonfat dry milk powder
- 2 tablespoons bacon-flavored bits, optional
- 1 tablespoon Butter Buds
- 1 teaspoon dried chopped onion
- ½ teaspoon salt
- A pinch of each: black pepper, cayenne pepper, dried thyme

Carry separately:
- 1 whole raw egg*
- Oil, bacon grease or clarified butter for frying

At camp:

In bowl, combine mix with 1 cup boiling water; stir well. Blend egg into potato mixture. Form into patties; fry until browned on both sides.

*If you're frying fish breaded with an egg wash, use the egg that's left over from breading.

Tabouli Salad *(photo page 156)*

4 servings

This delicious Mideastern salad makes a wonderful side dish with any type of meat or fish. For a simple, satisfying lunch, serve with some jerky.

Place in a small plastic bag and seal with a twist-tie:
- 2 tablespoons crumbled dried parsley leaves
- 2 teaspoons crumbled dried mint leaves
- ½ teaspoon salt
- ¼ teaspoon crumbled dried oregano leaves
- ⅛ teaspoon black pepper

Combine in freezer-weight quart plastic zipper bag:
- 1 cup medium or fine bulgur
- ¼ cup dried sliced green onion
- ¼ cup dried diced tomato

Carry separately:
- A fresh lemon, or 3 tablespoons lemon juice
- 3 tablespoons olive oil
- The small plastic bag with the spices

At camp:

Add 2½ cups boiling water to the zipper bag (see page 155); seal and let stand 30 minutes or longer. While the bulgur is soaking, squeeze 3 tablespoons lemon juice into a small bowl. Add the spices and oil; blend well with fork. When bulgur is done soaking, drain water, squeezing out excess. Pour dressing over soaked bulgur; mix well. Let stand 5 minutes or longer.

Rice, Anchovy and Olive Salad

4 to 6 servings

 In Northern Italy, you may see a dish like this served as a first course, or as a light meal at a **trattoria**. *If you have someone in your group who hates anchovies, don't try to trick them into eating this; even when they're dried, anchovies have a way of flavoring the entire dish.*

1	can (2 ounces) anchovy fillets
⅓	cup drained sliced green olives (often called "salad olives")

Drain anchovies; blot well with paper towels. Arrange anchovies and olive slices in a single layer on drying rack covered with mesh. Dry at 140°F until completely dry, about 2½ hours. The anchovies will be very lightweight and brittle, and will look whitish; the olives will be leathery.

Combine in quart plastic zipper bag:

	Half of the dried anchovy/olive mixture*
¾	cup converted or long-grain rice
2	tablespoons dried diced red bell pepper
1	teaspoon crumbled dried parsley leaves
¾	teaspoon crumbled dried basil leaves
⅛	teaspoon black pepper

Carry separately:

Olive oil, 1-2 tablespoons total
Fresh lemon, or 2-3 tablespoons lemon juice or vinegar

At camp:

Boil 1¾ cups water. Add mix; stir well. Cover; remove from heat and let stand about 10 minutes. Add 1 tablespoon olive oil, and return to boiling. Reduce heat and simmer, stirring frequently, until the rice is almost tender and most of the liquid is absorbed, about 15 minutes. Remove from heat; let stand, covered, 5 minutes. Fluff with fork. Allow to cool completely. Squeeze the juice of half the lemon over the mixture, or add lemon juice or vinegar to taste. Add additional olive oil to taste, or if the mixture seems sticky.

*Use the remaining anchovy/olive mixture for another batch of this recipe; or marinate in oil-and-vinegar dressing and toss with mixed greens for a tangy salad. Keep anything with the olive-anchovy mix in the refrigerator until you're packing for your trip.

Macaroni with Cheese Sauce

2 to 4 servings

At home, I don't use shelf-stable pre-grated cheese (the kind that sits on the supermarket shelf without refrigeration); I use real, fresh-grated Parmesan or Romano. But I make an exception for this recipe. The mixture can be carried in a pack, unrefrigerated, without spoiling or getting funky. It's quick and easy to fix, and satisfying to eat. Comfort camping food!

Place in a small plastic bag and seal with a twist-tie:

¼	cup shelf-stable grated Parmesan cheese
1	tablespoon nonfat dry milk powder
2	teaspoons all-purpose flour
1	teaspoon Butter Buds
⅛	teaspoon salt
	A pinch of nutmeg
	A pinch of cayenne pepper

Place in another plastic bag:

1¼	cups macaroni
	The small sealed bag with the sauce mix

At camp:

In medium pot, boil 1¾ cups water. Add macaroni; cook over medium-high heat, stirring frequently to prevent sticking, until just tender; there should be some water left in the pan. Stir in sauce mix; cook over medium-low heat, stirring constantly, until sauce is thick and creamy, about 1 minute.

Blue-Cheese Macaroni

2 to 4 servings

Once in a while, I find a convenience mix that really suits me. One that I use a lot is Hi Mountain Jerky's Blue Cheese Dressing Mix (see page 199 for ordering information). I've used it to make an unusual variation on **Macaroni with Cheese Sauce,** *above. You could substitute any dry blue-cheese (or ranch) dressing mix you can find at the supermarket, although it might not be as good!*

Place in a small plastic bag and seal with a twist-tie:

1½	teaspoons dry blue-cheese (or ranch) dressing mix
2	teaspoons all-purpose flour
2	teaspoons nonfat dry milk powder
1	teaspoon dried snipped chives
⅛	teaspoon salt

Place in another plastic bag:

1¼	cups macaroni
	The small sealed bag with the sauce mix

At camp:

Follow cooking instructions for **Macaroni with Cheese Sauce,** above.

Chili Mac 4 or 5 side-dish servings; 2 or 3 main-dish servings

The name "Chili Mac" means something different in various regions of the United States. In Wisconsin, where I attended college, it was a soup of ground-beef chili with beans and macaroni. In the East, chili mac means thick beef-and-bean chili poured over cooked macaroni. This easy camping version is a one-pot vegetarian dish that combines the best of many styles. Cooked as directed, it makes a hearty main dish or side dish. If you prefer a soupy chili mac, simply add an additional ¾ cup of water.

Combine in quart plastic zipper bag:

1	cup macaroni
⅓	cup dried diced tomatoes
¼	cup dried canned or cooked pinto beans
3	tablespoons nonfat dry milk powder
3	tablespoons freeze-dried corn, optional
2	tablespoons dried diced green bell pepper
2½	teaspoons chili powder blend
1	teaspoon dried chopped onion
¾	teaspoon celery salt
½	teaspoon cornstarch
¼	teaspoon garlic powder
¼	teaspoon sugar
	Half of the leather from an 8-ounce can tomato sauce

Carry separately:

3	tablespoons grated Parmesan cheese, optional

At camp:

In medium pot, combine mix with 2½ cups cold water. Bring to a boil over medium-high heat, stirring frequently to reconstitute tomato leather. Reduce heat and simmer, stirring frequently, until macaroni is almost cooked, about 10 minutes. Cover and remove from heat; let stand 5 to 10 minutes, until macaroni is tender. Stir in Parmesan cheese just before serving, or sprinkle on individual servings.

Ramen-Cabbage Salad

2 or 3 servings

I adapted this recipe from Dressing & Cooking Wild Game, *a book I co-authored for* The Hunting & Fishing Library. *The original recipe is written for use with wild duck. I've adapted it for lightweight camping by using freeze-dried chicken and home-dried vegetables. It's a surprising dish that makes a great lunch or light supper.*

Place in a small plastic bag and seal with a twist-tie:

½ of the seasoning packet from a 3-ounce package of ramen soup, any flavor (mushroom is particularly good)
½ of the uncooked noodles from a 3-ounce package of ramen soup
1 tablespoon almond slices
1½ teaspoons sesame seeds

Combine in gallon plastic zipper bag:

1 cup dried green cabbage (cut into 1-inch chunks before drying)
1 cup dried red cabbage (cut into 1-inch chunks before drying)
1 tablespoon dried green onion pieces (cut into 1-inch lengths before drying)
1 package (1 ounce) freeze-dried diced chicken
The smaller bag with the ramen noodles

Mix in a small bottle and carry separately:

2 teaspoons red-wine vinegar
2 teaspoons peanut or vegetable oil
1 teaspoon sugar
½ teaspoon sesame oil
½ teaspoon soy sauce

At camp:

Remove and set aside the bag with the ramen noodles. Add 2 cups cold water to the cabbage mixture in the zipper bag. Seal and let stand 30 to 45 minutes, or until the cabbage is tender-crisp; move the bag occasionally, redistributing the contents, to ensure even rehydration. Drain water, squeezing out excess (see page 155). If you're also making something like soup or stew, use this liquid as the cooking liquid in that recipe; the drained cabbage can stand for an additional 30 minutes or so while you prepare the other dish. If you're not making any other dish that can make use of the soaking liquid, discard it and proceed as directed with the Ramen-Cabbage Salad.

Five minutes before you're ready to eat, break up the ramen noodles into 1-inch pieces; it's easiest to break up the noodles while they're still in the small plastic bag. Add the broken-up noodles with the seasoning, almond slices, and sesame seeds to the drained cabbage. Shake the dressing well, and add to the cabbage. Toss well; let stand about 5 minutes.

Potatoes with Bacon and Onions

3 or 4 servings

This hearty shore-lunch classic is a natural accompaniment to grilled meat or foil-cooked fish; it's also great for breakfast, accompanied by some fruit. It provides a generous helping of the fat that is usually lacking in dried camping food, and provides great body fuel, especially in cold weather. To serve a few more people, simply cut up an additional potato; there will be enough bacon fat for the additional potato.

Carry separately:

½   pound slab bacon, sliced just before using, or bacon slices*
1   large Idaho baking potato
1   medium yellow onion
     Salt and pepper
     Ketchup, optional (but traditional)

At camp:

Cut bacon slices into ½" pieces. Begin frying bacon in cast-iron or cast-aluminum skillet over medium heat, stirring occasionally to break up slices. While bacon cooks, peel potato and cut into rough chunks or slices; the pieces can be any shape you like, but shouldn't be any thicker than ¼". Add the potato pieces to the skillet; there should be enough bacon grease to keep the potatoes from sticking, but the bacon should be no more than half-cooked (if the bacon is more than half cooked, remove it from the skillet before adding the potatoes, then add it back in with the onion). Cook, stirring occasionally, until potatoes are crusted with brown; this could take as long as 15 minutes. In the mean time, peel the onion and cut into 1" cubes. Add to the browned potatoes. Cook, stirring occasionally, until the onions are tender-crisp, about 5 minutes. Salt and pepper to taste. Serve with ketchup, if available.

*Bacon can be carried for a day or two in cool weather if it's frozen before packing into the center of your pack. Whole bacon slabs keep better than pre-sliced bacon.

The experienced woodsman or back-country cook would probably cut the potatoes and onions directly into the skillet as shown, rather than using a cutting board. Don't try this technique unless you've done it before and are very comfortable with knives; the back country is no place for a nasty cut!

Teresa's "Weetamoo" Stew

3 servings as a side dish

This is my version of a recipe in Trailside's Trail Foods, *an excellent book published by Backpacker Magazine. You can also serve this as a vegetarian main dish; it provides 2 generous servings.*

Combine in quart plastic zipper bag:

⅓ cup converted or long-grain rice
¼ cup broken cashew pieces
¼ cup mixed dried green vegetables
¼ cup dried mushroom slices
3 tablespoons bulgur
1 tablespoon dried chopped onion
½ package leek soup mix (I use Knorr's)
½ teaspoon salt
¼ teaspoon garlic powder
¼ teaspoon black pepper

Carry separately:

1 tablespoon butter, optional

At camp:

In medium pot, boil 2 cups water. Add mix; stir well. Cover; remove from heat and let stand about 10 minutes. Stir well, and return to boiling. Reduce heat and simmer, stirring occasionally, until the rice is almost tender and most of the liquid is absorbed, about 10 minutes. Remove from heat; let stand, covered, about 5 minutes. Stir in butter. Fluff with fork before serving.

How to Rehydrate Dried Vegetables *(photos pages 154, 155)*

These directions tell you how to rehydrate vegetables for a simple side dish; after soaking and cooking, just add some butter or lemon juice, and salt and pepper or other seasoning to taste. To save the water-soluble nutrients, use the leftover vegetable-soaking liquid to make soup or another side dish.

Vegetables rehydrate more quickly in hot or boiling water, although cold water can be used. In the drying instructions on pages 22-41, ranges are given for rehydration times. Vegetables that are listed as "quick to rehydrate" need only a few minutes soaking. If the specific directions say that the vegetable takes a moderate amount of time to rehydrate, plan on soaking 15 to 25 minutes. If the instructions indicate that the vegetable takes a long time to rehydrate, start soaking at least an hour before cooking. Properly rehydrated vegetables are tender and plump, with no hard, dry spots.

Potatoes that you'll be frying after soaking, vegetables for a stir-fry, or vegetables that you'll be eating without cooking are perfect for soaking right in their plastic zipper bags; after rehydrating, drain the liquid and squeeze the bag gently to remove excess moisture as shown on page 155.

If vegetables are to be served hot, it's easiest to just soak them right in the cooking pot; after the vegetables are properly rehydrated, simply heat to boiling and cook for a minute or two. Drain with a square of bridal-veil netting (page 47), and season to taste.

Carrot-Apple-Raisin Salad with
Blue Cheese Dressing *(color photo page 155)*   3 or 4 servings

This crunchy, fresh-tasting salad is the perfect accompaniment to grilled meat or fried fish. It requires no hot water to make. The dried mix can soak longer if that's the way your schedule is going; and once everything is mixed together, it can sit in a bowl until you're ready to eat.

Combine dressing mix in a small plastic bag and seal with a twist-tie:
 2   teaspoons powdered blue-cheese dressing mix (I use Hi Mountain Jerky's Blue Cheese Dressing Mix; see page 199)
 2   teaspoons nonfat dry milk powder

Combine in quart plastic zipper bag:
 ⅔   cup dried julienned carrots
 ¼   cup dried apple slices, cut into ½" dice before measuring
 2   tablespoons raisins
     The small bag with the dressing mix

At camp:

Set aside the bag with the dressing mix. Add enough cold water to the bag with the carrot mixture to cover generously. Seal the bag; set aside for at least 20 minutes to rehydrate. When carrots are plump, drain water, squeezing out excess (see page 155); reserve 2 tablespoons of the soaking water. In a cup or small bowl, blend the reserved water with the dressing mix. Pour over the carrot mixture, tossing well to coat.

Corn Fritters

These go great with many dishes: fried fish, grilled burgers or sausage, or a simple bacon and egg breakfast (maple syrup is delicious on these fritters). Leftovers make a tasty trail snack to be eaten at "room temperature."

Place in a small plastic bag and seal with a twist-tie:
⅔ cup freeze-dried corn kernels (1-ounce package)*

Combine in quart plastic zipper bag:
¼ cup nonfat dry milk powder
¾ teaspoon salt
⅔ cup all-purpose flour
1 tablespoon sugar
1 teaspoon baking powder
¼ teaspoon paprika
¼ teaspoon ground black pepper
2 tablespoons bacon-flavored bits, optional
The small sealed bag with the corn

Carry separately:
1 whole raw egg
Oil, bacon drippings or clarified butter for frying

At camp:

In medium pot, boil 1¼ cups water. Add corn; remove from heat and let stand about 10 minutes, stirring occasionally to cool water. Add mix and egg; beat with fork just until batter is no longer lumpy. Heat skillet or griddle over medium heat; oil lightly. Pour about ¼ cup batter per fritter onto skillet. When surface is bubbly, turn and cook the other side until browned.

Backpacker's Corn Fritters

Egg powder replaces the fresh egg; perfect for lightweight camping.

Follow above recipe, but add ¼ cup powdered egg to batter mix; omit fresh egg. Increase water to 1½ cups. Soak, mix and fry as directed.

Car Camper's Corn Fritters

In this recipe, canned corn replaces the more expensive freeze-dried corn.

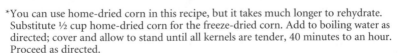

Carry a can (8½ ounces) of corn kernels instead of the dried corn; the batter mix is the same as the main recipe. To prepare, drain juice from the corn into a measuring cup; add water to equal ¾ cup. Blend liquid with egg. In bowl, combine liquid with dry ingredients; beat with a fork just until batter is no longer lumpy. Stir in canned corn; if batter is too thick, add a little more water. Fry as directed.

*You can use home-dried corn in this recipe, but it takes much longer to rehydrate. Substitute ½ cup home-dried corn for the freeze-dried corn. Add to boiling water as directed; cover and allow to stand until all kernels are tender, 40 minutes to an hour. Proceed as directed.

Maque Choux

Almost every Creole cook has a special way of preparing Maque Choux. *(pronounced "mock shoe"). Some cooks use tomatoes; others claim they spoil the dish. One thing most recipes rely on is slow frying of the corn, which develops the traditional rich, roasted taste. In this recipe, powdered vegetables are roasted at home to give that special flavor.*

2	tablespoons dried corn
2	teaspoons dried onion flakes
1	teaspoon dried celery slices

In spice/coffee grinder or blender, process corn, onion and celery until finely powdered. Heat a small heavy-bottomed frying pan (cast iron works best) over medium heat until hot. Add the powdered vegetable mix. Cook over medium heat, stirring constantly, until powder is lightly browned and fragrant, 2 to 3 minutes. Remove from heat; continue to stir until the powder has cooled (it will continue to brown in the hot skillet, and should end up a deep golden brown color). Set aside to cool completely.

Place in a small plastic bag and seal with a twist-tie:

¼	cup nonfat dry milk powder
1	teaspoon sugar
½	teaspoon salt
½	teaspoon paprika
½	teaspoon garlic powder
¼	teaspoon dry mustard
⅛	teaspoon black pepper
	The powdered vegetables

Combine in freezer-weight pint plastic zipper bag:

⅔	cup dried corn kernels
¼	cup dried diced tomato
2	tablespoons dried onion flakes
2	tablespoons dried diced green bell pepper
	The small sealed bag with the powdered vegetables and spices

At camp:

Remove small bag with the powdered vegetables; set aside. Add 1 cup boiling water to the bag with the corn (see page 155); let stand for 30 to 50 minutes, or until corn is almost tender. If there is more than a few tablespoons of water remaining in the bag, drain and discard excess. Transfer corn and remaining water to medium pot; add powdered mix. Cook over medium heat, stirring occasionally, until corn is tender and liquid has thickened, 5 to 10 minutes.

Quicker Maque Choux

Reduce dry milk powder to 2 tablespoons; substitute freeze-dried corn for the regular dried corn. You'll also need to carry 1 tablespoon butter or oil.
At camp: Eliminate pre-soaking of corn; instead, fry corn mix in 1 tablespoon butter until golden. Add ¾ cup water. Heat to boiling; cook about 4 minutes. Stir in powdered mix. Cook until thickened, about 5 minutes.

Beets and Carrots with
Lemon-Thyme Sauce *(photos pages 153, 154)*   2 or 3 servings

Beets are one of my favorite vegetables. They're colorful, sweet and tasty, and just looking at them seems to make me feel healthier. Combined with julienned carrots in a light lemon-thyme sauce, they make a delightful, elegant side dish that adds color to any camping menu.

Place in a small plastic bag and seal with a twist-tie:
- 1   teaspoon regular (*not* sugar-free) powdered lemonade mix (I use Country Time)
- ½   teaspoon cornstarch
- ½   teaspoon Butter Buds
- ¼   teaspoon crumbled dried thyme leaves
    A pinch each of powdered ginger, black pepper

Combine in quart plastic zipper bag:
- 1   cup dried julienned beets
- ½   cup dried julienned carrots
    The small sealed bag with the spices

At camp:

In medium pot, boil 1 cup water. Add vegetables; stir well. Cover; remove from heat and let stand about 20 minutes. There should be a little water left in the pan; add more if necessary. Return to boiling. Stir in seasonings. Cook, stirring frequently, until vegetables are hot and sauce is thickened, 3 to 5 minutes.

Minnesota Green Bean Casserole   3 to 4 servings

This dish seems to be in the repertoire of every old-fashioned cook in Minnesota. Surprisingly, it adapts easily to the back country. The French-fried onions are a traditional topping that provides nice crunch.

Place in a small plastic bag and seal with a twist-tie:
- 1   package (1.8 ounces) Knorr white cream sauce mix
- 2   tablespoons sliced almonds
- 2   tablespoons nonfat dry milk powder

Combine in quart plastic zipper bag:
- ⅔   cup dried French-cut green beans
- 2   tablespoons broken-up dried mushroom slices
- 1   teaspoon dried chopped onion
    The small sealed bag with the sauce mix

Carry separately:
- ¼   cup Durkee French-fried onions, optional (found in the snack aisle)

At camp:

In medium pot, boil 1½ cups water. Add vegetables. Cover; remove from heat and let stand about 10 minutes. Blend in sauce ingredients with a fork. Return to boiling. Reduce heat and simmer, stirring occasionally, until sauce thickens, about 2 minutes. Top with French-fried onions.

Stir-Fried Vegetables

2 to 4 servings

Use whatever vegetables you prefer for this dish; the combinations below will give you some ideas. When packing the ingredients, divide dried vegetables into two batches if necessary: those that rehydrate quickly, and those that take a moderate or long amount of time to rehydrate. Choose vegetables with a variety of colors for an attractive stir-fry.

Prepare the sauce (enough for three batches):
   2   tablespoons hoisin sauce*
   1   tablespoon soy sauce
   1   tablespoon Chinese plum sauce*
   1   tablespoon black bean paste with garlic*
  ½   teaspoon sesame oil
  ⅛   teaspoon 5-spice powder*

Blend ingredients well; spread evenly on a dryer tray lined with plastic wrap, or a solid liner sheet that has been sprayed with non-stick cooking spray. Dry at 150°F until leathery, about 5 hours; midway through drying, peel the leather from the tray and flip it over to help dry the bottom side. When dry, there should be no soft spots. Cut leather into 3 equal pieces; roll them up and wrap individually in plastic wrap. Refrigerate until you're packing for your trip.

Pack dried vegetables into two freezer-weight plastic bags according to their rehydration time. Some sample combinations are given below, or make up your own combinations. Quantities can be varied depending on the number of people you're cooking for.

	Bag 1: slow to rehydrate	*Bag 2: quick to rehydrate*
Combination A	⅓ cup carrot slices ¼ cup red bell pepper strips	⅓ cup zucchini slices ¼ cup diced red onion
Combination B	½ cup julienned carrot 2 tablespoons sliced celery	½ cup French-cut green beans ¼ cup sliced green onion
Combination C	⅓ cup red bell pepper strips	⅓ cup peapods ¼ cup sliced mushrooms ¼ cup sliced Chinese cabbage
Combination D	⅓ cup carrot slices ¼ cup diced green pepper	½ cup French-cut green beans ¼ cup sliced leek

In quart plastic zipper bag, combine:
  ¼   cup sliced or slivered almonds
      One wrapped roll of the sauce
      The two bags containing one of the above vegetable combinations

Carry separately:
      Raw rice, optional (use whatever type you prefer, and base the
         amount on the number of people you'll be cooking for; ½ cup raw
  rice generally makes 1 cup cooked, enough for 2 or 3 people)
      Peanut oil or clarified butter for frying (about 2 teaspoons)

At camp:

Boil some water, and start rehydrating the vegetables in bag 1; they'll take the most time (see page 155). Generally, 1½ cups of water will be enough for soaking. If you're cooking brown rice, start it now; wait until later if you're cooking white rice. While the first vegetables are soaking, start rehydrating the sauce by blending it with 3 tablespoons water in a small cup. When the first vegetables are close to tender (probably 30 to 40 minutes), add the other vegetables (bag 2). If you're cooking white rice, start it at this time.

When all the vegetables are tender, drain water, squeezing out excess. Heat a few teaspoons of oil in a skillet (the larger the skillet, the easier it will be to cook this dish). Add the drained vegetables to the hot oil and cook, stirring very frequently, for about 3 minutes. Add the almonds and cook, stirring constantly, for another 2 minutes or so. Add the rehydrated sauce and cook, stirring constantly, for another minute.

*Hoisin sauce, Chinese plum sauce, black bean paste with garlic, and 5-spice powder can be found in the Asian-foods section of larger grocery stores, or at ethnic markets or specialty stores. See page 139 for information on choosing hoisin sauce.

Lemony Harvard Beets

2 servings; easily doubled

I usually don't carry vinegar on camping trips, so I developed this version of Harvard beets using lemon rather than vinegar. It may not be totally authentic, but it's a good back-country substitute. It can be served hot, cold, or anything in between, so it fits into almost any schedule. The cooked beets can stand, covered, while you fix the rest of the meal.

Combine the sauce mix in a small plastic bag and seal with a twist-tie:

1   tablespoon regular (*not* sugar-free) powdered lemonade mix (I use Country Time)
½   teaspoon cornstarch
¼   teaspoon Butter Buds
¼   teaspoon salt
    Dash of ground cloves

Combine in pint plastic zipper bag:

⅓   cup dried diced beets
    The small bag with the sauce mix

At camp:

In medium pot, boil ⅔ cup water. Add beets. Cover; remove from heat and let stand until tender and plump, 20 to 25 minutes. Add sauce mix, stirring well to blend. Return to boiling. Reduce heat and simmer, stirring occasionally, about 2 minutes.

Herbed Vegetables Roasted in Foil

2 servings per foil packet

Almost any fresh vegetable can be cooked this way. Combinations are also good; try carrots and bell peppers for an attractive side dish.

½   teaspoon crumbled dried tarragon, thyme, or herb blend
⅛   teaspoon lemon pepper, garlic pepper or coarse pepper

Choose herbs to complement the vegetables. If you're not sure what to use, try a blend like *fines herbes* or *bouquet garni* (in the spice aisle). Place the herbs and pepper in the middle of an 18" square of heavy-duty foil. Fold foil in half, then in half again to make a square. Hold by the unfolded corners and tap gently to jostle all the herbs into the folded corner, then fold the open edges to seal the herbs in the center.

Carry separately:
   Fresh vegetables: carrots, zucchini, bell peppers, onion, etc.
2   teaspoons butter per packet

At camp:

You'll need a campfire, with the coals burned down and ready for cooking. Cook only one type of vegetable, or a mix, as you prefer. Peel vegetables if necessary; slice or cut up as you prefer. Smaller, thinner pieces cook more quickly. Place the cut-up vegetables on the foil with the herbs. Top with the butter; sprinkle with a few drops of water. Seal the packet as shown on page 56. Place wrapped packets onto grate above the coals, or directly in the coals. Turn and rotate every 10 minutes; total cooking time will be 20 to 30 minutes.

Potato-Carrot-Onion Packets   *(photo page 156)*

2 servings

In this variation on the above recipe, potatoes are cooked with a vegetable blend to produce a wonderful side dish with a roasted flavor.

Carry separately:
1   Idaho baking potato
1   carrot
1   small yellow onion
4   teaspoons butter
    Salt and pepper (garlic pepper is very good)
    An 18" x 24" piece of heavy-duty foil

At camp:

You'll need a campfire, with the coals burned down and ready for cooking. Peel vegetables. Cut potato into quarters lengthwise, then into ⅛" slices. Cut carrot into ⅛" slices. Cut the onion into chunks. Distribute half the butter, cut into smaller pats, over the center of the shiny side of the foil. Top with half the potatoes. Add the carrot and onion; sprinkle generously with salt and pepper. Top with the remaining potatoes; distribute the remaining butter, cut into smaller pats, over the potatoes. Seal the packet as shown on page 56. Place wrapped packets onto grate above coals, or directly in coals that are burned down for cooking. Turn and rotate every 15 minutes; total cooking time will be 35 to 50 minutes. This dish is best when the potatoes are well browned.

Roasted Corn-on-the-Cob *(photos page 157)* Per serving

Whole ears of corn-on-the-cob can be a bit of a nuisance for campers. They're bulky, they lose their freshness quickly even if kept cool, and they make a lot of messy garbage. But cooked in this manner, they're absolutely worth the trouble. Buy your corn at a roadside stand on your drive to the campsite, for the freshest possible corn. A note: many recipes I've seen advise you to peel the husks down and remove the silk, then fold the husks back before roasting. This is totally unnecessary; the silk will pull away with the husks after the corn is cooked this way. And you will never get the husks to seal properly once you've pulled them back.

Carry separately:

>   Fresh corn-on-the-cob, unhusked
>   Butter, salt and pepper for seasoning the cooked corn

At camp:

One of the secrets to cooking corn this way is to soak the whole ears in water before tossing them onto the coals. If you're camping by a clean lake or stream, tie the ears together with string or put them in a mesh bag; place into the water and weight down with a rock to keep them submerged (see photo on page 157). If there isn't a clean body of water nearby, soak the ears in a large pot, clean bucket, dishpan, or whatever you can come up with. The corn should soak for at least 30 minutes, but can stay in the water up to 3 hours. Watch out for raccoons and other woodland critters; they'd just love some fresh sweet corn to munch on, and can run off with your dinner when you're not looking.

Prepare a campfire; let the coals burn down for cooking. Remove the corn from the water, and shake off the excess. Toss the corn directly onto the coals (you can also place them on a grate above the coals if you have one; they will take a little longer to cook). The outer husks will eventually burn, but the inner husks should remain mostly intact. Turn the corn frequently to prevent excessive scorching. The corn will probably be done in 15 to 25 minutes; it should feel slightly soft when pressed (shield your hand with an old potholder to prevent burns).

Peel back the husks and silk; you can use the peeled-back husks as a handle to hold the corn while eating. Butter, salt and pepper to taste.

Chapter Eight

Main Dishes

Whether you take your main camping meal in the evening or at mid-day, it should be food you'll genuinely enjoy – not just fuel for the next hurdle. Food is more than fuel for the body; it should also be exciting and pleasing to eat.

Many recipes in this section benefit from accompaniment by a side dish, but they can also be eaten as a stand-alone dish. Number of servings depends on what else is served; a dish that serves three or four when accompanied by a side dish will probably only serve two if served alone. Individual appetites also vary, so take that into account when planning your menus; and remember that during cold weather or strenuous activity, your caloric needs increase.

Clam Sauce with Pasta   2 servings

This easy, flavorful dish gets a bit of kick from the black pepper.

Place in a small plastic bag and seal with a twist-tie:

2	tablespoons nonfat dry milk powder
1½	teaspoons crumbled dried parsley leaves
1	teaspoon cornstarch
½	teaspoon Butter Buds
¼	teaspoon onion powder
¼	teaspoon black pepper, preferably freshly ground
⅛	teaspoon crumbled dried marjoram leaves
½	Knorr fish bouillon cube, crushed, or 1 teaspoon chicken bouillon granules

Carry separately:
   1   cup (3.5 ounces) fine-cut egg noodles
   1   can (6.5 ounces) chopped clams in clam juice

At camp:

In medium pot, boil 1¼ cups water. Add pasta. Simmer, stirring occasionally, for about 5 minutes; most of the water will be gone, but the pasta will still be slightly underdone. While pasta cooks, drain clam juice into a small bowl. Add sauce ingredients; stir well to blend. When pasta has cooked for 5 minutes, stir the sauce into the pasta. Simmer, stirring occasionally, until sauce thickens and pasta is just cooked (it should still be slightly firm). Stir in the clams.

Upside-Down Sloppy Joes

This all-in-one dish combines fresh-cooked biscuits with a tasty sloppy Joe mixture. A wide pot is better for cooking this than a tall, narrow pot; the biscuits need some room.

Place in a small plastic bag and seal with a twist-tie:
- 1 cup biscuit mix (pages 78-80)

Combine in quart plastic zipper bag:
- 1 cup dried cooked ground beef
- ½ package (1.4 ounces) French onion soup mix (I use Knorr's)
- 2 tablespoons dried celery slices
- 2 tablespoons dried diced green bell pepper
  Half of the leather from an 8-ounce can tomato sauce
  The small sealed bag with the biscuit mix

Carry separately:
  A little flour for dusting your hands

At camp:

In medium pot, boil 2 cups water. Add beef mix; stir well. Cover; remove from heat and let stand about 20 minutes. While beef is soaking, combine biscuit mix with ¼ cup water; mix with a fork just until moistened. With floured fingers, pat biscuit mix into four large, flat biscuits, shaped to fit snugly in the cooking pot; set aside.

After beef has soaked for 20 minutes, stir well and return to boiling. Arrange biscuits on top of mix. Cover pan; cook over medium-low heat for 10 minutes, or until biscuits are puffy and no longer moist in center. To serve, scoop out of pot and place on plate with the biscuit on the bottom.

Placing the formed biscuits on top of the soaked ground beef mixture

The finished dish

Ground Beef Paprikash

2 to 4 servings

 A hearty hot dish that makes a quick, satisfying meal. This dish uses part of a sauce packet from a commercial boxed potato mix. See the footnote for recipes that use the other half of the sauce mix, as well as recipes that use the dried potato slices.

Place in a small plastic bag and seal with a twist-tie:
1   cup biscuit mix (pages 78-80)

Combine in quart plastic zipper bag:
1⅓   cups dried cooked ground beef
¼   cup dried mushroom slices
¼   cup nonfat dry milk powder
3   tablespoons dried diced red or green bell pepper
2   tablespoons dried onion flakes
2   teaspoons paprika, preferably Hungarian
½   package sour cream and chive sauce mix from a boxed potato side dish
1½   teaspoons Butter Buds
1   teaspoon dry mustard
½   teaspoon salt
¼   teaspoon black pepper
    The small sealed bag with the biscuit mix

At camp:

In medium pot, boil 2 cups water. Add beef mix; stir well. Cover; remove from heat and let stand about 15 minutes. Stir well, and return to boiling. Reduce heat and simmer, stirring occasionally, about 5 minutes. While the mixture simmers, combine biscuit mix with ¼ cup cold water; mix with fork until moistened. When beef mixture has simmered for 5 minutes, drop large spoonsful of biscuit mix on top of beef mixture. Cover pan; cook for 10 minutes longer, or until biscuits are puffy and no longer moist in center.

The other half of the sauce-packet mix can be used in the following recipe:
   Ground Beef Stroganoff, page 124

The dried potato slices can be used in the following recipes:
   Easy Goulash, page 122
   Easy-Does-It Beef Hash, page 127
   Artichokes and Potatoes alla Campagnola, page 144
   Indian Chicken with Potatoes, page 149

Chicken with Stuffing and Gravy

The inspiration for this recipe comes from the book Trailsides Trail Foods, *published by Backpacker Magazine. It's easy, quick, and about as close as you can get in the woods to comfort food.*

Place in a small plastic bag and seal with a twist-tie:

⅓ cup dried sliced mushroom pieces
2 tablespoons dried onion flakes
1 tablespoon dried diced green bell pepper, optional
1 teaspoon crumbled dried parsley leaves

Place in a larger plastic bag and seal with a twist-tie:

2 cups herb-seasoned crumb stuffing mix (half of an 8-ounce bag; I use Brownberry brand)

Carry separately:

1 can (5 ounces) chunk chicken
1 envelope (⅔ ounce) chicken gravy mix
The small bag containing the mushroom mixture
The bag with the stuffing mix

At camp:

In small saucepan, blend the gravy mix with 1 cup cold water; set aside.

In medium pot, boil 1 cup water. Add mushroom mix. Cook 5 minutes, stirring occasionally. While the mushroom mixture cooks, open the canned chicken; break up the chunks slightly with a fork. When mushroom mixture has cooked for 5 minutes, add chicken and juice. Cook for about a minute. Remove from the heat. Add stuffing mix; stir well. Cover and set aside.

Heat gravy mixture to boiling. Cook, stirring constantly, until smooth and thickened, about 1 minute. Serve gravy over chicken and stuffing.

Sweet and Sour Chicken

A colorful and tasty dish that is quite a treat in the back woods. Fresh celery and carrot sticks, or a fresh cucumber, are a great accompaniment.

Place in a small plastic bag and seal with a twist-tie:
    1   cup converted or long-grain rice

Place in another small plastic bag and seal with a twist-tie:
    Half   of a 2-ounce package sweet & sour sauce mix (available in the grocery store with the packaged gravy mixes)

Combine in freezer-weight quart plastic zipper bag:
    1   package (1 ounce) freeze-dried diced chicken
    ¾   cup dried peapods
    ¼   cup dried mixed-color bell pepper strips
    ¼   cup diced dried pineapple
    2   tablespoons dried onion flakes
    2   teaspoons dried celery slices (preferably de-stringed; see page 32)
    The small sealed bags with the rice and the sauce mix

Carry separately:
    A small amount of peanut oil or clarified butter for frying

At camp:

Remove bags of rice and sauce mix from zipper bag. In medium pot, boil 3½ cups water. Add about 1½ cups boiling water to chicken mix in zipper bag (see page 155). Let stand 15 minutes. While chicken mix is soaking, add rice to pot with remaining boiling water. Cover and return to boiling. Reduce heat and simmer, stirring frequently, until the rice is almost tender and most of the liquid is absorbed (this will take about 15 minutes; while the rice cooks, you will be preparing the sauce and chicken).

After the chicken mix has soaked for about 15 minutes, drain the liquid into a measuring cup, gently squeezing the bag to remove excess moisture; add water to equal ½ cup. Set zipper bag with chicken mix aside. In small saucepan, blend sauce mix with liquid. Bring to boil over medium heat, stirring frequently; cook about 1 minute, stirring constantly. Cover and set aside.

In medium skillet, heat enough peanut oil to just coat the bottom of the skillet. Add the drained chicken mix. Cook, stirring occasionally, until lightly browned. At this point, the rice should be almost tender and most of the liquid should be absorbed; remove rice from heat and let stand, covered, for 5 minutes or so while you finish cooking the chicken.

When the chicken is browned, stir in the sauce mixture. Continue to cook, stirring occasionally, until the sauce is bubbly. Fluff rice with a fork. Serve chicken over rice.

Easy Sweet and Sour Chicken

2 or 3 servings

The **Sweet and Sour Chicken** *on the facing page requires three pans and a fair amount of "ditzing around." For a simpler version, follow the instructions below. The texture won't be quite as good, but the taste will!*

Follow all drying and packing instructions for **Sweet and Sour Chicken** on the facing page, but pack rice in same bag with chicken and vegetables; omit peanut oil.

At camp:

In medium pot, boil 3½ cups water. Add chicken/rice mix; stir well. Cover; remove from heat and let stand about 15 minutes. Stir well, and return to boiling. Reduce heat and simmer, stirring frequently, about 10 minutes. While mix cooks, blend sauce mix with ¼ cup water in small cup. When rice is almost tender, stir in sauce mix; cook, stirring frequently, until sauce is thick and bubbly and rice is tender, about 3 minutes.

Spaghetti with Sausage Sauce 2 batches; 2 or 3 servings per batch

If you like spicy spaghetti sauce, make this with hot Italian sausage.

8	ounces Italian sausage, bulk or with casings removed
⅓	cup chopped green pepper
⅓	cup chopped onion
⅓	cup chopped celery
2	cloves garlic, peeled and crushed or minced
1	can (8 ounces) tomato sauce
½	teaspoon dried crushed basil leaves
¼	teaspoon dried crushed oregano leaves
6	tablespoons tomato paste (half of a 6-ounce can)

In large skillet, cook sausage over medium heat, stirring frequently to break up, until no longer pink. Drain in colander; rinse quickly with hot water. Add green pepper, onion, celery, and garlic to skillet; sprinkle with a teaspoon water. Cook over medium heat, stirring occasionally, until tender-crisp, about 10 minutes. Add tomato sauce, basil, oregano, and drained sausage. Cook about 10 minutes, stirring frequently. Add tomato paste; stir well. Spread on dryer trays lined with plastic wrap or liner sheets. Dry at 150°F until brittle, 7 to 9 hours. Cool completely. Divide into 2 batches. Store in refrigerator or freezer until packing for your trip.

Carry separately:

1	cup fine-cut egg noodles
1	batch of the dried sausage sauce, in freezer-weight plastic zipper bag Parmesan cheese

At camp:

Add ½ cup boiling water to sauce mix in zipper bag (see page 155). Let stand 15 minutes. In medium pot, boil 1¼ cups water. Add pasta. Simmer, stirring occasionally, for about 5 minutes; the pasta will still be slightly underdone. Add sauce; cook for about 5 minutes, stirring frequently. Top each serving with Parmesan cheese.

Chicken Fried Rice

2 servings; easily doubled

The best fried rice is an amalgam of a previously served dinner, coupled with fresh crunchy bean sprouts and other crispy vegetables. As campers, we usually don't have the luxury of such fixings, and have to make do with some easy substitutes. You'll be surprised at how good this easy-to-prepare meal tastes in the back country!

Place in a small plastic bag and seal with a twist-tie:

- ½ teaspoon beef bouillon granules
- ⅛ teaspoon 5-spice powder*

Combine in freezer-weight quart plastic zipper bag:

- ¾ cup instant rice
- 1 package (1 ounce) freeze-dried diced chicken
- 3 tablespoons dried sliced green onion
- 3 tablespoons freeze-dried green peas
- 2 tablespoons sliced almonds
- 1 heaping tablespoon dried shredded carrot
- ⅛ teaspoon garlic chips
  The small sealed bag with the spices

Carry separately:

A tablespoon or so of oil or clarified butter for frying
A small packet of soy sauce if available,** or additional salt to taste

At camp:

Remove bag of spices from zipper bag; set aside. Boil 1½ cups water. Add to ingredients in zipper bag (see page 155). Let stand 10 to 15 minutes. Drain water, squeezing out excess. In medium skillet, heat oil over medium-high heat. Add drained rice mixture. Fry, stirring frequently, until lightly browned, 5 to 10 minutes. Near the end of cooking, add contents of the small plastic bag and a small take-out size packet of soy sauce, or salt to taste.

*5-spice powder is a spice blend used in Asian cooking. Check in the Asian-foods section of a large supermarket for this seasoning.

**Save the soy sauce from an order of Chinese carryout; I've never seen individual packets of soy sauce offered for sale.

Rice with Mushrooms and Sausage

2 or 3 servings

Use spicy or mild Italian sausage to suit your own tastes. You could also try chorizo, or any other bulk sausage you enjoy. For a complete meal, accompany this dish with slices of sharp Gruyère or Cheddar cheese, apple slices and carrot sticks.

Combine in pint plastic zipper bag:

- 1 cup converted or long-grain rice
- ¼ cup dried cooked, crumbled bulk sausage
- ¼ cup dried mushroom slices
- 2 tablespoons dried onion flakes
- 1 tablespoon Butter Buds
- ½ teaspoon salt
- ¼ teaspoon crumbled dried sage leaves
  A dash cayenne pepper, or to taste

At camp:

In medium pot, boil 2 cups water. Add mix; stir well. Cover; remove from heat and let stand about 15 minutes. Stir well, and return to boiling. Reduce heat and simmer, stirring frequently, until the rice is almost tender and most of the liquid is absorbed, about 15 minutes. Remove from heat; let stand, covered, 5 minutes or longer. Fluff with fork before serving.

Chicken Chili

2 or 3 servings

We first had this on a damp, cold spring evening, and it really hit the spot. The lentils and rice make this a very hearty, satisfying one-pot meal. If you have some sharp cheese along, it will complement the chili very nicely, either on top or on the side.

Combine in pint plastic zipper bag:

- 1 package (1 ounce) freeze-dried diced chicken
- ⅓ cup lentils
- 3 tablespoons converted or long-grain rice
- 2 tablespoons dried diced green bell pepper
- 4½ teaspoons dried chopped onion
- 4 teaspoons chili powder blend
- 2 teaspoons vegetable bouillon granules
- ½ teaspoon garlic chips
- ½ teaspoon crumbled dried oregano leaves

At camp:

In medium pot, boil 2½ cups water. Add mix; stir well. Cover; remove from heat and let stand about 15 minutes. Stir well, and return to boiling. Reduce heat and simmer, stirring occasionally, until lentils and rice are tender and most of the liquid is absorbed, 15 to 20 minutes. Remove from heat; let stand, covered, 5 minutes. Fluff with fork before serving.

Salmon Patties *(photo page 156)*   4 patties

When we're fishing and camping in an area where there are no restrictions on cans, I carry the fixings for these patties. That way, if we don't catch any fish, I've still got the makings of a quick, tasty main dish.

Combine in pint plastic zipper bag:

     ½   cup Italian-style bread crumbs or other seasoned variety
     ½   cup powdered egg
     1   teaspoon dried chopped onion
     ½   teaspoon dry mustard

Carry separately:

     1   can (14¾ ounces) red salmon
        Clarified butter or oil for frying (about 1 teaspoon)
        Ketchup

At camp:

Drain juice from canned salmon into measuring cup. Add or subtract water to equal ½ cup. In medium bowl, combine measured juice with dry ingredients; stir well to mix. Let stand 5 minutes to rehydrate the onion. While the mix is standing, pick out and discard bones and skin from salmon if desired, although you can leave them in; the canning process softens them so they're edible (however, many people – especially kids – find them objectionable). Flake salmon into bowl with other ingredients. Mix well, and form into 4 equal patties. Melt a little butter in a skillet over medium heat. Fry patties until well browned, about 5 minutes per side. Serve with ketchup.

Easy Goulash   2 or 3 servings

Easy to assemble at home, and equally easy to cook at camp, this is a great dish for a quick, tasty lunch or light supper.

Combine in quart plastic zipper bag:

     1   package (1 ounce) freeze-dried diced beef
     1½   cups dried potato slices from a boxed potato side dish*
     ¼   cup lentils
     4   dried tomato halves, cut into ½" pieces
     ½   package Knorr spring vegetable soup mix
     1   tablespoon dried onion flakes

At camp:

In medium pot, boil 1¾ cups water. Add mix; stir thoroughly. Cover and allow to stand for 15 minutes. Return to boiling. Reduce heat and simmer, stirring occasionally, until the potatoes are tender, about 15 minutes.

*See page 116, including the footnote, for recipes that use the sauce mix from the boxed potato mix.

Mushroom Spaghetti

2 or 3 servings

For the best flavor in this vegetarian entrée, combine two or more types of mushrooms: sliced dried Shiitake mushrooms, broken-up Oriental black mushroom caps, Chanterelle pieces, or whatever you have. This also works great as a side dish; it will serve 3 or 4.

Combine in quart plastic zipper bag:

1	cup dried mushroom slices and pieces, mixed varieties if possible
¼	cup dried diced green bell pepper
3	tablespoons dried onion flakes
1	envelope (1⅛ ounces) spaghetti sauce mix
½	teaspoon garlic powder
½	teaspoon salt

Carry separately:

3	cups thin, flat spinach noodles (loosely packed)
	Parmesan cheese

At camp:

Boil 4 cups water. Drain 1 cup into smaller pot and add mushroom mixture to the smaller pot; stir well. Add noodles to remaining 3 cups water in the larger pot; return to boil. Cook, stirring occasionally, until almost tender, 5 to 7 minutes. Cover and remove from heat; let stand while you finish cooking the mushroom sauce.

Over medium heat, bring mushroom mixture to simmer (if mixture is too thick, add a bit of additional water). Cook, stirring occasionally, for about 3 minutes. To serve: drain water from noodles (they should be tender before draining). Cover with mushroom sauce. Sprinkle with Parmesan cheese.

One-Pot Mushroom Spaghetti

2 or 3 servings

For those times when one-pot cooking is preferable, use this simpler method. The consistency is just slightly less interesting, but when you're miles from nowhere, I bet you won't even notice; it's still delicious.

Follow packing instructions above, except add noodles to same zipper bag with mushroom sauce mixture. Carry Parmesan cheese separately.

At camp:

In medium pot, boil 4 cups water. Add mix. Cook, stirring frequently, about 5 minutes; if noodles are sticking too much, add a little bit of additional water. Cover pot and remove from heat; let stand about 5 minutes, or until noodles are tender. Stir well, and sprinkle with Parmesan cheese before serving.

Ground Beef Stroganoff

This dish uses some convenience foods, like pre-packaged sauce mixes, to save work and make preparation easy and quick. You'll need to buy a box of Sour Cream and Chives potato side dish; half of the sauce packet is used in this recipe.*

Combine in quart plastic zipper bag:

1	cup dried cooked ground beef
1	package (1.8 ounces) Knorr white cream sauce mix
½	package sour cream and chive sauce mix from a boxed potato side dish*
¼	cup dried onion flakes
¼	cup dried mushroom slices or broken-up caps
1	tablespoon crumbled dried parsley leaves
1	teaspoon beef bouillon granules
¼	teaspoon garlic powder

At camp:

In medium pot, boil 2 cups water. Add mix; stir well. Cover; remove from heat and let stand about 15 minutes (you could cook some rice, pasta or mashed potatoes as a side dish during the standing time). Stir well, and return to boiling. Reduce heat and simmer, stirring occasionally, about 10 minutes. Serve with rice, noodles, mashed potatoes or biscuits on the side.

*See page 116, including the footnote, for recipes that use the other half of the sauce mix, and the potato slices, from the boxed potato mix.

Beef Stroganoff with Freeze-Dried Beef

For easier at-home preparation, substitute 1 package (1 ounce) freeze-dried diced beef for the home-dried ground beef in the above recipe. Follow all other packing and cooking instructions.

Lentil-Bulgur Chili

Lentils, bulgur and shredded cheese combine to make a complete protein in this delicious vegetarian chili. The sunflower seeds add great texture.

Combine in quart plastic zipper bag:

½	cup lentils
⅓	cup bulgur
⅓	cup dried shredded carrot
2	tablespoons dried celery slices (preferably de-stringed; see page 32)
2	tablespoons husked, salted sunflower seeds
1	tablespoon dried diced green bell pepper
1	tablespoon cornmeal
1½	teaspoons dried onion flakes
1	teaspoon crumbled dried parsley leaves
½	teaspoon crumbled dried oregano leaves
½	teaspoon garlic chips
½	teaspoon celery salt
⅛	teaspoon ground cumin
⅛	teaspoon cayenne pepper
⅛	teaspoon black pepper
4	sun-dried tomato halves, cut into ½" pieces
	Half of the leather from an 8-ounce can tomato sauce

Carry separately:

2	ounces Cheddar cheese (or ½ cup shredded)

At camp:

In medium pot, boil 2½ cups water. Add mix; stir thoroughly. Cover and allow to stand for 15 minutes. Stir well and return to boiling. Reduce heat and simmer, stirring occasionally, until the lentils are tender, 15 to 20 minutes; add additional water (up to ½ cup) if the chili begins sticking during cooking. While chili cooks, shred or coarsely chop the cheese. Sprinkle each serving with cheese.

Corned Beef Hash

2 servings

Try this for a lazy-day camp breakfast, or as a change-of-pace lunch. You can substitute any type of dried, pressed lunchmeat for the corned beef; try pressed ham for a delicious variation.

Place in a small plastic bag and seal with a twist-tie:

1	teaspoon beef bouillon granules
¾	teaspoon dry mustard
¼	teaspoon (scant) crumbled dried thyme leaves
⅛	teaspoon black pepper

Combine in freezer-weight quart plastic zipper bag:

1¼	cups crumbled dried pressed corned beef slices
¾	cup dried diced potatoes
3	tablespoons dried chopped onion
2	tablespoons dried diced green bell pepper
	The small bag with the spices

Carry separately:

	Bacon drippings, clarified butter or oil for frying
2	eggs, optional
	Ketchup, optional

At camp:

Remove small bag with spices and set aside. Boil 1½ cups water; add to zipper bag with potato mixture (see page 155). Let stand until potatoes are almost tender, 20 to 30 minutes. Drain excess water (tip: the leftover soaking water– about ½ cup – is a tasty broth that the cook may enjoy as a pre-meal snack!). Add spices; mix well.

In medium skillet, heat enough drippings to grease the skillet well. Add potato mixture. Fry, stirring occasionally, until lightly browned. When browned, push hash to side of skillet to keep warm; fry eggs over-easy, or as desired. Serve eggs over hash, with ketchup on the side.

One-Pot Corned Beef Hash (photo page 156) 2 servings

If you won't be carrying a frying pan on your trip, try this one-pot version of **Corned Beef Hash.** *Use a 1½-quart pot for 2 people. For 4 people, use a 3-quart pot, and double the ingredients.*

Follow drying and packing instructions for **Corned Beef Hash** on page 126, except pack all dry ingredients in one bag. You will not need any bacon drippings.

At camp:

In medium pot, boil 1¾ cups water. Add mix; stir well. Remove from heat; cover and let stand 25 minutes.

Simmer over medium-low heat about 5 minutes, stirring frequently. Make two small depressions on top of the hash. Gently break one egg into each depression. Cover pot; cook over medium-low heat until egg whites are no longer clear but yolks are still runny, about 5 minutes.

Easy-Does-It Beef Hash 2 servings

Don't have a food dehydrator, and don't feel like messing around drying meat and potatoes in your home oven? Try this easy version of hash. It uses freeze-dried diced beef, and boxed dried potato slices (you'll find them in the supermarket, next to the instant mashed potatoes). See the note below for ideas on what to do with the sauce packet that comes with the potatoes.

Follow packing and camp cooking instructions for **Corned Beef Hash** on page 126, or **One-Pot Corned Beef Hash**, above, except substitute 1 package (1 ounce) freeze-dried diced beef for the dried pressed corned beef slices; substitute ½ box sliced dried potatoes from a boxed potato side dish* for the dried diced potatoes (break the potato slices into quarters before packing); add an additional ½ teaspoon beef bouillon granules, for a total of 1½ teaspoons. Cook as directed for either recipe.

*See page 116, including the footnote, for recipes that use the sauce mix, and the other half of the potato slices, from the boxed potato mix.

Barbecued Beef Sandwiches

3 or 4 servings

Kids particularly enjoy this dish; it's similar to an "at-home" favorite.

1	pound extra-lean ground beef
½	cup diced onion
¼	cup diced green bell pepper, optional
¾	cup barbecue sauce
5	tablespoons tomato paste (half of a 6-ounce can)
	A pinch of sugar

In medium skillet, cook ground beef over medium heat until a little grease begins to accumulate. Add onion and pepper. Cook over medium heat until the ground beef is thoroughly cooked and onion and pepper are tender, stirring frequently to break up the ground beef. Scrape the meat mixture into a mesh colander placed in the sink. Allow to drain for a few minutes, then spray quickly with hot water to rinse off additional grease. This helps the meat keep longer on the trail without turning rancid.

Wipe out the skillet with paper towels to remove grease. Return the meat mixture to the skillet. Add barbecue sauce, tomato paste, and sugar; stir well to blend. Heat over medium heat for a few minutes. Spread evenly onto dryer trays lined with solid insert sheets or cookie sheets that have been sprayed with non-stick spray. Dry at 145°F, turning and breaking up every hour or so, until mixture is dry and crumbly, 5 to 7 hours. Cool completely; place into zipper bag. Store in refrigerator or freezer until you're packing for your trip.

Carry separately:
  3 or 4   hamburger buns, pita breads, or other bread

At camp:

In medium pot, boil ¾ cup water. Add mix; stir well. Cover; remove from heat and let stand 10 or 15 minutes. Stir well, and return to boiling. Reduce heat and simmer, stirring occasionally, about 5 minutes. Serve meat in buns.

Turkey Tetrazzini with Spring Vegetables 3 or 4 servings

When you look at the packaged freeze-dried dinners at the camping store, you'll often see a dish like this one. I think this home-made version has more flavor and texture than the commercially packed versions, and you can tailor it with whatever vegetables you like.

Combine sauce mix in a small plastic bag and seal with a twist-tie:
   3   tablespoons shelf-stable Parmesan cheese
   2   tablespoons all-purpose flour
   2   tablespoons nonfat dry milk powder
   1   tablespoon Butter Buds
   ¾   teaspoon chicken bouillon granules
   ⅛   teaspoon white pepper

Combine in quart plastic zipper bag:
   1   package (1 ounce) freeze-dried diced turkey
   ¼   cup broken-up dried mushroom slices
   ¼   cup dried carrot slices
   3   tablespoons dried sliced green onion
   2   tablespoons dried celery slices
       The small sealed bag with the sauce mix

Carry separately:
   2   cups fine-cut egg noodles

At camp:

Remove small bag with sauce mix and set aside. In medium pot, boil 2¾ cups water. Add turkey and vegetables; stir well. Cover; remove from heat and let stand 20 to 30 minutes. Stir well, and return to boiling. Add noodles. Cook over medium heat, stirring frequently, until noodles are almost tender, 8 to 10 minutes.

While noodles are cooking, blend sauce ingredients with ½ cup water in a small cup. When noodles are just tender, add sauce mix, stirring constantly to prevent lumps. Continue to cook, stirring frequently, until sauce has thickened, about 1 minute longer.

Turkey Tetrazzini with Dried Vegetable Mix 3 or 4 servings

For convenience, I sometimes buy a mix that is simply called "vegetable flakes" at the health-food store. It contains dried peas, tomatoes, celery, onions, parsley, green peppers and carrots. Other similar vegetable mixes are sometimes available if you scout co-ops and natural-foods stores. They're a great time-saver when you're rushing to pack before a trip.

Follow packing and cooking instructions in **Turkey Tetrazzini with Spring Vegetables**, above, but omit mushrooms, carrots, green onion and celery; substitute ¾ cup vegetable flakes. Reduce soaking time to 10 to 15 minutes. Proceed as directed.

Camp Pizza

4 small servings

Use your imagination – and whatever ingredients you have on hand – when planning and assembling this dish. This is perfect for cooking in the Outback Oven (page 46) or other camp oven, and could also be cooked in a campfire with some care and attention.

Carry separately:

- 2 teaspoons olive oil or other oil
- 1 batch **Bread-Machine Mix** blend (page 86) *or* **Rosemary-Parmesan Focaccia** blend (page 87)
- 1 batch of the dried sauce from **Spaghetti with Sausage Sauce** (page 119) *or* one batch **Ratatouille** (page 145)
    Optional toppings: fresh or rehydrated dried vegetables like chopped green peppers, chopped onion, or sliced mushrooms; sliced salami
- 2 ounces co-jack or other cheese (or ½ cup shredded)

At camp:

Lightly oil the pan you'll be using with your camp oven with a bit of the olive oil. Heat ¼ cup water until it is hot to the touch; the water temperature should be like a very hot, but still tolerable, bath. Add the hot water and remaining oil to the bag with the bread mix. Seal the bag, and mix the dough by squeezing and kneading the bag with your hands. The dough will form a mass that pulls away from the plastic bag; if it seems dry, add a few drops water. Knead for 5 minutes. Let the dough rest in the bag for 5 minutes. Form dough into a flat disk with your hands. Place in the oiled pan, and press to cover the bottom of the pan. Cover the pan, and set aside in a warm place to rise for 30-45 minutes (longer if the weather is cool). Normally, bread should rise until double in size; if you have the time, let it rise until doubled (this could take an hour or longer). However, the pizza will be fine even if the dough has not doubled.

While the crust rises, pre-heat the camp oven if necessary*. Re-hydrate the sauce by adding enough boiling water to the sausage sauce mix or ratatouille mix to make a thick sauce; let stand until you're ready to assemble the pizza, stirring occasionally. It's better to add too little water at the beginning, and add more as needed, than to have a sauce that is too thin.

At the end of the rising time, prick the crust in several places with a fork. Top with the sauce. Add any vegetables or other topping. Shred or coarsely chop the cheese, and sprinkle over the pizza. Bake, uncovered, until the crust is browned on the bottom and the cheese melts. Baking time will be from 20 to 40 minutes; check after 20 minutes, and continue cooking if necessary.

Note: This can also be baked in a campfire, in a covered skillet or pot. Soap the outside of the skillet or pot, including the lid; or, plan to wrap the entire skillet and lid with foil. Assemble the pizza as directed. Cover the skillet, and place directly on a small bed of campfire coals (see pages 58-59 for campfire cooking tips); shovel a few coals on top of the skillet. Bake as directed, moving the skillet around on the coals frequently.

*The Outback Oven requires no pre-heating. Box-style camp ovens should be pre-heated to 300°F-350°F before baking.

Tamale Pie

Tamales are a Mexican specialty. In the most typical version, seasoned shredded meat is surrounded by a rich cornmeal batter; the tamale is wrapped in corn husks and steamed. **Tamale Pie** *is a wonderful one-pot meal that is reminiscent of this classic dish, but is easy to make at camp. The inspiration for this recipe came from one of the same name in Stella Hughes' delightful book,* Bacon & Beans: Ranch-Country Recipes.

Combine in freezer-weight pint plastic zipper bag:
- ½   cup cornmeal
- 2   tablespoons dry buttermilk powder
- 1   teaspoon baking powder
- ½   teaspoon salt

Combine in quart plastic zipper bag:
- 1   cup dried cooked ground beef
- ¼   cup dried diced tomatoes
- ¼   cup dried diced red or green bell peppers
- ¼   cup freeze-dried corn kernels
- 1   tablespoon chili powder blend
- 1   tablespoon dried chopped onion
- 3 or 4   dried pickled jalapeño rings, broken up, optional*
- ½   teaspoon salt
-   The bag with the cornmeal mix

Carry separately:
- 3   tablespoons butter or margarine
- 2   ounces co-jack or other cheese (or ½ cup shredded), optional

At camp:

Pre-heat camp oven if necessary.** Place the butter into the bag with the cornmeal; set the bag in a bowl as shown on page 155. In medium pot, boil 2½ cups water. Add ½ cup of the boiling water to the bag with the cornmeal; stir with a spoon to blend. Seal the bag and set aside. Add the ground beef mix to the remaining 2 cups boiling water in the medium pot. Cover and let both items stand for 10 minutes, stirring the ground beef occasionally.

While the meat and cornmeal are standing, shred or coarsely chop the cheese. After the 10-minute standing period, sprinkle the cheese on top of the ground beef mixture. Pour the cornmeal batter over the cheese and meat. Cover and bake in the Outback Oven (page 46) or other camp oven until the cornmeal is springy when pressed lightly with your fingertip. This will take 30 to 45 minutes, depending on oven temperature.

*You could also substitute ⅛ teaspoon cayenne pepper.

**The Outback Oven requires no pre-heating. Box-style camp ovens should be pre-heated to 300°F-350°F before mixing and baking.

Blackened Steak *(photo page 156)*   Enough for 2 pounds of meat

When you're packing for your trip, wrap solidly frozen steak (wrapped tightly in plastic wrap before freezing) in layers of newspapers, then pack into a large plastic bag to contain leaks; tuck it into the center of your pack just before you leave. The meat will thaw gradually, and be ready for dinner on the first night, or second night, if the weather is cool. You'll need a stove that generates a lot of heat; a charcoal grill or campfire will also work well. A cast-iron skillet or grill is a must. This dish is a natural for outdoor cooking, because the smoke isn't a problem like it is in your home kitchen!

Mix well, then place in a small plastic bag and seal with a twist-tie:

1	tablespoon paprika, preferably Hungarian
2	teaspoons salt
2	teaspoons freshly ground black pepper
2	teaspoons dry mustard
1½	teaspoons crushed fennel seeds
1	teaspoon ground cayenne pepper (*not* chili powder)
1	teaspoon onion powder
½	teaspoon crumbled dried thyme leaves
½	teaspoon crumbled dried oregano leaves

Carry separately:

Round or loin steak, ¾ to 1¼ inches thick
Clarified butter (about 4 tablespoons per pound of steak)

At camp:

Heat cast-iron skillet or griddle over high heat until very hot (some say the skillet will turn white, but I've never gotten it quite *that* hot!). While skillet heats, melt butter in another pan. Dip the steaks in the melted butter, turning to coat on all sides. Sprinkle liberally with the seasoning mix on all sides.

When skillet is as hot as it will get, add steaks in a single layer. Allow to sear very well on the bottom. Turn and sear the other side (tip: if the steaks are sticking to the skillet, they aren't ready to turn; when properly seared, the meat will "release" from the skillet). The meat should be rare to medium-rare in the center, with a charred exterior.

Note: This will probably remove most of the seasoning from your cast-iron skillet. When the skillet is cool enough to handle, clean it with a paper towel, then coat lightly with vegetable oil to prevent rust from forming until you can re-season it.

Blackened Chicken

Follow **Blackened Steak** recipe above, except substitute skinless boned chicken breasts or thighs for steak. Unlike steak, which is best served rare or medium-rare, chicken should be cooked completely. Because chicken spoils more easily than steak, plan on using it the first night of your trip.

Bacon-Mushroom-Tomato Quiche   2 hearty main-dish servings

Many camping-supply stores sell pre-packaged quiche mixes designed for use with special camper's ovens. You can easily make your own mix with readily purchased ingredients. The home-packed mix is about half the cost of the pre-packaged mix; plus, you can use any ingredients you like. Here, I've combined bacon, mushrooms, and tomato for a hearty meal. If you're serving this for breakfast, or with other dishes for lunch or dinner, it will easily serve 4 people; it's very rich.

Combine in quart plastic zipper bag:

- ¾   cup powdered egg
- ¼   cup (scant) broken-up dried sliced mushrooms
- 3   tablespoons dried cooked bacon pieces
- 2   tablespoons dried tomato, chopped up before measuring
- 2   tablespoons nonfat dry milk powder
- ¼   teaspoon salt

Place in another quart plastic zipper bag:

- 1⅓   cups Betty Crocker pie crust mix (half of an 11-ounce package)

Carry separately:

- A little clarified butter or oil to grease the baking pan

At camp:

Pre-heat camp oven if necessary.* Lightly grease a 6½"-diameter** pot; set aside. Add 1¼ cups cold water to the bag with the egg mixture. Seal the bag; shake and knead with your hands until the egg powder is blended into the water. Set aside.

Add 2 tablespoons plus 2 teaspoons cold water to the bag with the pie crust. Seal the bag; knead with your hands to mix thoroughly, but don't overmix or the crust will be tough. Dump the crust into the greased pot. Press firmly and evenly in the pan and up the sides; the crust should extend at least 1½" up the sides. Shake the egg mixture again, then carefully pour into the crust. Cover the pot.

Bake in the Outback Oven (page 46) or other camp oven until the egg mixture is set; when you touch it lightly with your fingertip, it should be springy and completely set, 30 to 35 minutes. Check it after 20 minutes to make sure it isn't burning or cooking more quickly.

*The Outback Oven requires no pre-heating. Box-style camp ovens should be pre-heated to 300°F-350°F before mixing and baking.

**This is the diameter of my 1.5-quart Peak cookset pot. If your pot is wider than 6½", the crust doesn't have to extend quite as high up the sides of the pan; the quiche will cook more quickly. If your pot is narrower, extend the crust higher, and cook the quiche longer.

Mock Drumsticks

4 servings

When I was a kid, my mom used to buy "mock drumsticks:" ground veal shaped into rectangles like fat fish sticks, covered with cornflake crumbs. I saw a somewhat similar recipe in Dian Thomas' classic Roughing It Easy 2 *that inspired me to re-create this childhood favorite, using ground turkey instead of veal. These are cooked on a stick over an open fire, and can be eaten right from the stick (kids really enjoy this sort of stuff).*

Carry separately:

1	whole raw egg
¾	cup cornflake crumbs, divided
½	teaspoon celery salt or seasoned salt
1	pound extra-lean ground turkey burger
2	tablespoons barbecue sauce, optional

At camp:

You'll need a campfire, with the coals burned down and ready for cooking. Find four downed hardwood sticks (not softwoods like pine or fir), ½" in diameter and at least 3 feet long. The sticks should be as straight as possible, and have few side branches. Strip the bark from about 8 inches of one end of each stick (a pocket knife works well for this; strip the bark with a carving motion away from yourself).

In a bowl, blend the egg, 6 tablespoons of the cornflake crumbs, and the celery salt with a fork. Add turkey burger; mix well. Divide into 4 equal portions. Flatten one portion into a long patty, then shape it around the peeled end of a stick into a cylinder about 5 inches long; cover the end of the stick also (this helps the meat hold together during cooking). Brush with barbecue sauce; roll in the remaining cornflake crumbs. Repeat with remaining ingredients.

Each camper cooks their own drumstick. Hold the drumstick over the coals, turning frequently to prevent burning. The drumsticks will be firm when

 done; this will probably take from 10 to 15 minutes, depending on the coals. The drumstick can be pulled off the stick onto a plate, or can be eaten directly from the stick.

Bacon-Wrapped Drumsticks

Follow recipe above, except carry only 6 tablespoons cornflake crumbs; also carry 8 strips bacon and 8 toothpicks. Instead of rolling the drumstick in cornflake crumbs, wrap two pieces of bacon around each drumstick, securing with toothpicks. Cook as directed. These are juicier and more tender than the cornflake-coated version, and are less likely to fall apart during cooking.

Foiled Again Hamburger Dinner

1 serving per packet

This camping classic is easy to prepare, and contains meat, vegetable, and potato – all in one convenient wrapper. If you have some cole slaw or green salad, it makes a nice addition to this meal.

For each serving, carry:

	18" x 24" piece of heavy-duty foil
1	tablespoon barbecue sauce
¼	small onion
5	ounces lean ground beef or venison
¼	teaspoon seasoned salt or garlic salt
½	small Idaho baking potato
1	medium carrot

At camp:

You'll need a campfire, with the coals burned down and ready for cooking. For each serving: fold the foil in half to 18" x 12", shiny side in. Place the tablespoon of barbecue sauce in the center. Peel the onion and slice ⅛" thick; arrange over barbecue sauce. Combine ground beef and seasoned salt; mix well. Shape into oblong patty, approximately 4" x 3" x ¾". Place patty on top of barbecue sauce and onions. Peel potato and carrot, and slice both ⅛" thick. Top patty with potato and carrot slices. Fold foil over ingredients, using drugstore wrap (page 56); be sure to seal ends very well. Repeat with any remaining ingredients until all packets are prepared.

The coals of the fire should be hot enough that you can place your hand an inch above the grate for about 5 seconds, but no longer, without discomfort. Place wrapped packets onto grate. Turn and rotate every 10 minutes, rearranging packets on grate; total cooking time will be approximately 35 minutes. To check for doneness, open one packet carefully; vegetables should be tender and meat should be medium-well or well-done. To serve, carefully unwrap packet; flip meat, vegetables and juices onto individual plate. Or, serve directly from the foil packet to save dishwashing.

Chapter Nine

International Favorites

Following are a baker's dozen recipes that are adaptations of dishes from around the globe: Morocco, India, Italy, China, Israel, Mexico, and France. These are exciting, fully seasoned dishes – not pale imitations that sound interesting but fail to stimulate the taste buds. If you're travelling with kids (or other picky eaters) who are not familiar with these types of foods, you may want to try these dishes at home before planning them for a trip. On the trail, it's not so easy to fix a quick hot dog if the dish is too spicy or "weird" for kids.

Couscous with Chicken and Fruit   4 servings

Couscous (pronounced koos-koos) is often called Moroccan pasta. It's a type of granular pasta made from semolina, the same flour used to make the best Italian pastas. Because it cooks quickly, it's ideal for camping.

Place in a small plastic bag and seal with a twist-tie:
 ⅔ cup couscous

Combine in quart plastic zipper bag:
 1 package (1 ounce) freeze-dried diced chicken
 ¼ cup freeze-dried green peas
 ¼ cup dried diced red bell pepper
 ¼ cup dried diced tomato
 3 tablespoons diced dried apricot
 2 tablespoons currants
 2 tablespoon diced dried apple slices
 1 teaspoon chicken bouillon granules
 1 teaspoon crumbled dried mint leaves
 ½ teaspoon garlic chips
 ½ teaspoon curry powder
 ⅛-¼ teaspoon cayenne pepper
  A pinch of ground coriander seeds
  The small bag with the couscous

At camp:

Set aside bag of couscous. In medium pot, boil 2 cups water. Add chicken mix; stir well. Cover; remove from heat and let stand about 15 minutes. Stir well, and return to boiling. Reduce heat to simmer and cook 3 or 4 minutes, stirring occasionally. Stir in the couscous. Cover and remove from heat. Let stand 5 minutes. Fluff with fork before serving.

Garlic Chicken with Curry Spices

2 or 3 servings

Serve this Indian-inspired one-pot meal with fresh carrot sticks or cucumber wedges, if you have them. Hot tea provides a nice counterpoint to this mildly spicy dish.

Place in a small plastic bag and seal with a twist-tie:

- ¼ cup Durkee French-fried onions (found in the snack aisle)

Combine in quart plastic zipper bag:

- 1 package (1 ounce) freeze-dried diced chicken
- ¾ cup converted or long-grain rice
- ⅓ cup dried sliced green onion
- ¼ cup dried onion flakes
- 1 tablespoon currants
- 2 teaspoons dried snipped chives
- 1 teaspoon salt
- ½ teaspoon turmeric
- ½ teaspoon garlic chips
- ½ teaspoon ground cardamom
- ½ teaspoon cayenne pepper, optional
- ¼ teaspoon white pepper
- ⅛ teaspoon ground cloves

The small sealed bag with the French-fried onions

At camp:

Set aside bag of French-fried onions. In medium pot, boil 2 cups water. Add chicken mix; stir well. Cover; remove from heat and let stand about 15 minutes. Stir well, and return to boiling. Reduce heat and simmer, stirring frequently, until the rice is almost tender and most of the liquid is absorbed, about 15 minutes. Remove from heat; cover and let stand 5 minutes. Fluff with fork before serving. Top each serving with French-fried onions.

Trail Kung Pao Chicken

We first field-tested this trail version of the classic Szechuan dish on a Seagull Lake island campsite. It requires a bit of organization at the campsite, but really isn't difficult to cook; all the work is done at home, in advance. And the dish is absolutely worth it: bright green spring onions in a dark, spicy sauce paired with chicken and crunchy peanuts, all atop a heap of fluffy white rice. An astonishing feat to pull off when you're miles from civilization!

In a small bowl, combine the sauce ingredients:

4	teaspoons brown bean paste*
4	teaspoons hoisin sauce*
1	tablespoon rice vinegar
1	tablespoon soy sauce
2	teaspoons cornstarch
½	teaspoon garlic powder
½	teaspoon sugar
⅛	teaspoon cayenne pepper (or more, if you prefer it spicier)

Note: You will also need 6 or 7 dried green onions for this recipe. If you don't have a batch of them dried already, slice into half-inch slices and dry them at the same time as the sauce, following the instructions on page 33.

Blend sauce ingredients together with a fork. Line food-dryer tray, or cookie sheet if drying in your oven, with plastic wrap (see page 36 for information on drying tomato sauce or paste; this is the same technique). Pour the sauce over the plastic wrap, and spread evenly with a spoon; the depth should be ⅛" or less. Dry at 140°F until leathery and pliable; this will take 8 to 12 hours. Near the end of the drying, the sauce will be leathery enough to peel off the plastic wrap and flip over; this helps ensure even drying by exposing the bottom side to the dryer. *Tip:* Dry the sauce at 140°F for 6 to 8 hours, then let it sit overnight in a gas oven with a pilot light; it will continue to dry slowly, and the next day you can resume regular drying. When the sauce is leathery and dry but still pliable (it may be slightly sticky; this is OK), peel off the plastic wrap, cut into narrower pieces, and roll up. Re-wrap in a piece of the plastic wrap.

Place in a small plastic bag and seal with a twist-tie:

⅔ cup converted or long-grain rice

Place in another small plastic bag and seal with a twist-tie:

⅔ cup unsalted dry-roasted peanuts**
The plastic-wrapped dried sauce

Combine in freezer-weight quart plastic zipper bag:

1 package (1 ounce) freeze-dried diced chicken
⅔ cup dried sliced green onions
The small sealed bags with the rice and the peanuts/sauce

Carry separately:

Peanut oil or clarified butter for frying (about 1 tablespoon)

Trail Kung Pao Chicken (continued)

Here is an overview of the cooking procedure. Read this through and you'll see that it's not difficult, but does require several steps. Organization is the key to easy cooking of this dish.

1. Cook rice first, then set aside and keep warm while you prepare the Kung Pao. For this recipe, you will cook the rice in more water than is necessary; the extra water will be used to soak the chicken and re-hydrate the sauce.

2. Drain the rice-cooking water into the chicken to re-hydrate.

3. Use the water from the chicken to re-hydrate the sauce. While one person cooks the chicken, it's helpful to have a second person stir the sauce mix to blend it with the warm water.

4. Fry the chicken and peanuts, then add the sauce and cook briefly.

At camp:

In medium pan, boil 2 cups water. Add rice; cover and reduce heat. Simmer, stirring frequently, until the rice is almost tender, about 15 minutes. While the rice cooks, remove the bag with the peanuts and sauce mix; set aside. When the rice is almost tender, drain the cooking water into the zipper bag with the chicken and green onions (see page 155). If there isn't enough water left to cover the chicken and spring onions, add cold water as needed. Allow to stand for 10 minutes; wrap the rice pot in a towel to keep it warm.

While the chicken is soaking, unwrap the sauce leather and place into a medium bowl or pan. When the chicken is tender, drain ¼ cup of the soaking water into the sauce mix. Drain and discard the remainder of the soaking water from the chicken, gently squeezing out excess moisture.

In 7" or larger skillet, heat enough oil to coat the bottom of the skillet. Add the chicken, spring onions and peanuts. Cook over medium-high heat, stirring frequently, until the chicken and peanuts are lightly browned. While the chicken is cooking, stir and mash the sauce mix with a fork to blend it with the water. Add the reconstituted sauce mix to the browned chicken; cook, stirring frequently, for 1 or 2 minutes. Fluff the cooked rice with a fork. Serve the Kung Pao chicken over the rice.

*Brown bean sauce and hoisin sauce are Chinese staples that are usually available in the specialty-foods section of larger grocery stores, or from Asian markets. There isn't much difference between brands of brown bean paste, but hoisin sauce is another matter. My favorite brand of hoisin sauce is Koon Chun Sauce Factory brand; I buy it at a Hmong-run grocery, but have also seen it in gourmet shops (where it costs twice as much as from the Hmong grocer!). Lee Kum Kee brand, which is a decent substitute, is usually available in larger grocery stores, and is much better than the readily available China Bowl brand. If you have several brands to choose from, look for one that is dark and thick, almost like heavy barbecue sauce; it should not appear translucent, gummy or watery.

**The traditional recipe uses raw peanuts, which need proper stir-frying to make them taste correct. After much experimentation with other types of peanuts, I have settled on *unsalted* dry-roasted peanuts as the best choice for this recipe. *Do not* use regular (salted and seasoned) dry-roasted peanuts; the result will be disastrous in flavor. Instead, substitute lightly salted cocktail peanuts (no skins).

Siniya Burgers

4 servings; recipe can easily be halved or doubled

This Israeli dish is usually baked like a meatloaf, or in individual ramekins. It adapts quite well to the wilderness kitchen, and is a welcome change-of-pace from the usual camp burger.

Place in a small plastic bag and seal with a twist-tie:

2	tablespoons pine nuts
1	teaspoon crumbled dried parsley leaves
¾	teaspoon salt
¾	teaspoon ground cumin
¾	teaspoon ground coriander seeds
½	teaspoon crumbled dried mint leaves
½	teaspoon garlic powder
¼	teaspoon crumbled dried dill leaves
⅛	teaspoon black pepper

Carry separately:

1	pound ground lamb, beef, or lamb-and-beef mixture
1	whole lemon
⅓	cup tahini*
4	pita breads
4	12" x 12" squares of heavy-duty foil
	Fresh cucumber, optional
	Fresh yogurt, optional

At camp:

You'll need a campfire, with the coals burned down and ready for cooking. Mix dry seasoning and meat well. Form into 4 slightly oblong patties, each about 3" x 5". Place each patty on the center of a foil square. Squeeze the lemon juice evenly over the patties; top each with a quarter of the tahini (about 1½ tablespoons). Fold and seal as shown on page 56.

The coals of the fire should be hot enough that you can place your hand an inch above the grate for about 5 seconds, but no longer, without discomfort. Place wrapped packets onto grate. Turn and rotate after 10 minutes; total cooking time will be 15 to 20 minutes. Serve in split pita breads; garnish with cucumber slices and yogurt.

Make-ahead tip:

Mix the meat and dry seasoning at home and form into patties. Place a small piece of waxed paper between each patty; wrap well in plastic wrap. Freeze at least overnight. The frozen patties can be carried in a cooler or pack for your first night's supper. Add the lemon juice and tahini prior to cooking in foil.

*Tahini is a paste made of ground sesame seeds. It is like a very smooth, slightly thin, light-colored peanut butter. Look for this Mideastern specialty item with the peanut butter or in the specialty-foods sections of large grocery stores. Health-food stores or co-ops also carry tahini. Pack only the amount you need, in a leak-proof plastic container. If you're transporting it in a pack, double-bag the container with plastic bags; this stuff would make a real mess if it got into the rest of the items in your pack.

Frijoles Borrachos ("Drunken Beans") 4 side-dish servings

If you don't have a can of beer, or if you prefer not to use it, simply substitute water and chicken bouillon granules as indicated in the variation below for a very tasty Frijoles Refritos ("Refried Beans").

1   can (16 ounces) pinto beans, drained and rinsed,
      or 1⅔ cups cooked pinto beans
3   pickled jalapeño pepper rings

Arrange beans and peppers on dryer racks. Dry at 145°F until beans are completely dry and pepper rings are leathery, 3 to 4 hours. Cool. Break or cut the jalapeño rings into smaller pieces.

Combine in pint plastic zipper bag:

2   tablespoons dried cooked bacon pieces or bacon-flavored bits,
      optional
1   tablespoon dried chopped onion
¼   teaspoon salt
⅛   teaspoon garlic chips
⅛   teaspoon black pepper
      The dried beans and jalapeño slices (if you dry cooked beans in bulk, you will need 1¼ cups of dried beans for this recipe)

Carry separately:

1   cup beer, room temperature
      Flour tortillas, optional
      Shredded cheddar or Monterey Jack cheese, optional

At camp:

Pour the beer and the bean mix into a medium pan or skillet; stir thoroughly. Allow to stand for 10 minutes. Cook over medium-high heat until thickened, about 10 minutes, stirring frequently. Sprinkle with shredded cheese and serve with flour tortillas.

Frijoles Refritos

Follow recipe above, but add ½ teaspoon chicken bouillon granules to the mix; omit salt and beer. In camp, combine bean mix with 1 cup water. Proceed as directed.

Turkey with Mole-Inspired Sauce

2 servings

A true Mexican mole *(mo-lay) sauce is a complicated business – my favorite recipe for it takes up 4 pages in the cookbook it's in. In the "real" recipe, 3 varieties of dried chiles are fried in lard, then soaked overnight in water and ground to a paste, which is then fried in more lard before being blended with seasonings, green tomatoes, fried raisins, 3 types of toasted seeds or nuts, a piece of French bread, a stale tortilla … well, you get the idea. My camping rendition of this classic recipe is a lot simpler (and, I might point out, a lot less fatty), but still maintains the general flavor of the original. All the work is done at home; at camp, your meal will be ready in about 10 minutes. A menu-planning note:* **Frijoles Borrachos** *(page 141) go great with this dish. Warning:* this is spicy!

Make the mole *sauce:*

- ¼   cup blanched slivered almonds
- 2   tablespoons sesame seeds
- ⅛   teaspoon anise seeds
- ⅔   cup crushed tortilla chips (plain salted, not "nacho" flavored)
- 1   *chile ancho*, seeds, stem and veins removed, cut up* (see Note below)
- 1   *chile chipotle*, seeds, stem and veins removed, cut up* (see Note below)
- 2   dried tomato halves, cut up
- 2   teaspoons chicken bouillon granules
- 1   teaspoon cocoa powder (the kind used for baking)
- ¼   teaspoon garlic chips
- ⅛   teaspoon ground coriander seeds
- ⅛   teaspoon cinnamon
- ⅛   teaspoon black pepper
- A good pinch of ground cloves

Heat a small cast-iron or other heavy-bottomed skillet over medium heat. Add the almonds, sesame seeds and anise seeds. Toast over medium heat, stirring constantly, for about 5 minutes, or until the sesame seeds turn golden brown. Remove from heat and continue to stir until the pan is no longer hot.

In food processor or blender, combine cooled toasted nuts and seeds with remaining sauce ingredients. Process in on-and-off pulses until everything is finely chopped. The mixture will be slightly paste-like and crumbly. Transfer to a small plastic bag; seal with a twist-tie.

Combine in quart plastic zipper bag:

1   package (1 ounce) freeze-dried diced turkey (you can substitute freeze-dried chicken to make **Chicken with *Mole*-Inspired Sauce**)

1   tablespoon currants

2   teaspoons dried onion flakes

1   teaspoon cornmeal

      The small bag with the *mole* paste

Carry separately:

      Flour tortillas (usually 1 or 2 per person)

At camp:

In medium pot, boil 1⅛ cups water. Add contents of both bags; stir well. Cover; remove from heat and let stand about 5 minutes. Stir well, and return to boiling. Reduce heat and simmer, stirring frequently, until thickened, about 5 minutes. Serve with tortillas.

Note: If your tortillas have become slightly stale and need freshening, steam them by placing them for a few minutes over the pot in which you are cooking the *mole*. Or, heat a skillet over medium heat. Add the tortillas, and shuffle for a few minutes so each one gets warmed on the bottom of the pan. Sprinkle a few drops of water in the pan and quickly cover; remove from heat and let steam for about a minute.

*As mentioned, this dish is pretty spicy! If you want the flavor, but not all the heat, use chile halves rather than whole chiles, and scrape out the seeds and veins inside the chiles.

Note: Chile ancho is a large, flavorful dried chile that is probably the most commonly used chile in Mexican cooking. *Chile chipotle* is is actually a dried, smoked jalapeño chile. Look for these dried chiles in a Mexican market, or in the specialty or produce section of a large grocery store. Be very careful when removing the seeds and veins; most of the chile's "heat" is in the seeds and veins, and the oils can burn your skin. Wear rubber gloves if you have sensitive skin, and be careful not to touch your eyes, nose, or other sensitive areas. Cut the chiles up with a scissors to make chopping easier. If you can't find these chiles, don't despair. You can still make the dish; it will be a little less authentic, but still very tasty. The best substitute is 12 home-dried pickled jalapeño rings (see page 34), but you can also substitute ¼ to ½ teaspoon ground cayenne pepper (*not* chili powder).

Artichokes and Potatoes alla Campagnola ("Country-Style")

2 or 3 side-dish servings

This is based on a dish that's often served in Northern Italy.

Combine in quart plastic zipper bag:

½ cup dried sliced canned artichokes
1½ cups dried potato slices from a boxed-potato side dish*
2 tablespoons dried onion flakes
2 teaspoons beef bouillon granules
½ teaspoon garlic chips
½ teaspoon crumbled dried basil leaves
¼ teaspoon black pepper
Half of the leather from an 8-ounce can tomato sauce

Carry separately:
Parmesan cheese, optional

At camp:

In medium pot, boil 1¾ cups water. Add mix; stir thoroughly. Cover and allow to stand for 15 minutes. Return to boiling. Reduce heat and simmer, stirring frequently, until the liquid has reduced to a fairly thick sauce and the potatoes are tender, about 15 minutes. Sprinkle with Parmesan cheese, if available.

*See page 116, including the footnote, for recipes that use the sauce mix from the boxed potato mix.

Risi e Bisi (Rice and Peas)

4 side-dish servings

Don't be tempted to omit the dried celery from this recipe; the flavor it contributes is indescribable, but totally wonderful. This is based on a traditional recipe from Venice, Italy.

Combine in pint plastic zipper bag:

¾ cup converted or long-grain rice
½ cup dried green peas (from fresh or frozen peas)
2 tablespoons dried celery slices
1 tablespoon Butter Buds
1 teaspoon beef bouillon granules
1 teaspoon dried chopped onion
½ teaspoon crumbled dried parsley leaves
¼ teaspoon sugar

At camp:

In medium pot, boil 1⅔ cups water. Add mix; stir well. Cover; remove from heat and let stand about 15 minutes. Stir well, and return to boiling. Reduce heat and simmer, stirring frequently, until the rice is almost tender and most of the liquid is absorbed, about 15 minutes. Remove from heat; let stand, covered, 5 minutes or longer. Fluff with fork before serving.

Ratatouille

Makes 2 batches; 2 or 3 side-dish servings per batch

Prepare this classic French vegetable stew when vegetables are in season, then dry for later. It's great in camp as a side dish when you're enjoying a fresh fish fry, or as a topping for **Camp Pizza** *(page 130); you can also toss it with cooked pasta for a wonderful vegetarian main dish.*

1	eggplant (about 1 pound), cut into eighths lengthwise and then sliced ⅛" thick
3	small zucchini (about 1 pound total), halved and sliced ⅛" thick
2	tablespoons salt
2	tablespoons olive oil
2	large yellow onions (about 1 pound total), peeled, quartered, and sliced ⅛" thick
2	medium green bell peppers (about ¾ pound total), cored, seeded, and halved, then sliced ⅛" thick
3	cloves fresh garlic, peeled and minced
1	bunch parsley, chopped (about ¼ cup chopped parsley)
5	tablespoons tomato paste (half of a 6-ounce can)
1	can (28 ounces) crushed tomatoes in purée
2	tablespoons fresh chopped basil leaves (or 2 teaspoons dried)
2	teaspoons fresh thyme leaves (or 1¼ teaspoons dried)
2	teaspoons fresh oregano leaves (or 1 teaspoon dried)
½	teaspoon freshly ground black pepper

Toss eggplant and zucchini slices with salt in a ceramic bowl. Allow to stand for 30 minutes, tossing occasionally. Transfer to colander (set the colander in the kitchen sink) for 15 minutes to drain excess juice.

In stainless-steel or enameled stock pot, heat olive oil over medium heat. Add onions and green pepper; cook over medium heat, stirring occasionally, until vegetables begin to soften, 5 to 10 minutes. Add garlic, eggplant and zucchini. Cook, stirring occasionally, until pan juices evaporate, about 15 minutes. Add remaining ingredients. Cook over medium-low heat, stirring occasionally, until thick, 30 to 45 minutes.

Spread mixture on dryer sheets that have been sprayed with non-stick spray. Dry at 145°F until dry and leathery, stirring and turning mixture occasionally; this will probably take from 7 to 10 hours. Divide mixture into two batches; place each batch into a quart plastic zipper bag.

At camp:

In medium pot, boil 2 cups water. Add mix; stir well. Cover; remove from heat and let stand about 15 minutes, stirring occasionally to break up vegetables. Return to boiling. Reduce heat and simmer, stirring occasionally, until vegetables are tender and sauce is thick, about 10 minutes.

Red Beans and Rice
2 batches; 3 or 4 servings per batch

 It's said that every Cajun cook worth his or her salt has their own version of this recipe. This one uses tasso, which is a smoked, seasoned pork shoulder (I order mine from K-Paul's mail-order catalog; see page 199 for mail-order information). If you can't get tasso, a substitute method is listed in the footnote at the end of the recipe. Traditionally, this dish is served with lots of Tabasco sauce on the side.

- 1 pound dry red beans (*not* kidney beans; red beans are smaller and more flavorful)
- 6 cups water

In large pot, combine beans and water. Bring to boil. Cook for 2 minutes. Remove from heat; cover and let stand 1 hour.

- 4 ounces *tasso,** fat removed (approximately a 4" x 5" piece)
- 1 cup chopped onion
- ½ cup diced celery
- 1 tablespoon chopped pickled jalapeño peppers (use up to 2 tablespoons if you like really spicy food)
- 2 cloves garlic, peeled and chopped finely
- 1 bay leaf
- 2 cups water
- 2 tablespoons tomato paste
- 2 teaspoons Tabasco sauce
- 2 teaspoons salt

Add *tasso*, onion, celery, jalapeño peppers, garlic and bay leaf to beans. Bring to a boil; reduce heat slightly and cook until most of the liquid has evaporated, about 1 hour. Remove *tasso;* set aside to cool slightly. Add 2 cups water, the tomato paste and Tabasco sauce to the beans. Return beans to a gentle boil. When the *tasso* is cool enough to handle, slice thinly and shred; return to beans and stir well. Continue cooking beans until most of the liquid has evaporated, stirring frequently to prevent burning; this will take about 45 minutes. The beans will be thicker than the usual Red Beans and Rice. Stir in the salt; taste for seasoning, and adjust if necessary.

Spread beans on dryer sheets that have been sprayed with non-stick spray. Dry at 145°F until dry and crisp, rotating dryer trays and stirring the bean mixture every hour; total drying time will be 5½ to 7 hours.

When beans are completely cool, divide into two batches. Seal each batch in a quart plastic zipper bag; refrigerate or freeze until you're packing for your trip.

---

*If you can't get *tasso*, or prefer to use something else, substitute a well-smoked ham hock for the *tasso;* add ¼ teaspoon cayenne pepper and ¼ teaspoon black pepper to the bean seasoning, and proceed as directed. Or, use 4 ounces of chorizo or other spicy sausage links; remove skins and break up before adding to beans.

When you're packing for your trip, place in a small plastic bag and seal with a twist-tie:
> ¾   cup medium-grain rice

Carry separately:
> One bag of the red bean mix
> Tabasco sauce, optional (but highly recommended!)

At camp:

In medium pot, boil 1¾ cups water. Add bean mix; stir well to break up. Remove from heat; cover and let stand while you prepare the rice.

While the beans soak, prepare the rice: in another medium pot, boil 1½ cups water. Add rice; stir well. Cover and simmer 10 minutes. Remove from heat and set aside. The rice will finish cooking while you prepare the beans.

When you set the rice aside, return the beans to the heat. Return to boiling. Reduce heat and simmer, stirring occasionally, until the beans are tender, about 15 minutes.

When beans are tender, remove from heat. Fluff rice. To serve, pile a mound of rice on each plate. Top with a generous scoop of beans. For a truly authentic meal, douse liberally with Tabasco sauce.

Pasta e Fagioli (Pasta with Beans)   2 or 3 side-dish servings

This dish has as many variations as there are cooks in Italy. It can be served as either a hearty soup or as a side dish; simply vary the amount of water used. Since beans and pasta combine to form a complete protein, this dish also serves nicely as a vegetarian main dish for 2.

Combine in quart plastic zipper bag:
> ⅔   cup dried cooked cannellini or great northern beans
> ½   cup curly egg noodles, macaroni, or broken fettuccini
> ¼   cup dried diced tomato
> 2   teaspoons vegetable bouillon granules
> 1   teaspoon crumbled dried parsley leaves
> ½   teaspoon garlic chips
> ½   teaspoon crumbled dried basil leaves
> ¼   teaspoon crumbled dried rosemary leaves

Carry separately:
> Parmesan cheese

At camp:

In medium pot, boil 1¼ cups water (for side dish) or 2 cups water (for soup). Add mix; stir well. Cover; remove from heat and let stand 10 minutes. Return to boiling. Cook, stirring occasionally, until noodles are tender, 5 to 10 minutes. Sprinkle with Parmesan cheese. Note: If using the smaller quantity of water to make a side dish, you may need to add a bit more water during cooking if the mixture is sticking. The finished side dish should have a thick sauce.

Hunan-Style Lamb Stir-Fry

2 or 3 servings

For this dish, marinated lamb is dried at home; at camp, the lamb is soaked before stir-frying with rehydrated vegetables. The meat will be rather chewy in the finished dish.

8	ounces very lean lamb (from the leg or loin)
2	tablespoons soy sauce
1	tablespoon hoisin sauce (see note on page 139)
1	teaspoon sugar

Slice lamb ¼" thick. Pound lightly with meat mallet to flatten and tenderize. Cut into ¾" x 1½" strips. In medium bowl, blend the soy sauce, hoisin sauce, and sugar. Add lamb; stir to coat. Cover and refrigerate at least 4 hours; this can sit overnight in the refrigerator if that's how your schedule works out.

Arrange lamb slices on dryer racks. Dry at 145°F until leathery but still pliable, 4 to 6 hours. Store in refrigerator until you're packing for your trip.

Place in a small plastic bag and seal with a twist-tie:
½	cup dried green onion (cut into ½" pieces before drying)
¼	cup dried mushroom slices

Combine in quart plastic zipper bag:
>   The dried lamb pieces
>   The bag with the vegetables

Carry separately:
½	cup converted or long-grain rice
	Oil or clarified butter for frying (about 1½ teaspoons)
	A small packet of soy sauce if available,* or additional salt to taste

At camp:

Remove and set aside the bag with the dried vegetables. Add 1 cup cold water to the bag with the lamb. Seal and let stand 1 hour or longer. Add dried vegetables; re-seal and let stand 15 minutes longer.

While the vegetables soak, begin preparing the rice: in medium pot, boil 1 cup water. Add rice; stir well. Cover; remove from heat and let stand about 10 minutes. Return to boiling. Reduce heat and simmer, stirring occasionally, about 10 minutes. Cover and remove from heat; let the rice stand while you cook the meat.

Drain the soaking liquid from the bag (see page 155), pressing to remove excess moisture. Heat a medium skillet over medium heat; add enough oil to coat the skillet well. Add the meat and vegetables. Cook, stirring frequently, about 5 minutes. Serve meat over rice; season with soy sauce.

*Save the soy sauce from an order of Chinese carryout; I've never seen individual packets of soy sauce offered for sale.

Indian Chicken with Potatoes

2 or 3 servings

Indian cooks make their own individual blends of garam masala – *what most Americans think of as curry powder. This dish uses a typical yet simple spice mixture to provide a flavor that is very different from commercial curry.*

Place the sauce mix in a small plastic bag and seal with a twist-tie:

    2   tablespoons instant mashed potato flakes
    1   tablespoon dried-tomato-paste crumbles*
    2   teaspoons chicken bouillon granules
    ¼   teaspoon ground ginger
    ¼   teaspoon ground cinnamon
    ¼   teaspoon turmeric
    ¼   teaspoon cayenne pepper
    ¼   teaspoon black pepper
    ⅛   teaspoon ground cardamom

Combine in freezer-weight quart plastic zipper bag:

    1½ cups dried potato slices from a boxed potato side dish**
    1   package (1 ounce) freeze-dried diced chicken
    3   tablespoons dried onion flakes
    1   teaspoon garlic chips
        The small sealed bag with the sauce mix

Carry separately:

    1-2 tablespoons oil or clarified butter
        Pita breads, optional
        Plain yogurt to serve as a sauce, optional

At camp:

Remove small bag with sauce mix and set aside. Boil 2 cups water; add to zipper bag with potato mixture (see page 155). Let stand until potatoes are tender, 25 to 30 minutes, turning the bag occasionally to be sure that all the potatoes are exposed to the water. When potatoes are tender, drain water into a small pot or bowl. Add sauce mix to water; blend with fork.

In medium skillet, heat a tablespoon of the oil. Add potato mixture. Fry, stirring occasionally, until browned, 10 to 15 minutes; add additional oil if necessary. Stir the sauce mixture one more time and add to the potatoes. Cook, stirring occasionally, until the sauce has thickened, about 3 minutes. Serve with pita breads and yogurt.

*When you store dried tomato-paste or tomato-sauce leather in a plastic bag, you'll often end up with a bunch of "tomato-paste crumbs" at the bottom of the bag. This dish takes advantage of these bits. If your tomato paste hasn't crumbled up, just rip off a chunk that is about 1" x 2"; that will be close enough!

**See page 116, including the footnote, for recipes that use the remaining potatoes, and the sauce mix from the boxed potato mix.

Chapter Ten
Fish and Game Recipes

It's hard to imagine anything that tastes better than fish that's crisped up in the frying pan within an hour of being caught. The flavor is nature's reward for the angler who sits patiently through hours of steady drizzle, or rises before dawn to trade a warm sleeping bag for a cold boat seat or shoreline spot.

Most campers that are near water will wet a line; for others, fishing is the reason they're out there camping in the first place. We usually fall into the latter category, so our schedule is arranged around fishing periods.

Most anglers who use this book won't have access to conveniences like livewells, refrigerators, or even ice. It's more likely that fish will be eaten within an hour or two of being caught, and this is the best for flavor and texture. If the fish are really biting, don't keep more than you can eat immediately, unless you have a way to refrigerate it; fish spoils very rapidly, and it's not only illegal but unethical to kill fish that you later throw away because it's gone bad. Learn proper catch-and-release tactics, so the fish you don't keep will survive. If you are fishing for a meal *and the water is cool,* you can keep a fish alive for a short time on a stringer. Hook the stringer through the lower lip of large fish, rather than running the stringer through the gills, then tie it to a shoreline rock or to an *unmoving* boat. Small fish like sunnies and crappies can be kept in a wire basket that hangs in the water. Don't try to keep fish alive if the water is warm, as the meat will become soft and strong-tasting. Instead, kill the fish humanely, field-dress it immediately, and keep it as cool as possible until cooking (preferably within the hour). The bottom of a canoe, under a seat, is a cool spot; a wicker creel lined with damp grasses also works well. If you're fishing from a motorboat, carry a cooler with ice for your catch.

Trout and salmon 4 pounds or smaller can be field-dressed quickly and easily with the technique shown in the color photos on pages 158-159. Walleyes, northern pike, bass, and larger fish are usually filleted and skinned, unless the fish will be cooked whole. Panfish can be filleted and skinned also, although it's quite a lot of work if you have a mess of small fish. Many panfish anglers prefer to simply gut, gill, and scale the fish, then cook them whole.

No matter how you handle your fish-cleaning chores, follow local regulations and common sense when disposing of the remains. Don't leave fish parts scattered around the campsite; it will attract bears and other critters, and is smelly and unsightly. Many states prohibit dumping fish entrails into the water, so you'll have to pack them out or bury them away from campsites. Know and follow all state and local fishing regulations; for example, fish eaten during the day may count toward your daily limit.

Something-Like-Bouillabaisse

Bouillabaisse *is a dish of great controversy in France. Most experienced cook-gourmands have their own recipe for it, and each cook insists that no other recipe will do. To be truly authentic,* bouillabaisse *requires a half-dozen or more fish species, many of which have no freshwater substitute. Hence the name of this dish; it's reminiscent of the the garlicky, tomato-infused French classic, but can't really be called* bouillabaisse. *However, when you're on a remote lake miles from the nearest white-tablecloth restaurant, this dish goes down pretty well!*

Combine in pint plastic zipper bag:

- ¼   cup dried diced red bell pepper
- ¼   cup dried sliced leeks or diced onion
- 1   tablespoon crumbled dried parsley leaves
- 4   sun-dried tomato halves, cut into ¼" pieces
- 2   teaspoons all-purpose flour
- 1   teaspoon Butter Buds
- ½   teaspoon garlic chips
- ¼   teaspoon crumbled dried thyme leaves
- ⅛   teaspoon freshly ground black pepper
- 1   Knorr fish bouillon cube, or 2 teaspoons vegetable bouillon granules
      A pinch of cayenne pepper

Carry separately:

- 2   cloves fresh garlic
- 4   slices stale French bread
      (Fresh fish fillets, about 1 pound)
- 2   cups dry white wine, optional

At camp:

Peel garlic cloves; cut in half so you have two short, fat halves (not two long, skinny halves). Toast bread quickly over fire or in a dry skillet, until lightly browned. Rub bread with garlic on both sides; set aside.

Skin fillets, and remove ribs and any bones. Cut into 1-inch chunks and set aside. In medium-large pot, bring white wine and 2 cups water (or a total of 4 cups water) to boil over medium heat. Add dry mix; stir well. Cover; remove from heat and let stand about 15 minutes. Return to boiling. Reduce heat to simmer. Add fish chunks. Simmer until fish is just cooked, stirring occasionally, about 10 minutes (fish will be opaque, firm and flaky when cooked). Place one piece of toasted bread into each of 4 serving bowls. Divide soup evenly among bowls. Serve immediately.

Northwoods Guide's Fish Fry

2 to 4 servings

The "secret ingredient" that makes shore lunch taste so good is truly fresh fish, seasoned with the beauty of the setting! Fried fish is often accompanied by fried or foil-roasted potatoes (see **Potatoes with Bacon and Onions,** *page 104; or* **Potato-Carrot-Onion Packets,** *page 112); a can of baked beans is a simpler option that is equally good.*

Following are several breading options. With any of these, you'll need to carry several tablespoons of butter or cooking oil for frying, as well as salt and pepper for seasoning; seasoned salt or seasoning blends add interest. For a longer trip when you'll be eating fried fish more than once, carry several different types of breading so you'll have a little variety with your fried fish.

Simple Flour Dredge / *Place in a gallon zipper bag:*
- 1   cup all-purpose flour
- ¼   cup cornmeal
- 2   teaspoons onion powder
- 2   teaspoons celery salt
- 1   teaspoon garlic powder
- 1   teaspoon paprika

Easy Italian Fish / *Carry separately:*
- 2   cups Italian-style bread crumbs in a gallon zipper bag
- 1   whole raw egg (wrap in a paper towel and nestle in cook kit)

Crispy Coating with Egg Wash / *Carry separately:*
- 2   cups finely crushed cornflakes, Rice Krispies, or Ritz crackers in a gallon zipper bag
- 1   cup plain flour or Simple Flour Dredge in a separate bag, optional
- 1   whole raw egg (wrap in a paper towel and nestle in cook kit)

At camp:

For walleye, bass, pike, or large fish: fillet and skin fish, removing rib bones. For panfish: leave skin on if desired, but scale before cooking. Small fish can be simply gutted, gilled and scaled before cooking; larger panfish can be filleted and skinned if desired. Rinse all fish very well in cool, clean water. Pat lightly with paper towels; flour adheres best to fish that is slightly damp but not wet.

Simple Flour Dredge: Place prepared fish in the bag; seal and shake to coat.

Easy Italian Fish: Beat egg with a tablespoon of water in a bowl, pot, or flat dish. Dip the prepared fish into the egg mixture, then place, one piece at a time, into the bag with the crumbs; shake to coat. Transfer coated fish to a plate while you repeat with remaining pieces.

Crispy Coating with Egg Wash: The texture will be best if you first coat fillets with plain or seasoned flour as described in Simple Flour Dredge. Dip floured fish into beaten egg, then into breading as described in Easy Italian Fish.

For all versions: Heat a tablespoon of butter in a heavy skillet. Fry fish over medium-high heat, turning only once, until browned and crispy, about 5 minutes per side; add additional butter as necessary. Don't overcook; fish should just barely flake when probed with a fork. Season to taste.

A wonderful shore lunch on Seagull Lake in Minnesota's Boundary Waters Canoe Area Wilderness: **Potato-Dill Chowder** *(page 91),* **Beets and Carrots with Lemon-Thyme Sauce** *(page 109), and* **Northwoods Guide's Fish Fry** *(page 152).*

Vegetables, sauces, and spreads are easy to dry at home (see pages 22-41), and weigh just a fraction of their fresh weight, making them ideal for the lightweight camper. Most rehydrate fairly quickly. Dried vegetables are shown on the left, rehydrated vegetables on the right.
Top row: *French-cut green beans (for* **Minnesota Green Bean Casserole**, *page 109).*
Middle row: **Beets and Carrots with Lemon-Thyme Sauce** *(page 109).* ***Bottom row:*** **Hummus** *(a Mid-eastern spread made of ground garbanzo beans, page 189).*

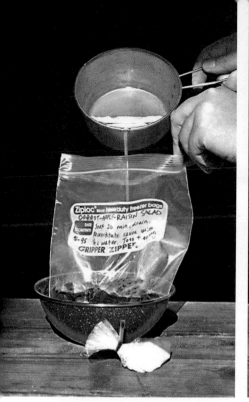

How to Soak Dried Foods in a Plastic Bag

Freezer-weight plastic zipper bags make convenient soaking containers, and are also handy for mixing pancake batter etc. **Top left photo:** *Support the bag in a bowl, pot lid, or other container (especially important if you're going to add boiling water), then add water. Seal the zipper top, and let the bag stand for the recommended amount of time, or until the food is rehydrated.* **Top right photo:** *Open a small corner of the zipper seal, and drain the soaking liquid; the small opening acts like a strainer to prevent the food from coming out with the liquid. Squeeze the bag gently to press out as much water as possible. Use the soaking water for cooking soup or other foods; it contains vitamins.* **Bottom photo:** *The rehydrated dish,* **Carrot-Apple-Raisin Salad with Blue Cheese Dressing** *(page 106).*

Meal Management with a Single-Burner Stove

If you're carrying a single-burner stove, it's difficult to cook two dishes at the same time. Here are several ways to make the best use of your stove to prepare a complete meal.

*Prepare a side dish that is cooked first, then can stand while you cook the main course; or, choose a side dish that doesn't require cooking. In the photo above left, **Blackened Steak** (page 132) is accompanied by no-cook **Tabouli Salad** (page 99), pita bread, and some fresh cucumber wedges. In the photo*

*above right, **Nutty Rice** (page 98), which can be served hot, cold, or anywhere in between, is the perfect complement to the **Salmon Patties** (page 122) being prepared. Some rehydrated julienned carrots (general vegetable instructions, page 106) need only quick heating after the salmon is cooked.*

*Some dishes, like **One-Pot Corned Beef Hash** (page 127), are complete meals by themselves. For variety, or to provide additional servings, accompany a one-pot dish with no-cook foods like cheese and crackers, or some fresh raw vegetables.*

*If you'll be having a campfire, use it to prepare some of your food. Here, fried fish was cooked on a camp stove while some **Potato-Carrot-Onion Packets** (page 112) and **Baked Apple** (page 181) were cooked in foil directly on the coals – no grate needed.*

How to Roast Corn-on-the-Cob on a Campfire

Corn-on-the-cob and hard vegetables like potatoes and winter squash are wonderful when roasted directly in the coals of a campfire, or on a grate above it. See pages 113 for full instructions. **Top photo:** *Soaking corn in the lake before roasting prevents burning.* **Middle photo:** *The unpeeled corn is placed directly on hot, but not flaming, campfire coals.* **Bottom photo:** *The dark spots on the roasted corn have a delicious, nutty flavor. In this photo, fish is cooking on the grate, while a pan of biscuits cooks directly in the coals (behind corn).*

The trout in the picture can be field-dressed with the method shown below; it works for trout and salmon up to 4 pounds.

How to Field-Dress Trout (pictured: 3-pound lake trout)

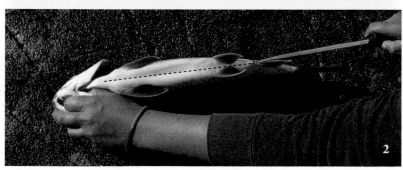

1/ Slip a fillet knife under the bony chin ridge (pictured), then cut toward the tip of the mouth to make a V-shaped flap. 2/ With the point of the knife, slit the belly from the vent (pictured) almost to the area where the head joins the body (dotted line). 3/ Grasp the lower lip and head of the trout firmly with your left hand as shown, then use your right hand to pull the V-shaped chin flap toward the tail. You'll need to use a fair amount of force, as you'll be pulling the gills away from the head. 4/ Continue pulling back to remove the entire intestinal contents; the gills and fins will be removed as shown. 5/ Slit the thin membrane covering the dark bloodline that runs along the backbone. Use the back of your thumbnail or a spoon to scrape the bloodline out; this is easiest if you hold the fish in the lake or stream while scraping. Rinse out the inside of the trout thoroughly.

Herbed Fish and Carrots in Foil (recipe on facing page)

Top photo: *Fresh carrots are sliced onto a piece of foil and topped with butter pats; a fillet of fresh fish (northern pike is pictured) is laid over the carrots. Note the herbs on the right side of the foil; they were folded into the foil while packing for easy transport (see page 112).*
Middle photo: *The dried herbs are sprinkled over the fish, which is then topped with a few more pats of butter. The sealed packet is roasted on a grate above the campfire or a grill.*
Bottom photo: *The finished dish.*

Herbed Fish and Carrots in Foil

2 servings per packet

*Fish and carrots cooked together over a campfire or grill make a tasty
combination. Complete this meal with some camp bread (pages 72-87),
some roasted whole potatoes, or a rice-based side dish.*

For each packet, you'll need:

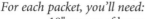

    18" square of heavy-duty foil*
 2   whole small carrots
 1   generous tablespoon butter or margarine
½   teaspoon mixed dried herb blend, like *fines herbes**
¼   teaspoon lemon pepper or garlic pepper
   (Fresh fish fillets, 4 or 5 ounces per serving)

At camp:

Light charcoal grill or start campfire. When coals are almost ready, prepare
the fish: skin fillets, and remove ribs and any bones. Each packet should
get enough fish for two servings. If you have a 1-pound fish, one side will
generally yield one serving, so you'll need both sides. A 2-pound fish yields
2 servings per side, so each packet should get a whole fillet. If you have
panfish, small bass, or other small fish, you'll need 3 or 4 fillets for 2 people.

For each packet: lay a piece of foil, shiny-side up, on a flat surface. Peel carrots
and slice ¼" thick; arrange down the center of the foil. Sprinkle carrot slices
with a few drops of water. Cut half of the butter into pats, and distribute
over the carrots. Place the fish on top of the carrots and butter. Sprinkle the
herbs and lemon pepper over the fish. Cut the remaining butter into pats,
and distribute over the fish. Fold sides of foil over the fish as shown in the
"drugstore wrap" on page 56. Roll the ends of the foil in securely.

Place the wrapped packets, fish-side up, on a grate over prepared campfire
coals or charcoal grill. Cook for about 15 minutes, moving the packet around
occasionally. Flip the foil packet, and cook the second side for another 8 to 10
minutes. To serve, carefully open the packet; serve directly from the foil, or
transfer fish, carrots, and all juices to individual plate for serving.

*When you're packing for your trip or shore lunch, sprinkle the herbs and lemon
pepper into the center of the foil and fold as described in **Herbed Vegetables Roasted
in Foil** (page 112). At camp, push the herbs and pepper off to the side while you
arrange the carrots and fish, as shown on the facing page.

Billy's Fish with Corn

I learned this simple method of cooking fresh fish while I was traveling as a professional "fish wrangler" and project manager for a series of fishing books by The Complete Angler (formerly The Hunting & Fishing Library). It's easy to fix if you have a grill or campfire, and very tasty.

For each serving, you'll need:

	18" square of heavy-duty foil
1	generous tablespoon butter or margarine
¼	cup drained canned "fiesta" corn*
	A generous pinch of crumbled dried thyme leaves
	A generous pinch of salt
	A generous pinch of black pepper
	A small pinch of cayenne pepper, optional
	(Fresh fish fillets, 4 or 5 ounces per serving)

At camp:

Light charcoal grill or start campfire. When coals are almost ready, prepare the fish: skin fillets, and remove ribs and any bones. Cut into individual serving-sized pieces if necessary. (If you have a 1-pound fish, one side will generally yield one serving. The fillets from a 2-pound fish should be cut into 2 servings per side. Small fish won't need to be cut up.) Set aside.

For each serving: lay a piece of foil, shiny-side up, on a flat surface. Place half of the butter, cut into small pieces, on the foil. Place the fish piece on top of the butter. Sprinkle the drained corn over the fish. Sprinkle with thyme, salt, pepper and cayenne. Top with the remaining butter. Fold sides of foil over the fish as shown in the "drugstore wrap" on page 56. Roll the ends of the foil in securely. Repeat with remaining fish and other ingredients.

Place the wrapped packets, corn-side up, on a grate over prepared campfire coals or charcoal grill. Cook for 5 to 7 minutes; you should hear the butter sizzling several minutes before you turn it. Flip the foil packets, and cook the second side for another 5 minutes or so. To serve, carefully open the packet; serve directly from the foil, or transfer fish, corn and all juices to individual plate for serving.

*An 11-ounce can of "fiesta" corn will make 4 fish packets. You can also carry ¾ cup of dried corn kernels and 3 tablespoons of dried diced bell peppers instead of the canned corn; cover with boiling water and rehydrate for 45 minutes before using.

Easy Rack-Grilled Fish

Up to 4 servings per rack

Gourmet stores, and some camping stores, sell special fish-grilling racks. I don't like them for several reasons: they're bulky, expensive, and only work for a fish "in the round." I use two inexpensive cake-cooling racks (from any discount store), which I wire together with the twist-ties that come in a box of plastic bags. My racks take up very little room, and allow me to cook fillets – even those from small fish.

For each batch, you'll need:

      Butter or margarine (about 1 teaspoon per serving)
      Seasoned salt, or salt and pepper
  2 cake-cooling racks (mine are 10" x 14")
6-8 twist-ties
      (Fresh fish fillets, 4 or 5 ounces per serving)

At camp:

Light charcoal grill or start campfire. When coals are almost ready, prepare the fish: skin fillets, and remove ribs and any bones unless you're cooking panfish (you may leave panfish ribs attached to help hold the fillet together).

Lightly butter the flat side of the cooling racks (the side without feet). Arrange fillets snugly on one rack, placing any fillets that are slightly thicker in the center. Thinner parts, like the rib area, can be overlapped slightly to fit all the fillets on the rack; this also helps prevent overcooking of the thin areas.

Place the second rack, buttered-side down, on top of the fillets. Wire the long sides together tightly with twist-ties (if the short ends are gapping, you can wire them together also, but this usually isn't necessary).

Place the racks on a grate over the prepared coals. As soon as the fish fillets are warmed by the fire, flip the rack and rub butter* over the warmed fillets. When the second side is warmed, flip and butter. Continue flipping and buttering frequently until fish is done; this is really the secret of making this dish (if you don't flip-and-butter enough, the fish will be horribly dry).

To serve, un-twist or cut the twist-ties on one edge, and open the racks like a book. (You can leave the second side wired together; it will be easier to carry, and wiring will be faster next time you use it.) Season fish to taste.

*The easiest way to do this is to use a stick of butter that is still wrapped; unwrap just the end, hold the stick by the other end, and rub the open end over the fish. If your butter is unwrapped or too soft, or if you're carrying clarified butter, you'll have to improvise by putting a glob of butter on a fork or knife. If you are carrying a more complete kitchen, melt the butter in a small pan and apply with a pastry brush.

Blackened Fresh Fish
Enough for 2 pounds of fillets

Even though pan-fried fresh fish is probably the most perfect food in the world, sometimes you need something different, just for variety. This is a nice change-of-pace for a longer fishing trip. Redfish is traditionally used, but any freshwater fish will work, as long as the fillets are at least ½" thick. Serve this spicy dish with rice or a starchy side dish.

Mix well, then place in a small plastic bag and seal with a twist-tie:

1	tablespoon paprika, preferably Hungarian
2	teaspoons salt
1	teaspoon onion powder
1	teaspoon white pepper
½	teaspoon freshly ground black pepper
½	teaspoon cayenne pepper
½	teaspoon crumbled dried thyme leaves

Carry separately:

Clarified butter (about 4 tablespoons per pound of fillets)
Cast-iron skillet or griddle
(Fresh fish fillets, 4 or 5 ounces per serving)

At camp:

Skin fillets, and remove ribs and any bones. Heat cast-iron skillet or griddle over high heat until very hot (some say the skillet will turn white, but I've never gotten it quite *that* hot!). While skillet heats, melt butter in another pan. Dip the fillets in the melted butter, turning to coat on all sides. Sprinkle liberally with the seasoning mix on all sides.

When skillet is as hot as it will get, add fillets in a single layer. Allow to sear very well on the bottom. Turn and sear the other side (tip: if the fillets are sticking to the skillet, they aren't ready to turn; when properly seared, the fish will "release" from the skillet). Check fish for doneness, and cook a bit longer if necessary; do not overcook.

Note: This will probably remove most of the seasoning from your cast-iron skillet. When the skillet is cool enough to handle, clean it with a paper towel, then coat lightly with vegetable oil to prevent rust from forming until you can re-season it.

Planked Fish *(color photo page 56)*   Servings depends on size of fish

This is a fun and different way to cook fish by a campfire. Salmon is traditionally used in this technique, although any fish weighing at least 3 pounds will work. Oily fish like salmon and trout are best, but leaner fish can also be used if you remember to baste frequently. Whole fish up to 8 pounds can be cooked with this method, but fillets from 3- to 6-pound fish are easier to prepare for the plank.

Carry separately:

  A wide, solid board (not plywood) or a split log
  A good handful of black roofer's nails (do *not* use galvanized nails)
3 to 5   bacon slices, optional (large fish need more bacon)
  Butter for basting
  Seasoned salt or regular salt, and pepper
  (Whole fish, skin-on, field dressed, head removed; or skin-on fillets)

Soak the board or split log for an hour or more in a lake or stream before preparing this dish. You'll also need a large bed of very hot coals. If using a whole fish, cut ribs along the inside backbone until you can spread the fish out flat. Nail the flattened fish, or fillet (skin-side down) onto the soaked wood. Nail bacon strips across the fish as shown below. Prop the board next to the campfire, and watch it carefully during cooking to be sure it doesn't catch fire. Cook the fish, basting occasionally with butter (especially if bacon hasn't been used), until it flakes when probed with a fork. Cooking time could be as short as 30 minutes, or as long as 2 hours. Season with seasoned or plain salt, and pepper. The wood can be burned in the campfire afterward; be sure to pick out the nails once the ashes have cooled completely, and pack them out with your trash.

Top: *A side of coho salmon is nailed to a split log.* **Above:** *A whole 3-pound lake trout has been split, and is nailed to a piece of solid board.* **Right:** *Bacon slices are nailed across the fish. The plank is propped up in front of the campfire.*

Cajun Venison Tenderloins · 2 main-dish or 6 appetizer servings

The tenderloins are two boneless pieces of meat you'll find inside the dressed deer cavity, at the end of the backbone. They're the most tender piece of meat on the animal, and are a traditional opening-day feast. If the deer was taken in the morning, you can enjoy the tenderloins for supper. If the deer was taken in the afternoon, let it hang overnight before removing the tenderloins; the meat needs a bit of time to relax before you cook it, or it will be tough.

Carry separately:

2   tablespoons **Blackened Steak** seasoning mix (page 132) *or*
       Chef Paul Prudhomme's Blackened Steak Magic (see page 199
       for mail-order address)
¾   cup milk (if you don't bring fresh milk to camp, you can carry
       ¼ cup nonfat dry milk powder, then add it to ½ cup water; or
       use ½ cup canned evaporated milk, diluted with ¼ cup water)
1   egg (or ⅓ cup powdered egg, mixed with ⅓ cup cold water)
½   cup all-purpose flour
1   small onion
     Bacon grease, clarified butter or oil for frying
     (2 deer or antelope tenderloins)

At camp:

In medium bowl or pot*, combine 2 teaspoons of the seasoning mix with the milk. Slice the tenderloins into 2-inch lengths; you'll probably get 4 pieces per tenderloin. Stand a chunk on end. Use the backbone (the edge that is opposite the cutting edge) of the heaviest non-folding knife you've got to pound the meat in criss-cross fashion; turn and criss-cross the other side as well. Be very careful not to cut yourself with the knife during the pounding; don't try this with a folding hunting knife. Whack the pounded meat with the flat of the blade also; you should end up with a piece of meat that is about ½" thick, and roughly 3 inches across. Place the pounded meat into the milk mixture; repeat with remaining meat. Let the meat soak in the milk for about an hour.

In a flat dish (a pie plate works great, if you have one) or pot, beat the egg with a tablespoon of water or milk. In another dish, mix the flour with a tablespoon of the seasoning mix (you can shake the flour and seasoning together in a paper bag to mix them). Peel the onion, and cut into quarters; slice about ¼" thick.

Put about 2 teaspoons bacon drippings in a heavy medium-sized skillet, and heat over medium-high heat. Working quickly, remove a piece of meat from the milk, shaking off excess milk. Dip into the egg mixture, then coat well with the flour mixture; add to the skillet immediately. Repeat with remaining meat. Cook just until the bottom is crisp and brown, 2 or 3 minutes. If the skillet is getting dry, add a little more bacon drippings. Turn the meat pieces over, and scatter the onion pieces over the meat. Sprinkle with additional seasoning mix. Cook until the second side is brown and crisp, another 2 or 3 minutes.

*You can use a large plastic zipper bag instead of a bowl to soak the meat. Place the meat slices in the bag, then add the milk. Seal the bag well. Turn the bag occasionally during the soaking.

Venison Loin with Cherry Sauce

4 servings

Also known as the backstrap, the loin is a tender strip of meat that runs along the deer's back, next to the blade of the backbone (there are two loin strips on each animal). It's a tender, delicious piece of meat if it's not overcooked. If you haven't butchered the deer yet, you can substitute tenderloins for the loin in this recipe. Accompany this elegant dish with biscuits or a rice side dish, and some colorful vegetables. A real feast!

Place in a small plastic bag and seal with a twist-tie:

- 1   teaspoon beef bouillon granules
- ½   teaspoon dry mustard
- ½   teaspoon crumbled dried thyme leaves
- ⅛   teaspoon black pepper

Carry separately:

- 1   can (16 ounces) pitted dark cherries in juice
- ½   cup port or red wine, optional
- 2   tablespoons clarified butter
- 2   teaspoons cornstarch
      The small bag with the spices
      (A piece of venison loin, 1 to 1¼ pounds)

At camp:

Drain and reserve juice from canned cherries. In small bowl, combine cherries with port; set aside to marinate while you prepare the venison. Remove all silverskin from the loin. Slice loin 1" thick.

In heavy medium or large skillet, melt butter over medium-high heat. Add loin slices. Brown well, 3 to 5 minutes per side; meat should still be pink in the center (it will feel slightly soft but not mushy when pressed with your fingertip). Transfer venison to a covered dish; set aside and keep warm.

Add ¼ cup water to the skillet, stirring to loosen any browned bits. Drain the port into the skillet (if not using port, add an additional ¼ cup water to the skillet). Add the reserved cherry juice and the spices to the skillet; stir well to blend. Heat to boiling; add cherries, and continue cooking over medium heat while you prepare the cornstarch thickener.

In a small bowl or cup, blend the cornstarch with 2 tablespoons cold water. Add the cornstarch to the mixture in the skillet, stirring well to prevent lumps. Cook over medium heat, stirring frequently, until sauce thickens and bubbles, about 3 minutes. Serve the cherries and sauce over the meat.

Venison Stir-Fry

When you butcher a deer or other big-game animal, you'll have lots of small meat scraps left. Use the scraps from the hindquarter or loin area to make a delicious stir-fry. Serve with plain cooked rice (page 95). If you don't want to carry fresh vegetables, follow the packing and re-hydrating instructions for the vegetables in **Stir-Fried Vegetables** *(Combination A) on page 110.*

In a small bottle, combine the following sauce ingredients:

- 2 tablespoons soy sauce
- 2 tablespoons dry sherry
- 2 tablespoons ketchup
- 1 tablespoon cornstarch
- 2 teaspoons white vinegar
- 1 teaspoon honey

Carry separately:

- 1 medium carrot
- 1 small whole red or green bell pepper
- 1 small zucchini, optional
- 1 small onion
- 2 whole cloves garlic
  (1 pound boneless tender venison scraps)
  Vegetable oil for frying (about 2 teaspoons)
  The bottle with the sauce mix

At camp:

Peel the carrot, and slice ¼" thick. Remove and discard core and stem from bell pepper; slice into ¼" strips. Remove and discard stem from zucchini. Cut in quarters lengthwise, then into ¼" thick slices. Peel onion and garlic; remove and discard root ends. Slice onion into quarters from top to root end, then into ¼" thick slices. Chop garlic finely. Remove any silverskin or gristle from venison, and slice into pieces no thicker than ¼".

Heat a heavy large skillet over high heat. Add enough oil to coat the inside well, then add the carrots. Cook, stirring constantly, for 2 or 3 minutes. Add the bell pepper and zucchini; cook and stir for another 2 minutes. Transfer the vegetables to a bowl; cover and set aside.

Re-heat the skillet over high heat. Add enough oil to coat the inside well, then add the venison. Cook, stirring constantly, for 2 or 3 minutes. Add the onion and garlic; cook and stir for another 2 minutes. Return the other vegetables to the pan; cook and stir for another 2 minutes. Shake the sauce mix well, then add to the pan. Cook, stirring frequently, until the sauce has thickened; the vegetables should be tender-crisp. Serve over rice.

Tenderloin Diane   2 to 4 servings, depending on size of tenderloins

We first had this with mule deer tenderloins, and it was delicious. See the information about tenderloins on page 166. If you prefer, substitute backstrap (loin) steaks for the tenderloin in this dish. Serve **Tenderloin Diane** *with rice or buttered noodles to catch all the savory juices.*

Place in a small plastic bag and seal with a twist-tie:
2	teaspoons crumbled dried parsley leaves
1	teaspoon beef bouillon granules
¼	teaspoon sugar

Combine in pint plastic zipper bag:
¼	cup dried sliced leek, *or* 2 tablespoons dried onion flakes
	The small bag with the spices

Carry separately:
	Coarsely ground black pepper
3	tablespoons butter
1	tablespoon peanut or vegetable oil
¼	cup brandy or cognac
1	tablespoon Worcestershire sauce or steak sauce, optional but good
	(2 deer or antelope tenderloins)

At camp:

Set aside the small bag with the spices. Add about a cup of cold water to the leeks in the zipper bag. Press out most of the air and seal the bag. Let the leeks soak in the bag until tender, 10 or 15 minutes. Open a corner of the bag and drain water, squeezing out excess. Set the drained leeks aside.

Cut tenderloin into 2"–3" lengths. Sprinkle both sides generously with coarse black pepper, pressing it into the meat with your fingers. In medium skillet (cast iron works best), melt the butter in the oil over medium-high heat. Add meat and sear well on both sides; it should still be rare (to judge doneness: relax your left hand and press the base of your left thumb with your right fingers; rare meat will feel like that when you press it). Remove the skillet from the fire so it cools slightly while you remove the steaks; if the skillet is too hot, you'll burn the leeks in the next step. Using a tongs or spatula to avoid piercing the meat, immediately transfer the meat to a plate or dish; cover and set aside.

Place skillet over medium heat. Add the drained leeks and the contents of the spice bag. Cook, stirring frequently, for about 2 minutes. Reduce heat to medium-low. Add the Worcestershire sauce and the brandy. When the brandy is warm, carefully ignite it by holding a long-handled match over the edge of the skillet; the fumes will catch fire, so you don't have to get the match right down into the skillet. Be very careful, as the fumes ignite with a powerful blast, and could easily burn you or anything nearby if you're not careful.

When the flames die down, return the meat to the skillet, turning to coat both sides with the sauce. Cook over medium heat for about a minute to warm the steaks, or a bit longer if medium doneness is desired. I recommend serving the meat medium-rare; if you cook it to well-done, it will be tough.

Grouse à la King

One year, our hunting party of seven got two deer right away on opening morning. I was one of the lucky ones, so the other guy and I grabbed our shotguns and went looking for ruffed grouse. We decided to fix the grouse for supper that night, with venison tenderloin as an appetizer. I drove to town to see what I could come up with to cook the grouse. "Town" consisted of a gas station/superette, a bar, and a seed/implement dealer (we were in a pretty remote area of northern Minnesota near the Canadian border). I came back with an odd assortment of cans and a box of Bisquick, and made this **Grouse à la King** *in our log cabin in the middle of the woods.*

Carry separately:

1	cup of any of the biscuit mixes on pages 78-80
4	tablespoons butter or margarine, divided
1	can (4 ounces) sliced mushrooms, drained
1	jar (2 ounces) diced pimientos, drained
2	tablespoons all-purpose flour
1	can (12 ounces) evaporated skimmed milk
2	teaspoons chicken bouillon granules
1	teaspoon crumbled dried parsley leaves, optional
	(The boned breast and thigh meat from 2 ruffed grouse,* cut into ¾" pieces)

At camp:

Prepare the biscuits according to the directions on pages 81-82. Set biscuits aside in a warm place.

In medium-large skillet, melt 2 tablespoons of the butter over medium heat. Add the grouse pieces. Cook, stirring occasionally, until lightly browned, 5 to 10 minutes. Add the drained mushrooms and pimientos. Cook, stirring occasionally, while you prepare the sauce.

In a small pan, melt the remaining 2 tablespoons butter over medium heat. Add the flour, stirring constantly with a fork to blend into a smooth paste. Cook, stirring constantly, for about 2 minutes (this removes the raw taste of the flour). Add ¼ cup water, stirring constantly with the fork to prevent lumps. Remove from heat.

Add the milk, chicken bouillon, and parsley to the flour mixture. Stir well. Add to the skillet with the grouse, stirring well to blend. Cook over medium heat, stirring frequently, until sauce is bubbly and thickened, about 3 minutes. Serve over split biscuits.

*You could also substitute the boned breast and thigh meat from one pheasant, or part of the boned meat from a wild turkey.

Lightweight Grouse à la King

2 to 4 servings

If you prefer to carry dried foods rather than cans, use this version of Grouse à la King. The sauce isn't quite as rich, but it's still very tasty. You may notice that this version uses freeze-dried peas, even though there aren't any peas in the other version, which uses canned foods. Personally, I'd rather have no peas than canned peas. Freeze-dried peas, however, are really nice; they're bright green, sweet, tender yet firm, and tasty. And since you're going to have to reconstitute dried vegetables for this version anyway, you might as well toss in some green peas; they add both color and taste to the dish.

Place in a small plastic bag and seal with a twist-tie:
   3   tablespoons nonfat dry milk powder
   2   tablespoons all-purpose flour
   2   teaspoons chicken bouillon granules
   1   teaspoon crumbled dried parsley leaves, optional

Combine in freezer-weight pint plastic zipper bag:
   ¼   cup dried mushroom pieces (morels are particularly good)
   ¼   cup dried diced red bell pepper
   2   tablespoons freeze-dried peas
       The small sealed bag with the flour mixture

Carry separately:
   1   cup of any of the biscuit mixes on pages 78-80
   4   tablespoons butter or margarine, divided
       (The boned breast and thigh meat from 2 ruffed grouse,
           cut into ¾" pieces)

At camp:

Remove the bag with the flour mixture and set aside. Add 1 cup boiling water to the zipper bag (see page 155). Let vegetables stand until tender, 15 to 20 minutes. Drain soaking liquid into a measuring cup; add water to equal 1 cup.

While the vegetables are soaking, prepare the biscuits according to the directions on pages 81-82. Set biscuits aside in a warm place.

In medium-large skillet, melt 2 tablespoons of the butter over medium heat. Add the grouse pieces. Cook, stirring occasionally, until lightly browned, 5 to 10 minutes. Add the drained vegetables. Cook, stirring occasionally, while you prepare the sauce.

In a small pan, melt the remaining 2 tablespoons butter over medium heat. Add the flour mixture, stirring constantly with a fork to blend into a smooth paste. Cook, stirring constantly, for about 2 minutes (this removes the raw taste of the flour). Add ¼ cup water, stirring constantly with the fork to prevent lumps. Remove from heat.

Add the cup of soaking liquid/water to the flour mixture. Stir well. Add to the skillet with the grouse, stirring well to blend. Cook over medium heat, stirring frequently, until sauce is bubbly and thickened, about 3 minutes. Serve over split biscuits.

Pheasant Kabobs Hangover-Style

2 or 3 main-dish servings

Lime juice and bitters is a combination that's sometimes offered to morning-after sufferers. It makes a wonderful, unusual marinade in this dish; the lime juice helps tenderize the meat, and the bitters adds an unusual, almost fruity, taste.. Serve with buttered noodles or rice, and a colorful vegetable. If you've got a crowd, serve **Pheasant Kabobs** *as an appetizer; it should be enough for 4 to 6 people.*

Carry separately:

- 3 tablespoons bitters
- 2 whole limes, or 3 tablespoons lime juice
- 1 medium onion
- 2 tablespoons butter
- 2 tablespoons soy sauce
- 2 tablespoons brown sugar
- 6 kabob skewers

(The boned breast and thighs from one pheasant)

At camp:

Cut pheasant into 1" chunks. If carrying fresh limes, squeeze out the juice (be sure to discard any seeds). In bowl or quart plastic zipper bag, combine bitters and lime juice; add pheasant chunks. Set aside to marinate for about an hour, stirring or rearranging the pieces occasionally.

While pheasant marinates, peel onion and remove ends. Cut in eighths from top to bottom; cut each wedge into 1" chunks. Melt butter, then blend in the soy sauce and brown sugar. Add the onion chunks and toss gently with the butter mixture, handling carefully to keep the onions from falling apart. Near the end of the marinating time, prepare charcoal grill or an open fire of clean hardwoods (if you're staying in a cabin that has a broiler, that will work too). Let burn down to a glowing bed of coals, with no open flame.

When the coals are ready, alternately thread pheasant and onion chunks on skewers. Grill until pheasant is just done, about 10 minutes, turning occasionally; onions will be tender-crisp.

Pan-Fried Duck Breast with Sherry Sauce

4 servings

This is a recipe I've been using for years because it's quick, easy, and delicious. A version of it appears in America's Favorite Wild Game Recipes, *a book I worked on for The Complete Hunter (formerly The Hunting & Fishing Library). This is good with served with noodles or rice, and some colorful vegetables.*

Carry separately:

    Celery salt
    Lemon pepper
1   small onion
2   tablespoons butter
¾   cup dry sherry
2   tablespoons raspberry jam or apple-mint jelly*
    (Boned, skinned breasts from one wild duck; you can also use the boned thighs in addition to the breast meat)

At camp:

Sprinkle duck breasts on both sides with celery salt and lemon pepper; set aside. Peel onion; cut off and discard ends. Chop onion and set aside.

In heavy medium skillet, melt butter over medium-high heat. Add duck breasts. Cook about 3 minutes. Turn breasts, and add onion to pan. Continue cooking for another 3 minutes.

While the second side cooks, blend the sherry with the jam in a small cup. When the duck has cooked for 3 minutes on the second side, pour the sherry mixture over the duck in the skillet, stirring well to mix. Cook for another 4 to 7 minutes, until duck is browned on the outside but still pink inside** and the sauce has thickened slightly. Slice breasts across the grain to serve.

*The little individual jam or jelly packets that you get at restaurants work great for this, if you don't happen to be carrying any jam. Use two packets of any flavor jam or jelly you can get.

**Wild duck is best when served medium-rare to medium. If cooked to well-done, it will be tough and dry.

Chapter Eleven

Beverages

For the most part, I'd rather devote my pre-trip time and attention to making mixes other than beverages. There are plenty of powdered drink mixes, instant cocoas, instant teas in a wide variety of flavors, and flavored coffee blends at the grocery store. However, there are a few mixes that I think are worth the time to pack. Following are some of my favorites.

Rick's Russian Tea

About 30 servings

One of the guys I went to college with used to make up jars of this stuff and give it to people as Christmas presents; I still have the tattered card with his recipe on it. It's a great hot drink for sitting around the campfire, and refreshing as a cold beverage also.

In quart glass jar, combine:
- 1 cup instant tea (unsweetened)
- ⅓ cup Tang or other orange-flavored breakfast drink crystals
- ¼ cup regular (*not* sugar-free) powdered lemonade mix (I use Country Time)
- ¼ cup sugar
- ½ teaspoon ground cinnamon
- ¼ teaspoon ground cloves

Combine all ingredients. Cover the jar and shake well to blend. Before your trip, pour as much as you'll use on the trip into a heavy plastic bag or other transportable container.

At camp:

For each serving: add a tablespoon (more or less to taste) to 1 cup boiling or cold water. Stir well.

Spicy Tomato Juice Mix/Bloody Mary Mix   5 or 6 servings

OK, I admit it: Bloody Marys are not traditional camping fare. But if you're car camping, or on a relaxing weekend boat trip where you have a cooler full of ice, these are mighty tasty, and a lot easier than bringing along a gallon of tomato juice, Worcestershire sauce, celery salt, Tabasco sauce, etc. etc. The mix also makes a tasty non-alcoholic tomato juice cocktail … a refreshing change from powdered orange drink for breakfast.

1	can (12 ounces) tomato paste
2	tablespoons Worcestershire sauce
2	tablespoons celery salt
1	tablespoon Tabasco sauce
1½	teaspoons prepared horseradish
½	teaspoon cayenne pepper, optional (for a very spicy mix)
¾	teaspoon onion powder
½	teaspoon white pepper

In a small bowl, mix all ingredients thoroughly. Line food-dryer tray, or cookie sheet if drying in your oven, with plastic wrap (see page 36 for information on drying tomato sauce or paste; this is the same technique). Pour the mixture over the plastic wrap, and spread evenly with a spoon; the depth should be ⅛" or less. Dry at 145°F until completely dry, 7 to 10 hours; the mixture should be cracking-brittle at room temperature. Near the end of the drying, the mixture will be leathery enough to peel off of the plastic wrap and flip over; this helps ensure even drying by exposing the bottom side to the dryer. *Tip:* Dry the sauce at 140°F for 4 to 6 hours, then let it sit overnight in a gas oven with a pilot light; it will continue to dry slowly, and the next day you can resume regular drying for a few hours.

When mixture is completely dry and crisp, allow to cool. Break into small chunks and grind to a powder in a blender or spice grinder. Store the mix in a glass jar in the refrigerator or freezer to prevent clumping. Before your trip, pour as much as you'll use on the trip into a heavy plastic bag or other transportable container.

At camp:

Per serving: boil ¼ cup water. Add 2 tablespoons mix; stir vigorously to blend and also to cool. When mixture has cooled, add ⅔ cup cold water, or to taste.

For Bloody Marys:

Reconstitute mix as directed above. Fill a glass with ice. Add a jigger of vodka (pepper vodka is great if you like a *really* spicy Bloody Mary). Fill with the spicy tomato mix. Garnish with anything you have (celery sticks, pickle wedges, lemon or lime wedges) or serve plain.

"Dreamsicle" Shake
Enough for 8 servings

When I was a kid, I just loved Dreamsicles – those orange-and-cream popsicles. This refreshing drink has a similar flavor.

1	cup instant malted milk powder
¾	cup nonfat dry milk powder
½	cup Tang or orange-flavored breakfast drink crystals
¼	cup sugar

Combine all ingredients and mix well. To serve, mix 5 tablespoons with 1 cup cold water. Shake in a jar to blend, or stir very well.

Spicy Cocoa
Enough for 8 servings

A creamy, spiced cocoa mix. Variation: add some crushed peppermints or red-hot cinnamon candies to each cup. Top with marshmallows.

1	cup nonfat dry milk powder
6	tablespoons cocoa powder
2	tablespoons sugar
¼	teaspoon cinnamon
⅛	teaspoon nutmeg

Combine all ingredients and mix well. To serve, mix 3 tablespoons with 1 cup boiling water. Stir very well.

Amaretto Cocoa
Enough for 8 servings

There are lots of flavored coffee creamers on the market now. This mix uses amaretto creamer; try other blends to suit your own taste.

½	cup nonfat dry milk powder
½	cup amaretto-flavored non-dairy coffee creamer
6	tablespoons cocoa powder
2	tablespoons sugar

Combine all ingredients and mix well. To serve, mix 3 tablespoons with 1 cup boiling water. Stir very well.

Mexican Coffee
Enough for 8 servings

Real Mexican coffee is made with ground bitter chocolate and spices, and is rich and creamy. This camping version is a good substitute.

½	cup nonfat dry milk powder
6	tablespoons cocoa powder
¼	cup instant coffee (I prefer Colombian)
4	teaspoons sugar
¼	teaspoon cinnamon

Combine all ingredients and mix well. To serve, mix 2 tablespoons plus a generous teaspoon with 1 cup boiling water. Stir very well.

Dried Orange Juice Concentrate

4 servings per batch

A word of warning: this is a fair amount of fooling around, just to get the taste of real orange juice in camp. But to me, the time spent is worthwhile. I haven't enjoyed powdered drink mixes since I was a kid (in fact, I'm not sure I enjoyed them very much even then); but until I worked out this method of drying frozen juice concentrates, the powdered mixes seemed to be the only option. Next time you've got a batch of stuff going into your dryer, make a tray of this; it isn't so much work if the dryer is already running.

1   can (6 ounces) frozen orange juice concentrate,* thawed

At home:

Line a dryer tray with plastic wrap.** My American Harvest dryer has round trays with a hollow tube in the middle, and are difficult to line properly; here's how I do it (adapt this technique to your own equipment). Put a solid liner sheet on the tray, then stretch two long overlapping pieces of plastic wrap over the tray. Cut a hole in the middle to fit snugly around the hollow tube. Trim the edges so the plastic isn't covering the vent holes around the edge of the tray, and secure the edges of the plastic wrap to the solid liner sheet in several places with freezer tape. Obviously, a square or rectangular dryer tray will be a lot easier; simply line the bottom and sides of the tray with plastic wrap, and secure with freezer tape.

Shake the thawed juice concentrate to distribute any pulp, then pour evenly onto the plastic wrap. Dry at 135°F-145°F until the concentrate is like a fruit leather. This will take between 8 and 14 hours, depending on your equipment. Near the end of the drying, the mixture will be leathery enough to peel off of the plastic wrap and flip over; this helps ensure even drying by exposing the bottom side to the dryer (be sure to put the flipped leather back onto the plastic wrap; if you put it directly onto the solid liner sheet, it will bond with the liner sheet and you'll never be able to peel it off). *Tip:* Dry the concentrate for 6 to 8 hours, then let it sit overnight in a gas oven with a pilot light; it will continue to dry slowly, and the next day you can resume regular drying.

When the leather is completely dry but still pliable, with no soft or sticky spots, peel it off the plastic wrap and cut into 4 equal pieces. Lay each piece onto a chunk of the same plastic wrap, and roll up. Store the rolls in a sealed plastic bag in the refrigerator until you're packing for your trip.

At camp:

For 2 servings: add 2 pieces of the leather to 1½ cups cold water. Let stand for about 10 minutes, stirring occasionally to dissolve the leather.

*This technique also works with other frozen citrus-juice concentrates. I've done this with lemonade and grapefruit juice concentrate, and both work well. You might want to try this with limeade, or some of the interesting blends of citrus and other fruits that are available these days.

**Don't be tempted to simply spray a solid liner sheet with non-stick spray; it doesn't work! The juice apparently absorbs the spray, and you'll be left with a sheet of oily leather that simply can't be removed except by soaking. I know, because I tried many techniques until I figured out the best way to dry concentrates.

Chapter Twelve

Desserts and Sweet Snacks

Camp dessert can be as simple and quick as a handful of dried fruit. But sometimes, you may want a more elaborate treat, especially if there are kids around. In addition to the recipes in this chapter, consider **Blueberry Scones** (pages 62-63) or **Miniature Cinnamon-Nut Rolls** (page 87).

Campfire Apple Crisp   2 to 4 servings, depending on sweet tooth

I adapted this recipe from one by Mary Carroll, who was a syndicated healthy-foods columnist at the time. A word of warning: if you don't watch this carefully, it scorches and makes a terrible mess in your pan. Remember that sand makes a good natural scrubber for a scorched pot.

Place in a small plastic bag and seal with a twist-tie:
¾	cup dried apple slices, cut into 1" pieces before measuring
4	teaspoons brown sugar
1½	teaspoons cornstarch
1	teaspoon Butter Buds, optional

Combine in quart plastic zipper bag:
¾	cup granola
2	teaspoons brown sugar
¾	teaspoon cinnamon
½	teaspoon nutmeg
	The small bag with the apples

At camp:

If you're cooking this over a campfire, either soap the outside of your pot to prevent blackening (page 56) or plan on wrapping the pot and lid with foil. In medium pot, combine apple mixture with ¾ cup cold water; stir well to blend cornstarch into the water. Squish the zipper bag between your fingers to mix the sugar and spices evenly with the granola. Sprinkle granola mixture over the apples. Cover pan. Cook over medium-low heat until bubbly, 10 to 15 minutes, rotating frequently; watch carefully, and if it is sticking badly, move the pot to a cooler part of the fire, or remove it temporarily from the stove or campfire. After the mixture is bubbly, remove the cover and cook for another 5 to 10 minutes to crisp up the granola. When the dessert has been dished out into individual serving bowls or plates, immediately add some cold water to the pan and allow to soak while you eat dessert; this makes clean-up easier.

Bananas Flambé

If you are on a relaxed trip and have a bit of rum or brandy in your grub box, try this adult-style treat. It's not the typical sugary dessert – just a little warm, sweet something to round out the evening. The alcohol burns off during the flaming, leaving only the taste.

Combine in pint plastic zipper bag:

1   cup dried banana slices
3   tablespoons chopped pecan pieces
3   tablespoons brown sugar
¼   teaspoon nutmeg
¼   teaspoon ginger
      A good pinch of cloves
      A pinch of salt

Carry separately:

2   tablespoons rum or brandy

At camp:

In medium pot, combine ½ cup cold water with mix. Let stand 15 minutes, stirring occasionally. Bring to a gentle boil over medium heat. Cook, stirring occasionally, until bananas are tender and sauce is syrupy, 5 to 8 minutes.

In small pot, heat rum gently until just warm. Pour over bananas. Ignite with long-handled match; allow flames to burn out completely before serving.

Cheesecake-in-a-Bowl

Re-package "no-bake" cheesecake mix for a simple trail dessert.

1   box (Jell-O brand is 11.1 ounces) no-bake cheesecake mix*
2   tablespoons sugar
4   tablespoons butter or margarine, melted
½   cup nonfat dry milk powder

Divide crumb mixture from the cheesecake mix into 2 pint plastic zipper bags. To each bag, add 1 tablespoon sugar and 2 tablespoons melted butter. Mix well. Divide cheesecake powder into 2 quart plastic zipper bags. To each bag, add ¼ cup nonfat dry milk powder. Store the mixes in the refrigerator until you're packing for your trip; carry one bag of each mix for 3 or 4 servings.

At camp:

Add ¾ cup plus 2 tablespoons cold water to the bag with cheesecake powder. Seal the bag, and shake well to mix. Place in a relatively cold location, like a cool stream (a cooler with ice is perfect if you have one along); let stand 30 minutes or longer. The cheesecake will thicken, but will not be firm like regular cheesecake. To serve, pour or spoon some cheesecake into individual bowls and top with the buttered crumb mixture.

*Some cheesecake mixes come with cans of fruit. Bring these along if you'll be making up both batches of cheesecake; a can of fruit is too much for 3 or 4 servings. Or, you could use the leftover fruit to top pancakes, cereal, or yogurt the next morning.

Paradell

I've had this old Italian recipe for so long, I don't even know where I got it, or what the name means. It adapts easily for camping, and makes a nice breakfast or brunch dish as well as a tasty dessert.

Combine in quart plastic zipper bag:
- ½ cup all-purpose flour
- 1 tablespoon nonfat dry milk powder
- 1 tablespoon Butter Buds
  A pinch of salt

Carry separately:
- 1 whole raw egg
  Medium Granny Smith apple
- 4 teaspoons butter or margarine, divided
- ⅓ cup powdered sugar, optional

At camp:

In bowl or pot, mix ¼ cup cold water with the egg. Add dry mixture; beat well with fork. The batter is best if it stands for up to an hour, although it can be used right away. If you're preparing this for dessert, mix the batter before you prepare the rest of the meal, then let it stand while you eat.

When you're ready to cook the Paradell, core and slice the apple (peel or not, as you prefer; I usually leave the peel on). Add to the batter, and stir gently to coat the apple with batter.

In medium skillet, melt 2 teaspoons butter over medium heat. Add the batter. Cook until browned on the bottom and slightly dry on top, about 5 minutes. Use a spatula to slide the Paradell onto a plate. Melt the remaining 2 teaspoons butter, then quickly flip the Paradell into the skillet, uncooked side down. Cook another 3 to 5 minutes, until the second side is brown. Sprinkle with powdered sugar and cut into 4 wedges.

Wilderness Paradell

Use this version when you want to travel as lightly as possible.

Follow packing instructions above, except add ⅓ cup powdered egg to flour mix. Omit the fresh apple and uncooked egg. Carry ⅔ cup dried apple slices in a freezer-weight pint zipper bag.

At camp:

Add ¾ cup boiling water to the apples in the bag (see page 155). Seal and let stand about 15 minutes. Drain soaking liquid into a measuring cup; let cool. Mix ½ cup of the liquid with the batter. Follow mixing and cooking instructions above, adding soaked apples to the batter when you're ready to cook the Paradell.

Baked Apple *(photo page 156)*

2 servings per apple

If you are having a campfire, toss one or two of these apples into the coals while you're cooking supper. You'll have a wonderful, warm, sweet treat for dessert, with almost no work.

For each 2 servings, carry:
- 1   whole apple*
- 1   tablespoon brown sugar**
- 1   teaspoon butter or margarine
  12" square of heavy-duty foil

At camp:

You'll need a campfire, with the coals burned down and ready for cooking. If you aren't cooking anything else on the campfire, you can scoop a small bed of coals off to the side of the main fire, and cook the apple in that area.

Cut the apple in half. Use a spoon or your pocket knife to remove the core, leaving a rounded hollow in the middle of the apple. Pack the brown sugar in a rounded heap in the hollow of one half of the apple. Put the butter in the hollow of the other half. Put the two halves together, and place on the shiny side of the foil. Fold sides of the foil over the apple as shown in the "drugstore wrap" on page 56. Roll the ends of the foil in securely, and mold the foil to the shape of the apple so there are no big gaps.

Place the wrapped apple onto the embers, near the edge where the fire is cooler. Cook for about 30 minutes, moving the apple around occasionally with a stick (be careful not to puncture the foil, or all the juice will get out). The apple should feel slightly soft when pressed with your fingers (protect your fingers with a potholder). To serve, carefully unwrap the apple; there will be some delicious juice trapped in the foil. Pour the juice equally over the apples on individual plates.

*Baking apples like Granny Smith are probably the best for this recipe, although Jonathans are also good. Don't use Delicious apples; they seem to have a soapy taste.

If you aren't carrying brown sugar in bulk, pack the brown sugar into the individual foil squares at home, as described in **Herbed Vegetables Roasted in Foil (page 112).

English Muffin Pies

Kids particularly love this tasty campfire treat. It's suited to car camping, because it requires bulky ingredients.

For each serving, carry:

2 teaspoons butter or margarine
1 English muffin, split
   12" square of heavy-duty foil
3 tablespoons canned pie filling, any flavor

At camp:

You'll need a campfire, with the coals burned down and ready for cooking. If you aren't cooking anything else on the campfire, you can scoop a small bed of coals off to the side of the main fire, and cook the pies in that area.

For each serving: Use half the butter to butter the outside of one of the English muffin halves (if the butter is cold, you can cut it up into chunks and simply put half of them onto the middle of the foil, then place the muffin half on top of the butter). Place buttered muffin half on the shiny side of the foil, buttered side down. Top with the pie filling. Butter the outside of the remaining English muffin half, and place on top of the fruit.

Fold sides of the foil over the muffin as shown in the "drugstore wrap" on page 56. Roll the ends of the foil in securely. Place the wrapped muffin onto the embers, near the edge where the fire is cooler. Cook for about 15 minutes, turning and moving the packet around in the coals every few minutes. The outside of the English muffin should be well browned. Be careful! The filling will be extremely hot; let it cool a bit before eating.

The buttered lower half has been topped with cherry pie filling. The top half will be placed on top of the filling before wrapping.

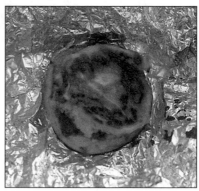

The finished cherry pie.

Skillet Snack Cakes

2 batches; 4 servings per batch

Look at the grocery store for muffin or snack-cake mixes that require no added oil or butter, then re-package the mix to make skillet cakes on the trail. This version is made with a popular muffin mix; it comes out like a high, light pancake. These are really good as a sweet, warm back-country snack or dessert.

1   box (17 ounces) Krusteaz Almond Poppyseed muffin mix, or any mix of your choice that doesn't require oil or butter

¼   cup powdered egg

Divide muffin mix evenly into 2 plastic quart-sized zipper bags. To each bag, add 2 tablespoons powdered egg. (Note: the Krusteaz mix I used here calls for 1 egg and 1 cup of water. I've substituted ¼ cup powdered egg for the fresh egg, dividing it between the 2 batches, and that's all I need to do. If the mix you use also requires added milk, use ¼ cup of nonfat dry milk powder for each cup of milk required, dividing it evenly between the 2 batches.)

Carry separately for each batch:

2   teaspoons butter or margarine
    A bag of the re-packaged mix

At camp:

In medium bowl, combine mix with ½ cup cold water. Stir well; let stand a few minutes before cooking.

To cook in a campfire: Melt butter in a heavy medium skillet that has a lid. Add the batter, and cover the skillet. Place the covered skillet onto the embers, near the edge where the fire is cooler. Shovel a few coals on top of the lid. Cook, moving pan frequently to prevent burning, until cake is springy to the touch, about 10 minutes. Cut into 4 pieces before serving warm.

To cook on a camp stove: Melt butter in a skillet over medium heat (if the skillet is small, melt only enough butter to coat the bottom). Pour the batter in ¼-cup batches onto the skillet; immediately reduce heat to low. Rotate the pan frequently, and occasionally remove it from the fire, to prevent burning; a diffuser plate (page 58) also helps. Cook until the bottoms are firm enough to flip the cakes (like pancakes), 3 to 5 minutes; the top will still be quite wet. Cook on the second side until the cakes are done, 3 to 5 minutes; they will feel springy to the touch. If your skillet is small, you may only be able to cook one or two cakes at a time; in a large skillet, you can cook all four at the same time.

To cook in a camp oven: Pre-heat the oven if necessary* before mixing the batter. Butter the inside of the dish you'll be baking in. Pour in the batter. Cover and bake until springy, 20 to 35 minutes. Cut into 4 pieces before serving warm.

*The Outback Oven requires no pre-heating. Box-style camp ovens should be pre-heated to 300°F-350°F before baking.

Chapter Thirteen

Omnium-Gatherum
(Miscellaneous Stuff!)

This catch-all chapter contains recipes that didn't seem to fit anywhere else. Included are a few sauces to dress up camp foods, a few appetizers that are great in the back-country, and some make-at-home goodies like jerky and fruitcake. Contrary to what I've seen in many camper's cookbooks, I haven't included basic bread-making or cookie-baking recipes, as I think that's beyond the scope of this book. If you're interested in this type of baking, there are many wonderful cookbooks available to guide you.

Camper's Salsa

Dried salsa is easy to carry into the back country, and rehydrates quickly and easily. Serve as a condiment with any Mexican-style dish, or use it to dress up scrambled eggs, fried potatoes, or grilled meats. Dry as much as you wish, then break up and store in plastic bags.

Homemade or bottled tomato-based salsa (*not* taco sauce)

Spread evenly on dryer trays that are lined with plastic wrap or solid liner sheets; cookie sheets lined with plastic wrap work well for drying in the oven. Dry at 135°F-145°F in dryer or oven. Peel the salsa off the liners after about 4 hours and flip it over, to speed drying. Properly dried salsa will be crispy with no soft spots, and will crumble easily. Total drying time will be 5 to 7 hours. One cup fresh salsa will yield about a cup of dried, broken-up pieces.

At camp:

Place some dried salsa in a bowl or small pot. Add some boiling water and stir; let stand for a few minutes, then stir again and add more water if needed for desired consistency. It's better to add too little water at the beginning than too much; start with ¼ cup boiling water to 1 cup dried, crumbled salsa. Let salsa stand, stirring occasionally, until completely rehydrated, 5 to 10 minutes.

Morel Sauce

About 1¼ cups sauce

Morel sauce over fresh walleye is springtime sorcery at its very best. However, the morel season is only a few weeks long, and if you want to enjoy this dish at other times, you'll have to dry the mushrooms so you can have the sauce any time you want. This recipe makes enough sauce to accompany fresh fish for 4 campers (or 2 campers, if they're true mushroom fans!). It also makes a wonderful pasta sauce; toss with enough cooked noodles to serve 4.

Place in a small plastic bag and seal with a twist-tie:

2	tablespoons all-purpose flour
2	tablespoons nonfat dry milk powder
2½	teaspoons Butter Buds
¼	teaspoon salt, or just a bit less
	A generous pinch of white pepper
	A generous pinch of paprika
	A pinch of nutmeg

Combine in quart plastic zipper bag:

½	cup dried morel pieces, broken into fingernail-sized pieces before measuring
1	teaspoon dried snipped chives
	The small bag with the flour mixture

At camp:

Remove the small bag with the flour mixture and set aside. In medium pot, boil 1¼ cups water. Add mushroom mixture; stir well. Cover; remove from heat and let stand about 5 minutes. Remove cover; return to boiling. Reduce heat to a gentle boil. Add the flour mixture while stirring vigorously with a fork to prevent lumps. Cook, stirring constantly, until sauce is thickened and smooth, 2 or 3 minutes.

Millionaire's Morel Sauce

About 1¼ cups sauce

If you don't have access to a morel woods, or if you've gobbled up all the ones you picked before you even took out the dryer, you can buy dried morels in many supermarkets and gourmet stores. Get ready for sticker shock, though; last I checked, they were selling for $19.99 for 1 ounce.

Follow above recipe, except substitute purchased dried morels for home-dried morels.

Garlic Heads Roasted in Foil

4 to 6 servings

Roasted garlic has the full flavor of garlic, with none of the bite. It's great as a spread for French or Italian bread, and also makes a delightful topping for a campfire-baked potato, roasted corn (page 113) or other vegetable. A campfire is ideal for preparing this savory treat.

Carry separately:

1   whole head of garlic, unpeeled
1   tablespoon extra-virgin olive oil (see footnote on page 187)
    12" square of foil

At camp:

You'll need a campfire, with the coals burned down and ready for cooking, or a prepared charcoal grill. Cut the top off the head of garlic, exposing the tops of the individual cloves; remove any skins that are very loose, but do not peel the garlic. Fold the foil in half with the shiny side in; both sides of the folded foil will be dull. Place the garlic head on the foil; bring the foil loosely around the garlic head to form a cup. Pour the olive oil over the cut top of the garlic head. Fold the sides of the foil in quickly in the drugstore wrap (see page 56). Roll the ends up tightly to enclose the garlic head and the oil, and mold the foil to the shape of the garlic so there are no big gaps.

Place the foil-wrapped garlic on a grate above the coals, or in the coals near the edge where it's slightly cooler. Cook the garlic, turning and moving around frequently, for about 20 minutes. Pull the foil package from the fire; with a potholder, squeeze the foil-wrapped garlic head (do not unwrap). When the garlic is done, it should feel slightly soft. If it's not soft, return the foil package to the fire and check again in 5 or 10 minutes; turn and move the garlic around frequently.

When the garlic is done, unwrap carefully to avoid escaping steam. Let cool slightly. Pull off individual cloves, and squeeze to remove the cooked garlic from the peel; or, dig the cooked garlic out with a fork or small knife.

Bruschetta

2 to 4 servings; easily doubled

Talk about good! When properly prepared, this classic Italian recipe is one of the best dishes around, and makes a great cocktail snack, side dish or evening fireside treat. Garlic haters need not *apply … in fact, they should probably travel to the next county when this dish is being served.*

Carry separately:

A partial loaf of *good* French or Italian bread*

8   cloves fresh garlic, unpeeled

¼   cup extra-virgin olive oil**

Salt to taste

At camp:

You'll need a campfire, with the coals burned down and ready for cooking, or a prepared charcoal grill. Build the campfire out of "clean" wood for cooking this dish – no moldy or painted wood should be used.

Slice bread about ¾" thick, on a diagonal if possible (the slices will be larger when cut diagonally). Each person will probably want 2 or 3 pieces. Peel the garlic cloves, and cut each in half the short way (so you have two short fat halves, not two long skinny halves); set aside. Pour the olive oil in a small bowl; set aside.

Set a grate above the prepared coals. Place the bread on the grate, and cook until toasted but not burned. Turn and toast the second side. Transfer the bread to a plate. Immediately, while the bread is still hot, rub each slice with one of the cut garlic cloves; depending on the size of the cloves, this could take one-half of a clove per side of bread. Quickly brush the bread on both sides with the olive oil; if you have a pastry brush, it would be ideal, but you can make do with a wadded-up clean paper towel.

Return the bread to the grate. Grill briefly until warm; flip quickly and warm the other side also. Salt lightly to taste.

*Don't try to make this recipe with *soft* French-style or Italian-style bread; it will be ripped apart during the garlic application. Authentic French or Italian bread is dense and almost chewy when fresh. You may need to go to a specialty bakery to get the real thing. If you can't find it, don't try to make this recipe; you'll be sadly disappointed.

**Extra-virgin olive oil is fruity and flavorful, with no acid bite. Unfortunately, I've read some other camping cookbooks (and regular cookbooks, for that matter) that give genuinely bad advice about olive oil. The good olive oil is not the colorless stuff in the little bottles; it's green, and will always be marked "extra-virgin." The best oil is from Italy, although Spain and France produce some good oil as well. Be wary of bargain-priced oils; good olive oil is expensive, but has many uses in good cooking. Although there are many wonderful brands available at specialty shops, I've noticed that many supermarkets also carry one or two good brands; Coltibuono is one of the best you're likely to find at a supermarket. Bella is not as exquisite, but is a brand I trust; I use it as my "everyday" olive oil at home.

Homemade Vegetable Broth Powder

12 servings

A similar recipe is featured in **The Meatless Gourmet** *by Bobbie Hinman. Use this as a quick pick-me-up in camp, or substitute for bouillon granules in any recipe in this book.*

1	tablespoon onion powder
1	tablespoon crumbled dried parsley leaves
2	teaspoons celery salt
1½	teaspoons garlic powder
½	teaspoon crumbled dried thyme leaves
½	teaspoon crumbled dried marjoram leaves
½	teaspoon crumbled dried rosemary leaves
½	teaspoon crumbled dried summer savory or tarragon leaves
½	teaspoon crumbled dried basil leaves
¼	teaspoon paprika
¼	teaspoon white pepper

Combine in a glass jar; shake well.

At camp:

Mix a heaping teaspoon with 1 cup boiling water. You can also add a teaspoon of this mix to the water used to cook rice.

Hummus *(color photo page 189)* 4 to 6 appetizer servings

A delicious Mideastern spread that adapts easily to the camping menu, and is particularly suited to a mid-sized, convivial group. Serve it with crackers and fresh, crunchy vegetables like carrot sticks, celery, and cucumber spears for dipping; cut-up pita breads are also a natural accompaniment.

- 1 teaspoon olive oil
- ¾ teaspoon minced garlic
- 1 can (15 ounces) garbanzo beans, drained, or 1⅔ cups cooked
- 1 tablespoon tahini*, optional
- 2 tablespoons fresh lemon juice
- 1¼ teaspoons salt
- ½ teaspoon black pepper
- ½ teaspoon crumbled dried parsley leaves

In medium skillet, heat oil over medium heat. Add garlic; cook, stirring constantly, about 2 minutes. Add garbanzo beans and tahini; cook, stirring frequently, 2 to 3 minutes, or until mixture is dry. Add lemon juice; cook, stirring frequently, about 1 minute. Remove from heat; add salt, pepper and parsley. Mash with potato masher until fairly smooth.

Spread on lightly greased drying sheets. Dry at 145°F for one hour. Reduce heat to 135°F and continue drying, rearranging and stirring occasionally, until completely dry and crumbly; total time will be about 5½ hours. Allow to cool completely, then place in a pint plastic zipper bag.

At camp:

In medium pot, boil ¾ cup water. Add mix; stir well to break up and blend (this can also easily be reconstituted in a freezer-weight zipper bag by adding the boiling water to the bag with the mix as shown on page 155, then kneading to combine; use a potholder around the bag so you don't burn your hands). Let stand until cool, stirring occasionally. If hummus is too thick, you can add an additional teaspoon or two of water or olive oil. Serve as a dip or spread.

*Tahini, also called sesame paste, is a flavorful Mideastern specialty. Look for it in the international-foods section of larger grocery stores, or with the peanut butter. Co-ops and health food stores often carry tahini.

Dried hummus

Reconstituted hummus, with cucumbers, carrots, and pita breads

Cold-Smoked Jerky

About ¾ pound

 This recipe makes traditional jerky – whole strips of meat, seasoned and slowly cold-smoked until dry. Several different marinades allow you to experiment to find the flavor you prefer. I'm going to assume that if you are reading this, you have a cold smoker and are familiar with its use.

For any of the marinades:

1½   pounds boneless beef or venison

Remove all fat and gristle from the meat. Slice with the grain into ⅛" thick strips (meat is easiest to slice if partially frozen).

Beer-B-Que Jerky Marinade

1   cup barbecue sauce
1   cup beer
2   tablespoons Morton TenderQuick salt
1   teaspoon black pepper

Combine all ingredients in non-metallic bowl; stir well to blend. Add meat. Cover with plastic wrap and refrigerate overnight. Drain meat; pat with paper towels before arranging on smoker racks. Smoke as directed.

Spicy Teriyaki Jerky Marinade

⅓   cup teriyaki sauce
⅓   cup pineapple juice
2   tablespoons brown sugar
2   tablespoons Morton TenderQuick salt
1   tablespoon dried chopped onion
2   teaspoons crushed dried hot peppers

Combine all ingredients in non-metallic bowl; stir well to blend. Add meat. Cover with plastic wrap and refrigerate overnight. Drain meat; pat with paper towels before arranging on smoker racks. Smoke as directed.

Dry Jerky Rub

1   tablespoon Morton TenderQuick salt
1   tablespoon pickling and canning salt (non-iodized)
2   teaspoons garlic powder
2   teaspoons onion powder
1½   teaspoons freshly ground black pepper

Combine all ingredients in empty spice bottle with shaker top. Sprinkle meat strips on both sides with seasoning mix as though salting heavily. Arrange seasoned meat on smoker racks; smoke as directed.

Smoking the jerky:

Spray the smoker racks with non-stick vegetable spray like Pam. Arrange the meat strips on the racks so the pieces don't touch each other. Smoke at 100°F-110°F until jerky is leathery but still pliable, 4 to 7 hours; replenish smoking wood as necessary. For the typical aluminum box smoker, use a total of 3 pans of sawdust (about 1 cup sawdust or "chips and chunks" per pan). Keep jerky refrigerated for long-term storage.

Easy Jerky

Even if you don't have a cold smoker, you can still make delicious jerky in your oven or home dryer. The flavor won't be quite as intense as true cold-smoked jerky.

1½	pounds boneless beef or venison
	Beer-B-Que Jerky Marinade, or Spicy Teriyaki Jerky Marinade (page 190)
2	teaspoons liquid smoke flavoring

Remove fat and gristle from the meat. Slice with the grain into ⅛" thick strips (meat is easiest to slice if partially frozen). Combine all marinade ingredients and liquid smoke in non-metallic bowl; stir well to blend. Add meat. Cover with plastic wrap and refrigerate overnight. Drain meat; pat with paper towels.

To dry in the oven: Spray several cake-cooling racks with non-stick vegetable spray like Pam. Arrange meat strips on the racks so the pieces don't touch each other. Place in oven with temperature at the lowest possible setting; prop the oven door ajar with a ball of foil or an empty can. Monitor the oven temperature; it shouldn't get above 120°F. Dry until jerky is leathery but still pliable, 3 to 5 hours. Keep jerky refrigerated for long-term storage.

To dry in a food dryer: Arrange meat strips on dryer racks so the pieces don't touch each other. Dry at 120°F until jerky is leathery but still pliable, 3 to 5 hours. Keep jerky refrigerated for long-term storage.

Ground-Beef Jerky

This jerky is more tender than jerky made from "whole" meat. If you want to soak jerky at camp so you can use it in a stew, this type is the best choice; it also makes a wonderful out-of-hand snack. It can be prepared in a cold smoker, oven, or home dryer.

1½	pounds extra-lean ground beef or venison
¼	cup cold water
1	tablespoon Morton TenderQuick salt
1½	teaspoons pickling and canning salt (non-iodized)
2	teaspoons onion powder
1	teaspoon garlic powder
1	teaspoon freshly ground black pepper
½	teaspoon dry mustard
½	teaspoon cayenne pepper

Combine all ingredients in large non-metallic bowl, mixing well with your hands. Cover with plastic wrap and refrigerate overnight.

To shape jerky: roll about 2 tablespoons meat into a short "rope" between your hands. Place on a piece of waxed paper. Use the back of a spatula, dipped in water, to smooth the rope into a flat strip.

Place strips on smoker or dryer racks. Smoke as directed in **Cold-Smoked Jerky** on page 190, or dry in oven or dryer as described in **Easy Jerky**, above.

Note: Hi Mountain Jerky (page 199) sells jerky racks, a wonderful slicing board that helps slice meat evenly for jerky, and a "jerky gun" that pumps out nice even strips from ground meat. They also sell excellent spice pre-mixes for jerky.

No-Citron Fruit Cake 1 loaf

Fruit cake has an undeserved reputation as a dreadful concoction foisted off by maiden aunts onto unsuspecting relatives at Christmas. A good fruit cake puts that reputation to shame: firm, tangy-sweet fruits, and rich nuts, held together with a dense, buttery cake, laced with brandy. It's great camping food, because it can take the rough handling without falling completely apart. And it's a great treat at the end of the day, or whenever your sweet tooth craves a little something. This recipe is very liberally adapted from one in The Joy of Cooking, *and contains no citron (I think citron is one of the things that gives fruit cake a bad name!). Properly wrapped loaves will keep for many months.*

Prepare the fruits:

⅔	cup glacé (candied) cherries*, cut into quarters before measuring
½	cup golden raisins
½	cup dried apricots, cut into ½" dice before measuring
½	cup Calimyrna figs, cut into ½" dice before measuring
½	cup diced dried pineapple* (I use dried, sugared pineapple bits)
¼	cup currants
½	cup apricot nectar
½	cup brandy or dark rum

In heavy stainless-steel pan, combine fruits with apricot nectar and brandy. Bring to a boil over medium-high heat. Cook, stirring frequently, 3 to 5 minutes; most of the liquid will be absorbed. Let stand 3 hours or longer; this can sit overnight if you cover the pan.

After the fruits have soaked 3 hours or longer, prepare the batter mix:

1¼	cups all-purpose flour
½	teaspoon nutmeg
½	teaspoon salt
¼	teaspoon cinnamon
¼	teaspoon allspice
¼	teaspoon baking soda
⅛	teaspoon ground cloves
⅛	teaspoon ground cardamom
¼	pound unsalted butter (1 stick), softened
½	cup packed brown sugar
3	eggs, at room temperature
1½	teaspoons pure vanilla extract
1¼	cups chopped pecan pieces

Line a standard-size loaf pan with waxed paper or parchment paper; set aside. Pre-heat oven to 275°F.

Sift together flour, nutmeg, salt, cinnamon, allspice, soda, cloves, and cardamom; set aside. In large mixing bowl, cream butter with high speed of electric mixer until light and fluffy. Add sugar; beat until smooth and fluffy. Add eggs, one at a time, beating well between additions. Add vanilla and beat well; mixture should be smooth, light and fluffy.

Add flour mixture to butter/egg mixture; stir with heavy wooden spoon until well-mixed. Add soaked fruits and pecan pieces, along with any remaining liquid, to batter; stir with heavy wooden spoon until fruit and nuts are incorporated. (The mixture will be fairly stiff by now, and could easily break a thinner-handled wooden spoon. I know, because *I* broke one while I was working on this recipe!)

Spoon the mixture into the prepared pan; force out any large air pockets with a spatula, and smooth the top. Bake in pre-heated oven until a toothpick inserted into the center of the loaf comes out clean and there are no soft spots, 2½ to 3 hours. Remove from oven. Cool in loaf pan for 30 minutes, then turn out onto cake-cooling rack. Remove paper, and let stand until completely cool.

For a richer fruit cake, pierce cooled loaf in about a dozen places with a skewer; sprinkle about 2 tablespoons brandy or dark rum over the cake. Let the brandy soak in before wrapping the loaf.

Wrap loaf well in cheesecloth, then in plastic wrap; overwrap with foil. Store in a cool place but do not refrigerate. You can open the plastic wrapping and drizzle the cheesecloth-wrapped loaf with brandy as described above once a week for a month or two, if you like; carefully re-wrap each time to prevent the fruitcake from drying out.

The fruit cake is best when it mellows for a few days after the brandy treatment before serving. Before you go on a trip, unwrap the loaf and slice off what you need; re-wrap the remainder of the loaf for the next time.

*The candied cherries may be difficult to get during spring or summer; many stores stock this item only during the pre-winter-holiday season. If you can't find the cherries at your grocer, try a specialty baking store, or check with a local bakery. I buy the dried, sugared pineapple bits at a health-food store; this item is often also carried by larger supermarkets with the trail mixes. If you can't find dried, sugared pineapple bits, you could dry your own (page 39); or, you could substitute candied pineapple, which is available from the same sources as the candied cherries. Candied pineapple will produce a sweeter, moister fruitcake.

Breakfast Cookies

*Carry these crispy, unusual cookies for a quick-start breakfast (great with **Mexican Coffee**, page 176), or tasty trail snack that's much better than a commercial granola bar. Pack them in one of those round canisters used to package potato crisps. They'll keep on the trail for a week or longer.*

½   pound bacon
½   cup chunky peanut butter
½   cup sugar
2   tablespoons unsalted butter or margarine, softened
2   tablespoons applesauce
1   egg
1   cup all-purpose flour
¼   teaspoon baking soda
2   cups cornflakes
½   cup raisins

In medium skillet, fry bacon over medium heat until very crisp. Drain and cool on paper towels. Break into pieces no larger than ½" and set aside.

Pre-heat oven to 350°F. In medium mixing bowl, beat peanut butter, sugar, butter and applesauce with electric beater on medium-high speed until well-incorporated. Add egg and beat until light and fluffy, about 2 minutes. Sift flour and baking soda into peanut butter mixture; beat with electric mixer at low speed just until flour is incorporated. Add bacon pieces, cornflakes and raisins; mix with your hands until combined (dough will be crumbly; this is OK). Form into walnut-sized balls; place on ungreased cookie sheets, 1" apart. Bake for 15 to 18 minutes, until browned. Cool on wire racks. Store cookies in an airtight container in the refrigerator until your trip; they may be frozen in a tightly sealed container up to 3 months.

Red-Wine Biscotti

About 20 biscotti

Biscotti is the Italian word for biscuit. These peppery, savory morsels are not biscuits in the American sense; they're almost cookie-like in texture. But the resemblance stops there! Serve these as a snack with coffee or tea, or if you're really camping in style, with a little cheese and red wine.

2¼ cups all-purpose flour
¼ cup sugar
1½ teaspoons baking powder
1¼ teaspoons freshly ground 5-pepper blend* or black pepper
1 teaspoon salt
¼ teaspoon powdered dried sage leaves
2 tablespoons sesame seeds
½ cup dry red wine
½ cup extra-virgin olive oil

Pre-heat oven to 350°F. Sift together the flour, sugar, baking powder, pepper, salt, and sage. In a large bowl, combine the sifted ingredients with the sesame seeds; mix well. In a 2-cup measuring cup, whisk together the wine and oil; quickly add it to the flour mixture. Stir with a wooden spoon just until the mixture forms a dough and no dry flour is left.

Pinch off a piece about the size of a whole walnut and roll into a fat cigar shape that is about 2" x ¾". Arrange on ungreased baking sheets, ½" apart. Bake until golden brown on the bottom and firm to the touch, 22 to 28 minutes. Cool on wire racks. Store biscotti in an airtight container.

*Five-pepper blend is usually available in the spice aisle or at gourmet stores. It is a mix of white, pink, green, and regular black peppercorns with whole allspice. Blended peppers like this have a milder, more fragrant flavor. Pepper is always best when freshly ground, by the way, but the fresh-ground taste and fragrance is particularly important for this recipe.

Glossary of Terms

Al dente: Literally, "to the teeth" in Italian; used to describe proper doneness of pasta and rice. When cooked *al dente,* pasta or rice is still slightly firm (but not crunchy) in the center; it should not be mushy.

All-purpose flour: I use unbleached white flour as my all-purpose flour, but bleached white flour will also work in these recipes (it is more highly processed than unbleached flour). Don't substitute whole-wheat, rye, bread flour, or other flours for the all-purpose flour unless you're experienced with this sort of thing; the results could be unpredictable.

Bacon-flavored bits: These imitation bacon pieces are made from soy, and really don't have the true flavor or texture of bacon. However, they won't spoil in even the hottest weather, and can be used to add flavor to many dishes. Dried cooked bacon pieces (see entry later in Glossary) are a better choice when you're camping in moderate weather.

Bacon drippings: Drippings are the fat left in the pan after bacon is cooked. Drippings become more solid as they cool, and are hard when cold (like butter). To transport drippings to your next campsite, let them cool slightly and pour into a container with a good seal. Carry the sealed container in a plastic bag. Drippings will keep a week or more, except in very hot weather.

Bouquet garni: A commercially packed dried herb mixture (not related to the true *bouquet garni,* a fresh herb bundle used in French cooking), generally including oregano, savory, marjoram, rosemary, basil, sage, thyme, dill, and tarragon. Look in the spice aisle for pre-mixed *bouquet garni.*

Bulgur: Whole wheat kernels are parboiled, dried and cracked to make bulgur, which is available in several finenesses. Medium or fine bulgur cooks more quickly than coarse bulgur, and works best for camping. Bulgur has a nutty taste.

Butter Buds: Butter-flavored sprinkles. Other brands are available (Molly McButter is fairly common), and can be substituted, although all recipes in this book were tested with the brand called Butter Buds. Because the sprinkles are fat-free, they can't be used for frying.

Buttermilk baking mix: Pre-mixed commercial blend used for making biscuits, pancakes, etc. Bisquick is a common brand, although many others are available and can be freely substituted.

Cayenne pepper: Finely ground dried hot red peppers, used to add "heat" to many dishes. Do *not* substitute chili powder blend.

Chili powder blend: This commercial blend generally includes cayenne pepper, ground cumin, garlic powder, oregano, and salt. It is commonly used to season chili.

Chorizo: A spicy Mexican sausage, usually unsmoked. Check at a Mexican or specialty market, or in the freezer case of larger grocery stores.

Clarified butter: Butter which has had the milk solids removed by melting and straining (see page 17 for directions). Unlike regular butter, clarified butter doesn't turn rancid when unrefrigerated, and also doesn't burn at high heat.

Dried canned or cooked shell beans: Used for camping mixes because they cook more quickly than regular uncooked dried shell beans. See page 30 for instructions on drying canned or cooked beans in a home dryer or oven.

Dried cooked bacon pieces: Real bacon pieces that have been dried after cooking, not "imitation bacon-flavored bits." Easy to dry in a home dryer or oven (see page 40); can also be purchased at grocery stores. Dried cooked bacon pieces are OK for up to a week in moderate weather.

Dried green peas: Frozen or fresh peas that have been dried (see page 34). Do *not* substitute dried split peas or other readily available dried peas from the grocery store; they will take longer to cook, and have a completely different flavor. Freeze-dried green peas can be substituted, but need less re-hydrating.

Fines herbes: A dried French-inspired herb blend, usually consisting of parsley, chives, tarragon, and chervil. Use to season vegetables, eggs, and fish dishes.

French-cut green beans: Green beans that have been thinly sliced along the length. They dry and rehydrate quickly, making them ideal for camping. The photos on page 154 show dried and re-hydrated French-cut green beans; page 29 gives drying instructions.

Garlic chips: Commercially dried coarsely chopped garlic. Chips have a better flavor than garlic powder, but need a bit of soaking or cooking to re-hydrate; garlic powder requires no soaking or cooking. Available in the spice aisle.

Garlic powder: Commercially dried garlic that's been ground to a powder; used to flavor foods that will get little or no cooking. Do *not* substitute garlic salt.

Green onions: Also called scallions or spring onions, these thin onions consist of a small bulb with green shoots. Use both the green and white parts (see page 33 for drying instructions).

Hoisin sauce: A Chinese sauce with a ketchup-like consistency. Look for it in the specialty-foods aisle of a large supermarket, or at an Asian grocery. See the footnote on page 139 for information on choosing hoisin sauce.

Imitation chicken (or other meat): Made from wheat gluten, imitation meat is a good substitute for more expensive freeze-dried meats. Look for imitation meats at an Asian grocer, co-op, or health-food store.

"Instant" beans: Commercially prepared dried cooked beans that have been chopped to a flaked consistency. They re-hydrate quickly, but don't have much texture. Fantastic Foods is a brand that is often available at grocery stores.

Instant rice: Often referred to as "minute rice" (which is also the name of a nationally available brand). This pre-cooked dried rice "cooks" very quickly in camp, but is mushy in texture and nutritionally poor compared to regular rice.

Julienned: Food (usually vegetables) which has been cut into matchstick-shaped pieces. See page 31 for photos of julienning.

Nonfat dry milk powder: Available in the baking aisle of any grocery store, this powdered milk doesn't need refrigeration because the fat has been removed.

Onion powder: Dried onions which have been finely powdered; available in the spice aisle at all grocery stores. Do *not* substitute onion salt.

Plastic zipper bags: Food-storage bags with a press-together seal that "zips" (you don't need the ones with the little sliding plastic tab, but they work fine too). *Freezer-weight* plastic zipper bags are sturdy enough to hold boiling water for re-hydrating dried foods (see page 155).

Powdered egg: Commercially dried eggs, used when fresh eggs aren't practical. Buy powdered eggs in bulk at camping-supply stores, where they may also be called "scrambled eggs"; some health-food stores and grocery stores also carry powdered eggs. Powdered egg keeps best when the original package is unopened; trail mixes using powdered egg are OK for a week or so, but should be stored in the refrigerator for long-term home storage.

Pressed beef slices (or other meat): Also known as "chipped" meat, this thinly sliced luncheon meat dries and re-hydrates quickly. Available in many varieties. See pages 39-41 for instructions on drying.

Provençal herb mixture: Also called *herbes de Provence*, this dry herb blend usually contains rosemary, marjoram, thyme, sage, anise, and savory. It is a good all-purpose herb blend for vegetables, potatoes, fish, or meat.

Re-hydrating: Dried vegetables, meats, and some fruits need to be re-hydrated by soaking in water before use; this returns them to a condition resembling fresh (see page 154 for photos of some foods before and after re-hydrating). Hot or boiling water re-hydrates foods more quickly, but isn't necessary for most foods. Page 155 shows how to re-hydrate foods in plastic bags.

Shelf-stable Parmesan cheese: Available in all grocery stores, this is found on the supermarket shelf (not in the refrigerated case) in glass or plastic jars. Unlike "real" Parmesan cheese, shelf-stable cheese can be carried in recipe pre-mixes without turning rancid; however, the flavor and texture is a poor substitute for the real thing.

Sun-dried tomatoes: These naturally dried tomatoes have a richer, smokier taste than regular tomatoes that have been dried in a food dryer. Look at a larger grocery store, a gourmet shop or specialty store for sun-dried tomatoes.

TenderQuick salt: Packed by Morton Salt Company; usually available in the spice aisle. TenderQuick contains chemicals that help prevent spoilage in cured meats like jerky. If you prefer to avoid these chemicals, substitute ⅔ the volume of canning/pickling salt for the TenderQuick (in other words, for each tablespoon of TenderQuick, substitute ⅔ tablespoon of canning/pickling salt).

Unsalted butter: Very different in flavor from regular salted butter; doesn't keep quite as long as regular butter. For trail use in warm weather, clarify unsalted butter (page 17) to keep it from turning rancid.

Mail Order and Website Addresses

These URLs and other contact information are current as of the date of publication of this book. If you can't get in touch with these companies using the information below, enter the company name in a search engine for more recent information.

Alpine Aire Foods • alpineaire.com
406-585-9324 • 8551 Cottonwood Road • Bozeman, MT 59718
Products: Freeze-dried chicken, beef, turkey; other dried foods

Chef Paul Prudhomme's Smoked Meats • chefpaul.com/meats
800-457-2857 • P.O. Box 23342 • New Orleans, LA 70183-0342
Products: Tasso and other smoked meats. Chef Paul's Magic Seasoning Blends (including blends especially for blackening meats, chicken and fish), and rice mixes are also available at larger supermarkets.

Cooke Custom Sewing • cookecustomsewing.com
651-784-8777 • 7290 Stagecoach Trail • Lino Lakes, MN 55014
Products: High-quality tarps (for kitchen fly), packs

Frieda's, Inc. • friedas.com
Products: A wide variety of freeze-dried fruits, mushrooms and vegetables

Hi Mountain Jerky • himtnjerky.com
800-829-2285 • 1000 College View Drive • Riverton, WY 82501
Product: Seasoning blends (pages 47, 97), jerky cures (page 191), sausage-making kits, bacon cures, powdered blue-cheese dressing mix (pages 101, 106), jerky-making supplies (pages 24, 191)

Just Tomatoes, Etc. • justtomatoes.com
800-537-1985 • P.O. Box 807 • Westley, CA 95387
Products: A wide variety of freeze-dried fruits and vegetables (also available in many supermarkets)

Melissa's/World Variety Produce • melissas.com
800-588-0151 • P.O. Box 21127 • Los Angeles, CA 90021
Products: Dried mushrooms, unusual varieties of dried beans, couscous, rices and other grains, some freeze-dried vegetables (also available in many supermarkets)

Penzeys Spices • penzeys.com • 800-741-7787
Products: Freeze-dried bell peppers and shallots; wide variety of herbs, spices and seasoning blends

Ty Ry, Inc. (Richmoor) • richmoor.com • 800-322-6325
Products: Freeze-dried beef, chicken and some vegetables, scrambled egg powder

Voyageur Trading Post • boundarywatersjournal.com
800-548-7319 • 9396 Rocky Ledge Road • Ely, MN 55731
Products: Cast-aluminum skillets (page 43), canoe packs, kitchen kits, saws, paddles, water jugs, and various supplies

White Earth Land Recovery Project • nativeharvest.com • 888-274-8318
Products: Truly wild rice that is hand-harvested and traditionally finished, maple syrup

Index

S